Cambridge School Shakespeare

T0159686

KING RICHARD III

Edited by Linzy Brady and Jane Coles
Series editors: Richard Andrews and Vicki Wienand
Founding editor: Rex Gibson

CAMBRIDGE
UNIVERSITY PRESS

CAMBRIDGE
UNIVERSITY PRESS

University Printing House, Cambridge CB2 8BS, United Kingdom

One Liberty Plaza, 20th Floor, New York, NY 10006, USA

477 Williamstown Road, Port Melbourne, VIC 3207, Australia

314–321, 3rd Floor, Plot 3, Splendor Forum, Jasola District Centre, New Delhi – 110025, India

103 Penang Road, #05-06/07, Visioncrest Commercial, Singapore 238467

Cambridge University Press is part of the University of Cambridge.

It furthers the University's mission by disseminating knowledge in the pursuit of education, learning and research at the highest international levels of excellence.

www.cambridge.org
Information on this title: www.cambridge.org/9781108456067

Commentary and notes © Cambridge University Press 2000, 2015
Text © Cambridge University Press 2000, 2015

First published 2000
Second edition 2005
Third edition 2015

20 19 18 17 16 15 14 13 12 11 10 9 8

Printed in Poland by Opolgraf

A catalogue record for this publication is available from the British Library

ISBN 978-1-108-45606-7 Paperback

NOTICE TO TEACHERS IN THE UK
It is illegal to reproduce any part of this work in material form (including photocopying and electronic storage) except under the following circumstances:
(i)   where you are abiding by a licence granted to your school or institution by the Copyright Licensing Agency;
(ii)   where no such licence exists, or where you wish to exceed the terms of a licence, and you have gained the written permission of Cambridge University Press;
(iii)   where you are allowed to reproduce without permission under the provisions of Chapter 3 of the Copyright, Designs and Patents Act 1988, which covers, for example, the reproduction of short passages within certain types of educational anthology and reproduction for the purposes of setting examination questions.

Cover image: Richard Dyson/Alamy Stock Photo

Contents

**Cambridge School
Shakespeare**

Introduction

This *King Richard III* is part of the **Cambridge School Shakespeare** series. Like every other play in the series, it has been specially prepared to help all students in schools and colleges.

The **Cambridge School Shakespeare** *King Richard III* aims to be different. It invites you to lift the words from the page and to bring the play to life in your classroom, hall or drama studio. Through enjoyable and focused activities, you will increase your understanding of the play. Actors have created their different interpretations of the play over the centuries. Similarly, you are invited to make up your own mind about *King Richard III*, rather than having someone else's interpretation handed down to you.

Cambridge School Shakespeare does not offer you a cut-down or simplified version of the play. This is Shakespeare's language, filled with imaginative possibilities. You will find on every left-hand page: a summary of the action, an explanation of unfamiliar words, and a choice of activities on Shakespeare's stagecraft, characters, themes and language.

Between each act and in the pages at the end of the play, you will find notes, illustrations and activities. These will help to encourage reflection after every act and give you insights into the background and context of the play as a whole.

This edition will be of value to you whether you are studying for an examination, reading for pleasure or thinking of putting on the play to entertain others. You can work on the activities on your own or in groups. Many of the activities suggest a particular group size, but don't be afraid to make up larger or smaller groups to suit your own purposes. Please don't think you have to do every activity: choose those that will help you most.

Although you are invited to treat *King Richard III* as a play, you don't need special dramatic or theatrical skills to do the activities. By choosing your activities, and by exploring and experimenting, you can make your own interpretations of Shakespeare's language, characters and stories.

Whatever you do, remember that Shakespeare wrote his plays to be acted, watched and enjoyed.

Rex Gibson
Founding editor

This new edition contains more photographs, more diversity and more supporting material than previous editions, whilst remaining true to Rex's original vision. Specifically, it contains more activities and commentary on stagecraft and writing about Shakespeare, to reflect contemporary interest. The glossary has been enlarged too. Finally, this edition aims to reflect the best teaching and learning possible, and to represent not only Shakespeare through the ages, but also the relevance and excitement of Shakespeare today.

Richard Andrews and Vicki Wienand
Series editors

This edition of *King Richard III* uses the text of the play established by Janis Lull in **The New Cambridge Shakespeare**.

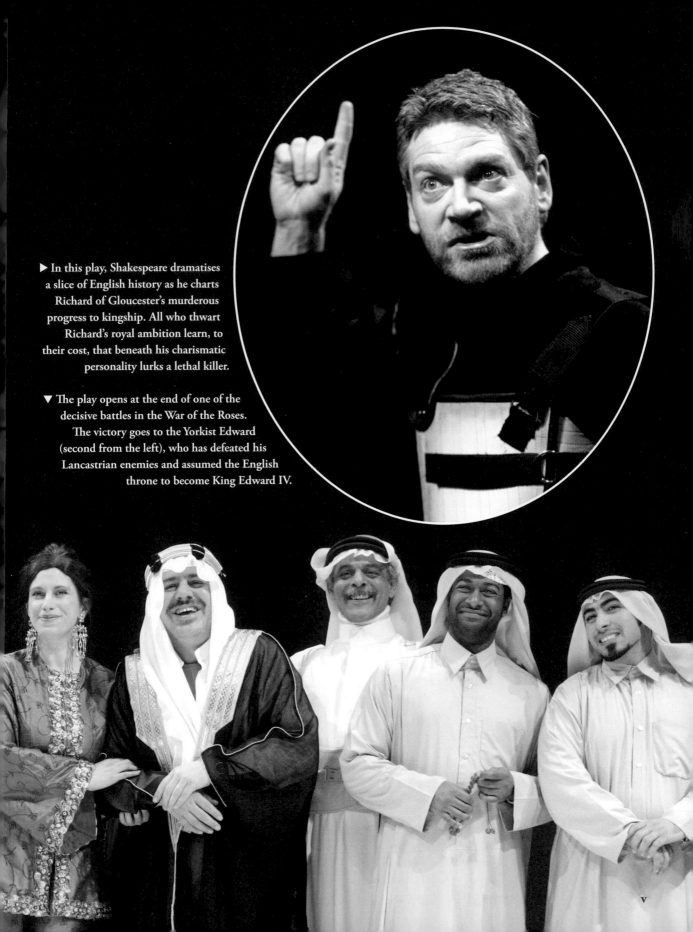

▶ In this play, Shakespeare dramatises a slice of English history as he charts Richard of Gloucester's murderous progress to kingship. All who thwart Richard's royal ambition learn, to their cost, that beneath his charismatic personality lurks a lethal killer.

▼ The play opens at the end of one of the decisive battles in the War of the Roses. The victory goes to the Yorkist Edward (second from the left), who has defeated his Lancastrian enemies and assumed the English throne to become King Edward IV.

Richard's first step to the throne is to get rid of his older brother George, Duke of Clarence, who stands between Richard and the crown. Edward and Clarence are at odds with each other, and Richard swears to help Clarence reconcile with the King. At the same time, Richard orchestrates Clarence's death.

The dying King Edward seeks to secure peace and stability for his family and country by continuing his royal line through his eldest son. But Richard plans to kill both of Edward's young sons and seize the crown for himself.

As part of his plan to take the throne, Richard persuades Anne Neville to become his wife. Richard admits that he killed Anne's husband and father-in-law, but gives such a dazzling performance in wooing Anne that her loathing turns first to confusion and then to acceptance.

Margaret is the widow of the Lancastrian Henry VI. Her long life and enduring memory remind certain characters – especially Richard – of their bloody past, as she calls for justice and revenge to redress old wrongs committed against her family.

When King Edward dies, his son is hailed as Edward V. However, the boy's mother fears for his safety because he is so young and under the protection of his manipulative and evil uncle.

Richard plays the jovial and harmless uncle with the young King and his brother. But secretly he plans their imprisonment and murder.

Richard's next steps to the throne involve getting rid of courtiers and nobles who do not support his claim to it. One of these is Lord Hastings, a faithful supporter of Edward IV and his sons. Hastings is unaware of Richard's plans to seize the throne and he is led into a trap and executed.

Richard also gathers support from influential nobles such as Buckingham, who is willing to do anything to ensure that Richard becomes King.

With the help of Buckingham, Richard stages a performance in which he plays a saintly man who is more concerned with praying than ruling England. He pretends to refuse the crown, but makes a show of being forced to take it for the sake of the country and its citizens.

▲ Richard finally fulfils his ambitions and gains the throne. In order to secure his position, he makes plans to murder the two young princes, Edward and Richard. He tests Buckingham's loyalty by asking him to kill them. Buckingham refuses and tries to flee, but he is captured and beheaded.

▲ Richard is still working out ways to secure his throne. With Anne dead, he seeks to marry the daughter of Edward IV and Elizabeth to consolidate his position as King. But Elizabeth is unimpressed and secretly makes plans to marry her daughter to someone else.

▼ News of Richard's villainy has reached the Earl of Richmond. He wages war to take back the throne and re-establish order, while also asserting the Lancastrian claim to the throne. Richard and his dwindling army prepare to defend the crown.

▼ On the eve of the decisive Battle of Bosworth, where he is to meet Richmond, Richard dreams that he is cursed by the ghosts of his eleven victims. Appearing in the order of their deaths, the ghosts make repeated demands for revenge on Richard. They are a forceful reminder of his past crimes and guilt.

▶ Richmond's defeat of Richard ends the cycle of murder and revenge that has fuelled the Wars of the Roses. Richmond unites the houses of Lancaster and York by marrying Princess Elizabeth. In doing so, he founds a new dynasty – the Tudors – and establishes peace in England.

Shakespeare's history plays
The movement of the English crown through the plays

King Richard III is the last of eight plays that Shakespeare wrote to dramatise the historical events leading up to the reign of the Tudors in England. The plays are Shakespeare's version of the struggle for the crown that culminated in the civil war known as the Wars of the Roses. These wars were skirmishes over the right to the throne between two branches of the House of Plantagenet, a royal dynasty in England: Lancaster (represented by a red rose) and York (represented by a white rose). The wars ended when the Lancastrian Henry Tudor defeated the Yorkist Richard III. Henry married Elizabeth of York so that their descendants would unite the two branches and ensure peace. This new Tudor line was symbolised by a red and white rose.

King Richard II
Richard II is a weak and ineffectual ruler. Henry Bullingbrook becomes Henry IV.

King Henry IV Parts 1 and 2
Henry IV's son Hal, after spending his youth with Falstaff in London taverns, turns over a new leaf when he becomes King Henry V.

King Henry V
King Henry V wins an important victory over the French at Agincourt. He extends England's territory and marries a French princess.

King Henry VI Parts 1, 2 and 3
Henry VI loses English possessions in France and sees his kingdom racked by civil war (the Wars of the Roses) as the house of York challenges his right to rule. Edward IV emerges from these wars as the new King.

King Richard III
When King Edward dies, the crown passes to his son, the young Prince Edward; the old King's brother, Richard, is made Lord Protector until Edward is old enough to rule. However, Richard seizes the throne and murders all who get in the way, including his young nephews. He is finally overthrown by the Earl of Richmond (Henry Tudor), who becomes King Henry VII. Henry unites the two warring families and begins the line of Tudor monarchs.

Crown taken by Henry IV, establishing the House of Lancaster on the throne

↓

Crown inherited by Henry V

↓

Crown held by Henry V

↓

Crown inherited by Henry VI

Crown taken by Edward IV

↓

Crown inherited by Edward V

Crown taken by Richard III

Crown taken by Henry VII

The world of the play

The royal rogue: a pre-reading activity

You are in the court of a new king towards the end of the Wars of the Roses. The crown has just been taken from the previous king, who died in battle along with his sons. Now a new king, with his newly made royal family and trusted courtiers, comes to London. Imagine there is a clever but isolated member of this new royal family. He is determined to become king one day – no matter what the cost. In groups, compile a list of actions this 'royal rogue' might use to manoeuvre his way to the throne. Start with the following: intimidate; flatter; seduce; murder; marry; imprison; bribe.

What else can you add? Remember, the royal rogue cannot be too obvious or his actions might alienate the people of London and start another civil war.

Assign roles to every member of the group so that you simulate this new court:

- the new king
- the new king's wife
- the new king's brother
- the new king's young son (the heir to the throne)
- the old king's wife
- the old king's daughter-in-law
- the new king's trusted courtier.

Then take turns as the royal rogue to decide which action you would use for each of the people listed above. Remember to give your reasons and to think about the consequences of the actions you take.

Tower of London

Crosby Place

Guildhall

Baynard Castle

St Paul's

Holborn (Ely House)

Whitefriars

List of characters

The royal family

RICHARD, DUKE OF GLOUCESTER (later King Richard III)

DUCHESS OF YORK his mother

KING EDWARD IV ⎱
CLARENCE ⎰ his brothers

ANNE his wife (earlier betrothed to Prince Edward, son of King Henry VI)

QUEEN ELIZABETH (wife of King Edward IV)

PRINCE EDWARD ⎱
DUKE OF YORK ⎰ her sons (the princes in the Tower)

BOY ⎱
GIRL ⎰ Clarence's children

QUEEN MARGARET (widow of King Henry VI)

EARL OF RICHMOND (later King Henry VII)

The Woodvilles

MARQUESS OF DORSET ⎱
LORD GREY ⎰ sons of Queen Elizabeth

LORD RIVERS (brother of Queen Elizabeth)

VAUGHAN

Nobles, church and court

LORD HASTINGS

DUKE OF BUCKINGHAM

LORD STANLEY, Earl of Derby

BRAKENBURY

LORD LOVELL

SIR RICHARD RATCLIFFE

SIR WILLIAM CATESBY

JAMES TYRREL

TRESSEL ⎱
BERKELEY ⎰ attendants of Lady Anne

BISHOP OF ELY

ARCHBISHOP OF YORK

LORD CARDINAL, Archbishop of Canterbury

SIR CHRISTOPHER URSWICK

EARL OF OXFORD

EARL OF SURREY

SIR WALTER HERBERT

SIR JAMES BLUNT

DUKE OF NORFOLK

The people

KEEPER OF THE TOWER	SCRIVENER
LORD MAYOR OF LONDON	SHERIFF
THREE CITIZENS	PURSUIVANT
TWO MURDERERS	PRIEST

Ghosts

(Who appear to Richard and Richmond at Bosworth)

PRINCE EDWARD (son of King Henry VI)	VAUGHAN
KING HENRY VI	HASTINGS
CLARENCE	ANNE
RIVERS	BUCKINGHAM
GREY	THE PRINCES IN THE TOWER

Lords, Attendants, Halberds, Messengers, Soldiers, Servants, Citizens, Gentlemen, Page, Guards, two Bishops.

The action of the play takes place in various locations in England.

Richard soliloquises on the end of the civil war and the pleasure of peace. He mocks his brother's sexual games and regrets he cannot enjoy similar pleasures.

Stagecraft

A dramatic opening (in pairs)

The play opens dramatically with Richard, Duke of Gloucester's **soliloquy**. He describes the change from war to peace that has taken place since his brother Edward, the new Yorkist king, has assumed the throne. He then goes on to paint a verbal portrait of himself.

a Read through Richard's soliloquy together, taking turns with the three main sections (lines 1–13, 14–27 and 28–41). Then work out how you would stage the lines to achieve the greatest dramatic effect, highlighting the following features in the script:

- His dramatic opening, capturing the audience's attention with the word 'Now'.
- His repetition of the word 'Our' and his use of **alliteration** (words with the same letter sounds at the start) in lines 6–8.
- His use of **personification** (giving human attributes to non-human things) – for example, describing war as a soldier who has replaced his warlike behaviour with that of a lover.
- From line 14 onwards, Richard repeatedly uses the personal pronoun ('I') and shifts the attention to himself.

b Choose a block of four lines to memorise. Explore different ways of saying it in order to bring out the drama and the meaning.

c In role as director, make notes to advise the actor playing Richard at the start of this scene. Keep a Director's Journal as an ongoing record of your ideas about this play in performance. This is where you will explore aspects of stagecraft, actors' perspectives and dramatic possibilities.

1 Visual images (in small groups)

Richard makes use of vivid visual **imagery** (see p. 250) through his choice of words.

a Look through the soliloquy and find examples of visual images of flirtation, deformity, pleasure and war. Then create a series of tableaux ('freeze-frames') to represent Richard's images for each example.

b Discuss which is more effective: Richard's description in words or your embodiment of the ideas in the form of frozen pictures? Give reasons for your decision.

this son of York King Edward IV, the new King and Richard's older brother

loured scowled, looked threatening

bruisèd arms battered weapons

monuments memorials, relics

alarums battle skirmishes

dreadful inspiring dread

measures dances

front brow, forehead

barbèd steeds war horses covered in armour

fearful full of fear

lascivious pleasing lewd attraction

sportive tricks playful games or sexual exploits

rudely stamped imperfectly shaped

want lack

wanton immoral

ambling sauntering

nymph attractive woman

curtailed cut short

fair proportion good appearance

Cheated of feature robbed of good form or shape

dissembling deceiving, disguising

before my time born prematurely and undeveloped

unfashionable not good-looking or stylish

halt limp

descant on comment on, sing about

King Richard III

Act 1 Scene 1

Outside the Tower of London

Enter RICHARD DUKE OF GLOUCESTER

RICHARD   Now is the winter of our discontent
Made glorious summer by this son of York,
And all the clouds that loured upon our house
In the deep bosom of the ocean buried.
Now are our brows bound with victorious wreaths,   5
Our bruisèd arms hung up for monuments,
Our stern alarums changed to merry meetings,
Our dreadful marches to delightful measures.
Grim-visaged war hath smoothed his wrinkled front,
And now, instead of mounting barbèd steeds   10
To fright the souls of fearful adversaries,
He capers nimbly in a lady's chamber
To the lascivious pleasing of a lute.
But I that am not shaped for sportive tricks
Nor made to court an amorous looking-glass,   15
I that am rudely stamped and want love's majesty
To strut before a wanton ambling nymph,
I that am curtailed of this fair proportion,
Cheated of feature by dissembling nature,
Deformed, unfinished, sent before my time   20
Into this breathing world scarce half made up,
And that so lamely and unfashionable
That dogs bark at me as I halt by them,
Why, I, in this weak piping time of peace,
Have no delight to pass away the time,   25
Unless to see my shadow in the sun
And descant on mine own deformity.

Richard resolves to be evil. He tells the audience that he has arranged for King Edward to see his brother Clarence as a threat and imprison him in the Tower. He jokes about Clarence's plight.

Stagecraft

Richard's soliloquy (in fours)

Richard's opening soliloquy falls into three main parts:

- **Lines 1–13** His comments about the change from war to peace and the character of the new monarch, Edward ('this son of York').
- **Lines 14–27** How Richard feels about the way he looks.
- **Lines 28–41** How he plans to gain power.

A major decision for any director of the play is how to stage this important speech. The conventional way of playing a soliloquy is for the actor to speak directly to the audience, as if inviting them to share his innermost thoughts. In the 1996 movie version starring Ian McKellen, however, Richard speaks the first ten lines as if making a public speech at a state banquet. The rest of the soliloquy is delivered in private in the men's toilet. What ideas do *you* have for staging this speech?

a One member of your group takes the role of director; the other members each choose one of the three sections listed above and read the lines aloud one after the other. Think about how you might create contrasts between voice, gesture and body language as you swap over from section to section.

b What particular words or images give you clues about how you might play the part? Compile a list in your groups.

1 Dramatic irony (in threes)

Richard has just told the audience how he is plotting to destroy his brother George, the Duke of Clarence, so almost all of what Richard says to Clarence's face is filled with **dramatic irony** (when the audience knows more than a character on stage, see p. 251). Richard pretends to be innocent, but he already knows the answers to the questions he asks.

- Two members of the group take the parts of Richard and Clarence and read through the script opposite from line 43. The third person voices Richard's hidden thoughts at appropriate points. For example, when Richard says, 'Brother, good day', does he mean this? What is he really thinking? Practise reading the script in this way up to line 61, then share your presentation with the rest of the class.

entertain spend, enjoy
determinèd decided, resolved

inductions preparations
libels lies about people

subtle crafty
mewed up imprisoned; caged like a hawk
About a prophecy by means of a prophecy
Dive descend
guarded surrounded by guards

Tend'ring caring for
conduct guard
the Tower the Tower of London (both a royal residence and a state prison)

belike maybe

cross-row alphabet

issue offspring, children

toys fancies
commit imprison

And therefore, since I cannot prove a lover
To entertain these fair well-spoken days,
I am determinèd to prove a villain   30
And hate the idle pleasures of these days.
Plots have I laid, inductions dangerous,
By drunken prophecies, libels, and dreams
To set my brother Clarence and the king
In deadly hate the one against the other.   35
And if King Edward be as true and just
As I am subtle, false, and treacherous,
This day should Clarence closely be mewed up
About a prophecy which says that 'G'
Of Edward's heirs the murderer shall be.   40
Dive, thoughts, down to my soul, here Clarence comes.

Enter CLARENCE *and* BRAKENBURY, *guarded*

Brother, good day. What means this armèd guard
That waits upon your grace?

CLARENCE   His majesty,
Tend'ring my person's safety, hath appointed
This conduct to convey me to the Tower.   45

RICHARD   Upon what cause?

CLARENCE   Because my name is George.

RICHARD   Alack, my lord, that fault is none of yours.
He should for that commit your godfathers.
Oh, belike his majesty hath some intent
That you should be new christened in the Tower.   50
But what's the matter, Clarence? May I know?

CLARENCE   Yea, Richard, when I know, but I protest
As yet I do not. But as I can learn,
He hearkens after prophecies and dreams,
And from the cross-row plucks the letter 'G',   55
And says a wizard told him that by 'G'
His issue disinherited should be.
And for my name of George begins with 'G',
It follows in his thought that I am he.
These, as I learn, and suchlike toys as these   60
Hath moved his highness to commit me now.

Richard claims that Queen Elizabeth has caused King Edward to imprison Clarence, and that she and Jane Shore have become powers behind the throne. Brakenbury's unease is dismissed with innuendo and sexual puns.

Themes

Richard's attitude to women

Richard comments that 'men are ruled by women' (line 62). He blames Queen Elizabeth and Clarence blames King Edward's mistress, Jane Shore, for having Clarence sent to the Tower. In line 64, Richard sneeringly refers to Queen Elizabeth as 'My lady Grey' because before her marriage to Edward in 1464 she was the widow of Sir Thomas Grey. Elizabeth used her position as Queen to gain power and influence for her large family, the Woodvilles, and in so doing aroused much jealousy. In the course of the play, Richard frequently refers to both Jane Shore and Elizabeth as sources of trouble, as if they pose a threat to him in his pursuit of power.

- Look through the script opposite and make a list of all the words Richard uses that are insulting to women. As you work through the play, keep in mind Richard's attitude to women and consider the true extent of women's power and influence in this society.

1 Making Brakenbury feel inferior? (in threes)

Brakenbury (the courtier who is taking Clarence to the Tower) addresses Richard and Clarence as 'your graces' (line 84) because they are royal dukes, but Richard calls him 'man' (line 90) and makes jokes at Brakenbury's expense. How might you show their different status on stage?

a Number each group member 1 to 3, where 1 is someone of very high status, 2 is someone of middle status and 3 is someone of low status. Experiment with how these people relate to one another:

- How do you look at one another?
- How do you say hello to one another?
- How do you sit down, walk around and so on?

b Take Richard's line 90 ('We speak no treason, man') and freeze the action in role as Richard, Clarence and Brakenbury. Show your tableau to the rest of the class. Can they guess who is who, using clues from positioning, body language and facial expressions?

c Compile a list of reasons why Richard might enjoy trying to make Brakenbury feel inferior. Do you think he succeeds?

worship honour

kindred family
night-walking heralds secret messengers
trudge trail back and forth
suppliant beggar of favours
delivery Hastings's release from prison
her deity her god (King Edward or Jane Shore's evil spirits)
Lord Chamberlain Hastings
livery uniform
o'er-worn worn out, second-hand
widow Queen Elizabeth, whose first husband died
dubbed created
straitly given in charge strictly ordered
conference conversation
Of what degree soever no matter what their social status

Well struck advanced

cherry lip red lips (a sign of beauty)
bonny pretty
passing pleasing tongue exceptionally well spoken
nought nothing
Naught naughtiness (with sexual overtones)

RICHARD	Why, this it is when men are ruled by women.
	'Tis not the king that sends you to the Tower.
	My lady Grey, his wife, Clarence, 'tis she
	That tempts him to this harsh extremity. 65
	Was it not she and that good man of worship,
	Anthony Woodville, her brother there,
	That made him send Lord Hastings to the Tower,
	From whence this present day he is delivered?
	We are not safe, Clarence, we are not safe. 70
CLARENCE	By heaven, I think there is no man secure
	But the queen's kindred and night-walking heralds
	That trudge betwixt the king and Mistress Shore.
	Heard you not what an humble suppliant
	Lord Hastings was for her delivery? 75
RICHARD	Humbly complaining to her deity
	Got my Lord Chamberlain his liberty.
	I'll tell you what, I think it is our way,
	If we will keep in favour with the king,
	To be her men and wear her livery. 80
	The jealous, o'er-worn widow and herself,
	Since that our brother dubbed them gentlewomen,
	Are mighty gossips in our monarchy.
BRAKENBURY	I beseech your graces both to pardon me;
	His majesty hath straitly given in charge 85
	That no man shall have private conference,
	Of what degree soever, with your brother.
RICHARD	Even so. And please your worship, Brakenbury,
	You may partake of any thing we say.
	We speak no treason, man. We say the king 90
	Is wise and virtuous, and his noble queen
	Well struck in years, fair, and not jealous.
	We say that Shore's wife hath a pretty foot,
	A cherry lip, a bonny eye, a passing pleasing tongue,
	And that the queen's kindred are made gentlefolks. 95
	How say you, sir? Can you deny all this?
BRAKENBURY	With this, my lord, myself have nought to do.
RICHARD	Naught to do with Mistress Shore? I tell thee, fellow,
	He that doth naught with her (excepting one)
	Were best to do it secretly alone. 100

Richard promises to do any service he can to ensure Clarence's release. Alone on stage, Richard reveals that he really seeks Clarence's death. Hastings swears vengeance on those who caused his imprisonment.

1 Saying one thing but meaning another (in pairs)

A major feature of Richard's language is that his words frequently have double meanings. Listeners hear one thing, but he means something else. Most of what he says to Clarence has a meaning that Clarence does not perceive. For example, when Richard says 'Brother, farewell', Clarence probably hears a friendly voice, but Richard may mean 'Goodbye for ever because you'll soon be dead'.

• As one person slowly speaks lines 107–16, pausing frequently, the other person says in each pause what Richard probably means.

Characters

Who's who? (in pairs)

• Draw up a list of who's who in the play so far and show their relationships to one another. Use the list of characters on pages 4–5 and devise symbols, or a colour code, to show status and relationships between the people who have appeared so far in the scene.

• Where would you fit Lord Hastings? Hastings is a faithful supporter of the House of York, but he is much opposed to Queen Elizabeth and the rest of the Woodville family. Hastings' influence weakened during the illness of his patron King Edward, and that loss of power may have led to his imprisonment. Hastings was Jane Shore's lover, however, and she may have used her influence with the King to secure his early release from prison.

Language in the play

Birds of prey (by yourself)

Throughout the play, the imagery of birds and animals is often used to describe Richard.

a Who is Hastings referring to when he talks of 'the eagles' (line 133) and 'kites and buzzards' (line 134)?

b Write a paragraph describing Shakespeare's use of animal imagery in this part of the play and its effect on characterisation and atmosphere. Remember to refer to the script in detail and to use embedded quotations.

withal also
Forbear stop

abjects despised outcasts or servants (Richard's joking pun on 'subjects')

widow (Queen Elizabeth – Richard again mocks her)
enfranchise free (from prison or from life)

perforce without choice ('Patience perforce' was a common proverb for a condition that had no remedy)

new-delivered recently released from prison

brooked endured

to give them thanks to be revenged on them
cause of my imprisonment (Hastings refers to the Woodville clan)

BRAKENBURY	What one, my lord?
RICHARD	Her husband, knave. Wouldst thou betray me?
BRAKENBURY	I do beseech your grace to pardon me, and withal
	Forbear your conference with the noble duke.
CLARENCE	We know thy charge, Brakenbury, and will obey.
RICHARD	We are the queen's abjects and must obey.
	Brother, farewell. I will unto the king,
	And whatsoe'er you will employ me in,
	Were it to call King Edward's widow 'sister',
	I will perform it to enfranchise you.
	Meantime, this deep disgrace in brotherhood
	Touches me deeper than you can imagine.
CLARENCE	I know it pleaseth neither of us well.
RICHARD	Well, your imprisonment shall not be long.
	I will deliver you or else lie for you.
	Meantime, have patience.
CLARENCE	I must perforce. Farewell.

Exeunt Clarence[*, Brakenbury, and guards*]

RICHARD	Go, tread the path that thou shalt ne'er return.
	Simple, plain Clarence, I do love thee so
	That I will shortly send thy soul to heaven,
	If heaven will take the present at our hands.
	But who comes here? The new-delivered Hastings?

Enter LORD HASTINGS

HASTINGS	Good time of day unto my gracious lord.
RICHARD	As much unto my good Lord Chamberlain.
	Well are you welcome to this open air.
	How hath your lordship brooked imprisonment?
HASTINGS	With patience, noble lord, as prisoners must.
	But I shall live, my lord, to give them thanks
	That were the cause of my imprisonment.
RICHARD	No doubt, no doubt, and so shall Clarence too,
	For they that were your enemies are his
	And have prevailed as much on him as you.
HASTINGS	More pity that the eagles should be mewed
	While kites and buzzards play at liberty.
RICHARD	What news abroad?

Line numbers: 105, 110, 115, 120, 125, 130, 135

Hastings says Edward is near to death. Richard blames the King's lifestyle. Alone on stage, Richard hopes that Edward will not die until Clarence has been executed. He reveals his plan to marry Anne.

1 What is King Edward like?

On every page of the play so far, there have been clues to King Edward's character. 'Oh, he hath kept an evil diet long' (line 140) suggests that for a long time Edward has lived wildly.

- Look back at what Richard, Clarence and Hastings have said about Edward so far in Scene 1. Compile a list of between six and ten words that sum up your impression of the King.

fear him fear for his life

by Saint John (Richard swears an oath)

diet way of life

Characters

Richard's revelations (in pairs)

The soliloquy that ends this scene (lines 146–63) offers many oportunities to explore Richard's wicked revelations through a range of dramatic choices regarding changes in voice inflection, emphasis, tone, pitch, pause and gesture.

a Sometimes actors play the lines with a lot of humour. In line 153, 'bustle' (be busy) often gains a laugh as it catches the obvious rogueishness of Richard's character. Take turns to speak the lines with actions that might be used to provoke laughter.

b Sometimes actors play the lines with a sense of outrageous evil. Lines 149–58, in particular, provoke a response in audiences. Take turns to speak the lines in a way that will most shock the audience.

c In role as an actor, write notes about how you intend to speak this soliloquy and what aspects of Richard's character you want to portray at each line or two.

packed with post-horse sent as quickly as possible

steeled strengthened

deep profoundly crafty, subtle

bustle be active

Warwick's youngest daughter Anne Neville

her father her father-in-law (Henry VI in the play)

wench girl

secret close intent hidden purpose

I run ... market I am getting too far ahead of myself

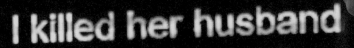

I killed her husband

HASTINGS	No news so bad abroad as this at home:
	The king is sickly, weak, and melancholy,
	And his physicians fear him mightily.
RICHARD	Now by Saint John, that news is bad indeed.
	Oh, he hath kept an evil diet long 140
	And over-much consumed his royal person.
	'Tis very grievous to be thought upon.
	Where is he, in his bed?
HASTINGS	He is.
RICHARD	Go you before, and I will follow you. 145

Exit Hastings

He cannot live, I hope, and must not die
Till George be packed with post-horse up to heaven.
I'll in to urge his hatred more to Clarence
With lies well steeled with weighty arguments,
And if I fail not in my deep intent, 150
Clarence hath not another day to live:
Which done, God take King Edward to his mercy
And leave the world for me to bustle in!
For then I'll marry Warwick's youngest daughter.
What though I killed her husband and her father? 155
The readiest way to make the wench amends
Is to become her husband and her father,
The which will I, not all so much for love
As for another secret close intent
By marrying her which I must reach unto. 160
But yet I run before my horse to market.
Clarence still breathes, Edward still lives and reigns;
When they are gone, then must I count my gains. *Exit*

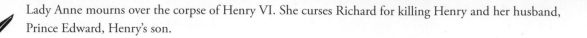

Lady Anne mourns over the corpse of Henry VI. She curses Richard for killing Henry and her husband, Prince Edward, Henry's son.

Stagecraft

'The corpse of KING HENRY VI is carried in'

The dead body of the former King is on stage throughout Scene 2 as a dramatic reminder of Anne's grief and loss. Imagine you are the stage designer. How do you deal with the body on stage? Compile notes and/or sketches in your Director's Journal. Remember that the body:

- is royal (but this is not a state funeral)
- is of the Lancastrian dynasty
- has been on view for some time as Anne grieves over it
- has to be transported across the stage.

HALBERDS soldiers carrying battle-axes

hearse bier or coffin

obsequiously as a mourner

Th'untimely the premature

key-cold very cold (i.e. as cold as a metal key)

figure form, shape

blood family

Be it let it be

invocate pray to

Language in the play

Anne's grief and anger (in pairs)

a Together, read Anne's speech and pick out one key word or short phrase per line. Keeping these key words or phrases in their original order, devise a dramatic presentation of your shortened script. Experiment with different drama strategies, such as tone of voice, choral speech, mime, movement or tableaux. Remember, you cannot add any other words. Share your performances with the rest of the class. Which one is the most effective and why?

b As an extension to this activity, you could choose some background music that you feel captures the mood and tone of the speech. Be prepared to explain why you think it is suitable.

the selfsame the very same

windows wounds

helpless balm tears (bodies would traditionally be embalmed prior to burial)

holes wounds

More direful hap betide a more dreadful fate fall upon

abortive premature

Prodigious abnormal

Write about it

Curses

During the course of the play, several prophecies and curses are made – some of which come true in bitterly ironic ways. In lines 14–28, Anne utters a series of vengeful curses against the man who murdered her husband and his father.

- Write two paragraphs summarising Anne's curses and commenting on the language she uses. For example, think about the kinds of creatures she refers to and which words she repeats in the course of her speech.

thee (line 28) Henry VI

Chertsey a town south-west of London, where there is a monastery

Paul's St Paul's cathedral (the former King is not afforded a state funeral)

interrèd buried

Act 1 Scene 2
Near the Tower of London

The corpse of KING HENRY VI *is carried in accompanied by* LADY
ANNE, HALBERDS, TRESSEL, BERKELEY *and other gentlemen*

ANNE   Set down, set down your honourable load,
If honour may be shrouded in a hearse,
Whilst I awhile obsequiously lament
Th'untimely fall of virtuous Lancaster.
Poor key-cold figure of a holy king,   5
Pale ashes of the house of Lancaster,
Thou bloodless remnant of that royal blood,
Be it lawful that I invocate thy ghost
To hear the lamentations of poor Anne,
Wife to thy Edward, to thy slaughtered son,   10
Stabbed by the selfsame hand that made these wounds.
Lo, in these windows that let forth thy life,
I pour the helpless balm of my poor eyes.
Oh, cursèd be the hand that made these holes,
Cursed the heart that had the heart to do it,   15
Cursed the blood that let this blood from hence.
More direful hap betide that hated wretch
That makes us wretched by the death of thee
Than I can wish to wolves, to spiders, toads,
Or any creeping venomed thing that lives.   20
If ever he have child, abortive be it,
Prodigious, and untimely brought to light,
Whose ugly and unnatural aspèct
May fright the hopeful mother at the view,
And that be heir to his unhappiness.   25
If ever he have wife, let her be made
More miserable by the death of him
Than I am made by my young lord and thee.
Come now towards Chertsey with your holy load,
Taken from Paul's to be interrèd there.   30
And still as you are weary of this weight,
Rest you while I lament King Henry's corpse.

Richard orders the guards to set down the coffin. He threatens violence if they disobey him. Anne accuses Richard of being a devil. Henry's wounds open and begin to bleed. Anne calls for Richard's death.

Stagecraft

Power-play (in large groups)

Richard's entrance changes the mood of the scene and creates a moment of dramatic tension between Richard, Anne and the men accompanying her.

a Create a series of three tableaux using the following lines:

- 'Stay, you that bear the corpse' (line 33)
- 'Unmannered dog, stand thou when I command' (line 39)
- 'What do you tremble? Are you all afraid?' (line 43)

Think about the ways in which various characters react to these lines – what gestures might the speaker make? Who looks at whom and in what way? Where is each character positioned – at a distance or closer together? Place a line of chairs to denote where the corpse is stationed at each line and consider what difference it makes if Anne is accompanied by three or four men, or ten.

b Share your tableaux with the class. Class members can take it in turn to tap various characters on the shoulder and ask them to voice their thoughts at this precise moment.

c Discuss which tableau suggests the highest moment of dramatic tension and why. Then write a note in your Director's Journal explaining how you would stage this part of the scene.

Characters

Anne's view of Richard

Read through the script opposite, paying particular attention to all the different words Anne uses to describe Richard. List Anne's descriptions in a table similar to the one below, and then consider what impression this gives of Richard. Add to this table as you continue working through Scene 2.

Description	Line	Impression of Richard
'fiend'	34	He's evil
'devil'	45	He's a creature from hell

halberd battle-axe
to my foot to the ground
spurn stamp

Avaunt be gone (used to banish supernatural beings)
minister agent
but only
curst spiteful
hence go away
exclaims outcries
heinous evil

Henry's wounds … afresh the scabs on Henry's wounds bleed again (people believed that a body would start to bleed again in the presence of the murderer)
exhales draws out

deluge flood
mad'st made, created

quick alive

charity Christian belief

Enter RICHARD DUKE OF GLOUCESTER

RICHARD	Stay, you that bear the corpse, and set it down.
ANNE	What black magician conjures up this fiend
	To stop devoted charitable deeds? 35
RICHARD	Villains, set down the corpse, or by Saint Paul,
	I'll make a corpse of him that disobeys.
GENTLEMAN	My lord, stand back and let the coffin pass.
RICHARD	Unmannered dog, stand thou when I command.
	Advance thy halberd higher than my breast, 40
	Or by Saint Paul, I'll strike thee to my foot
	And spurn upon thee, beggar, for thy boldness.
ANNE	What, do you tremble? Are you all afraid?
	Alas, I blame you not, for you are mortal,
	And mortal eyes cannot endure the devil. 45
	Avaunt, thou dreadful minister of hell.
	Thou hadst but power over his mortal body;
	His soul thou canst not have. Therefore be gone.
RICHARD	Sweet saint, for charity, be not so curst.
ANNE	Foul devil, for God's sake hence, and trouble us not, 50
	For thou hast made the happy earth thy hell,
	Filled it with cursing cries and deep exclaims.
	If thou delight to view thy heinous deeds,
	Behold this pattern of thy butcheries.
	O gentlemen, see, see, dead Henry's wounds 55
	Open their còngealed mouths and bleed afresh.
	Blush, blush, thou lump of foul deformity,
	For 'tis thy presence that exhales this blood
	From cold and empty veins where no blood dwells.
	Thy deeds inhuman and unnatural 60
	Provokes this deluge most unnatural.
	O God, which this blood mad'st, revenge his death.
	O earth, which this blood drink'st, revenge his death.
	Either heav'n with lightning strike the murd'rer dead,
	Or earth gape open wide and eat him quick, 65
	As thou dost swallow up this good king's blood,
	Which his hell-governed arm hath butcherèd.
RICHARD	Lady, you know no rules of charity,
	Which renders good for bad, blessings for curses.

Language in the play

Tennis-match language (in pairs, then whole class)

In lines 68–118, Anne's and Richard's words move rhythmically back and forth like the ball in a tennis rally. The technical term for this rapid alternating exchange of lines is **stichomythia** (see p. 249). The same words are sometimes repeated, or words with opposite meanings are flung back at the first speaker.

a Draw two columns on a sheet of paper, one headed 'Anne', the other headed 'Richard'. Collect examples of matched repetitions or contrasts. Three have been given below – how many more can you find?

Anne	Richard
'No beast so fierce, but knows some touch of pity' (line 71)	'But I know none, and therefore am no beast' (line 72)
'devils tell the truth' (73)	'Angels are so angry' (line 74)
'Vouchsafe, diffused infection of a man' (line 78)	'Vouchsafe, divine perfection of a woman' (line 75)

b Collate a whole-class version of this table. Divide the class into two lines (A and B), facing each other as if opponents: line A is Anne, line B is Richard. The line taking the role of Anne starts by saying together 'No beast so fierce…'. Richard's line then answers it. Experiment with different ways of saying the lines – for example, whispered, shouted, hissed, angrily hurled, calmly stated and so on. Try changing the pace, just as in a real tennis rally, and see how your opponent reacts.

c As a class, discuss which style of delivery works best and why.

Vouchsafe allow

leave permission

circumstance evidence

diffused widespread (like an infection)

èxcuse current genuine excuse

slew killed

Edward (Richard's brother)

falchion broadsword

smoking in his blood steaming with his still-hot blood

bend aim

sland'rous spreading malicious lies

aught anything

hedgehog (an insulting term for Richard, see p. 66)

ANNE	Villain, thou know'st nor law of God nor man.	70
	No beast so fierce but knows some touch of pity.	
RICHARD	But I know none, and therefore am no beast.	
ANNE	Oh, wonderful, when devils tell the truth!	
RICHARD	More wonderful, when angels are so angry.	
	Vouchsafe, divine perfection of a woman,	75
	Of these supposèd crimes to give me leave	
	By circumstance but to acquit myself.	
ANNE	Vouchsafe, diffused infection of man,	
	Of these known evils but to give me leave	
	By circumstance to curse thy cursèd self.	80
RICHARD	Fairer than tongue can name thee, let me have	
	Some patient leisure to excuse myself.	
ANNE	Fouler than heart can think thee, thou canst make	
	No èxcuse current but to hang thyself.	
RICHARD	By such despair I should accuse myself.	85
ANNE	And by despairing shalt thou stand excused	
	For doing worthy vengeance on thyself,	
	That didst unworthy slaughter upon others.	
RICHARD	Say that I slew them not.	
ANNE	Then say they were not slain.	90
	But dead they are, and, devilish slave, by thee.	
RICHARD	I did not kill your husband.	
ANNE	Why, then he is alive.	
RICHARD	Nay, he is dead, and slain by Edward's hands.	
ANNE	In thy foul throat thou liest. Queen Margaret saw	95
	Thy murd'rous falchion smoking in his blood,	
	The which thou once didst bend against her breast,	
	But that thy brothers beat aside the point.	
RICHARD	I was provokèd by her sland'rous tongue,	
	That laid their guilt upon my guiltless shoulders.	100
ANNE	Thou wast provokèd by thy bloody mind,	
	That never dream'st on aught but butcheries.	
	Didst thou not kill this king?	
RICHARD	I grant ye.	
ANNE	Dost grant me, hedgehog? Then God grant me too	105
	Thou mayst be damnèd for that wicked deed.	
	Oh, he was gentle, mild, and virtuous.	

Anne wishes Richard in hell but he offers himself as her new husband. He claims that her beauty caused him to kill. She curses her beauty and him, hoping for revenge.

1 An unlikely wooing scene (in pairs)

Act 1 Scene 2 is often referred to as 'the wooing scene' because this is where Richard attempts to propose marriage to Anne.

- Read through the whole script opposite. Then list all the ways that this scene differs from conventional 'wooing scenes' in which a lover talks of marriage. In particular, consider such scenes in any other Shakespeare plays you are familiar with. Think about setting and context, as well as the words spoken by the couple.

2 'Your bedchamber' (in pairs)

Look again at Richard's line 115, where he tells Anne he wants to share her bed. On stage this can be a truly shocking moment. Think carefully about what Anne's reaction might be to Richard's advances. For example, might she be:

- visibly repulsed
- wrong-footed and confused
- angry and confident
- fearful and intimidated
- sexually attracted to Richard (despite not liking him)?

a Try different ways of acting out this part of the scene (from line 109 up to Richard's 'I know so' at line 119).

b It is easy to forget that, according to the stage directions, Richard's proposition takes place in public, with pall bearers, soldiers and others all looking on. Do you think that makes it more or less shocking?

▼ How would you interpret this moment between Anne and Richard?

holp helped

Ill rest betide may bad sleep visit

timeless untimely

Thou wast ... effect you were the reason

To undertake ... world I would have killed the whole world
homicide murderer
rend tear
wrack ruin

Black night ... thy life (notice two antitheses in line 136: night/day, death/life)

bereft robbed

22

RICHARD	The better for the king of heaven that hath him.
ANNE	He is in heaven, where thou shalt never come.
RICHARD	Let him thank me, that holp to send him thither,
	For he was fitter for that place than earth.
ANNE	And thou unfit for any place but hell.
RICHARD	Yes, one place else, if you will hear me name it.
ANNE	Some dungeon.
RICHARD	Your bedchamber.
ANNE	Ill rest betide the chamber where thou liest.
RICHARD	So will it, madam, till I lie with you.
ANNE	I hope so.
RICHARD	I know so. But gentle Lady Anne,
	To leave this keen encounter of our wits
	And fall something into a slower method,
	Is not the causer of the timeless deaths
	Of these Plantagenets, Henry and Edward,
	As blameful as the executioner?
ANNE	Thou wast the cause and most accursed effect.
RICHARD	Your beauty was the cause of that effect:
	Your beauty, that did haunt me in my sleep
	To undertake the death of all the world,
	So I might live one hour in your sweet bosom.
ANNE	If I thought that, I tell thee, homicide,
	These nails should rend that beauty from my cheeks.
RICHARD	These eyes could not endure that beauty's wrack.
	You should not blemish it if I stood by.
	As all the world is cheerèd by the sun,
	So I by that. It is my day, my life.
ANNE	Black night o'ershade thy day, and death thy life.
RICHARD	Curse not thyself, fair creature; thou art both.
ANNE	I would I were, to be revenged on thee.
RICHARD	It is a quarrel most unnatural
	To be revenged on him that loveth thee.
ANNE	It is a quarrel just and reasonable
	To be revenged on him that killed my husband.
RICHARD	He that bereft thee, lady, of thy husband
	Did it to help thee to a better husband.
ANNE	His better doth not breathe upon the earth.

110

115

120

125

130

135

140

145

Richard tells Anne that he could love her better than Edward, her former husband. He claims that Anne has the power to make him weep when other griefs leave him unmoved. He continues to woo her.

1 Why Plantagenet?

Plantagenet was the family name of the kings of England between 1154 and 1485. Both the houses of York and Lancaster, which fought in the Wars of the Roses, were Plantagenets. This is the second time in this scene that Richard has used his family name (the first is in line 123).

- Why do you think he uses the name Plantagenet again here to refer to himself?

2 'Why dost thou spit at me?' (in small groups)

Richard's 'Here' (line 149) seems to be the trigger for Anne's strong reaction. Is it this word alone that so angers Anne, or are there other reasons for her contemptuous response?

a Carefully read the three or four lines leading up to Anne's reaction and discuss what you think they mean.

b What gesture do you think Richard makes as he says 'Here'? Try out a few and see which you think works best.

c Pool your ideas on what the action of spitting at someone means and how this might vary in different cultures. How might some of the items on your list help you to advise Anne how to play her line 150? Add your notes to your Director's Journal.

3 Richard's audacity

Richard's quick-witted wordplay continues. His lines 156–71 turn Anne's image of the eyes of a monster into his own eyes, which weep for Anne's beauty but are unable to weep at tragic events such as the death of Rutland and of his own father. (Rutland was Richard's younger brother, murdered in 1470.)

- Look again at lines 150–9, which show how Richard reverses Anne's intended insults ('poison', 'infect', 'dead', 'die', 'kill' and 'eyes') in his audacious attempt to win her affection. Make two lists – one of Anne's insults and another of Richard's clever answers.

mortal fatal

basilisks monster serpents that killed with a look

aspècts appearances

Rutland Richard's dead brother

bedashed drenched

sued to asked favours of
smoothing flattering
proposed offered as
sues begs, implores, pleads with

RICHARD	He lives that loves thee better than he could.
ANNE	Name him.
RICHARD	Plantagenet.
ANNE	Why, that was he.
RICHARD	The selfsame name, but one of better nature.
ANNE	Where is he?
RICHARD	Here.

[She] spits at him

       Why dost thou spit at me?

ANNE	Would it were mortal poison for thy sake.	150
RICHARD	Never came poison from so sweet a place.	
ANNE	Never hung poison on a fouler toad.	
	Out of my sight. Thou dost infect mine eyes.	
RICHARD	Thine eyes, sweet lady, have infected mine.	
ANNE	Would they were basilisks', to strike thee dead.	155
RICHARD	I would they were, that I might die at once,	
	For now they kill me with a living death.	
	Those eyes of thine from mine have drawn salt tears,	
	Shamed their aspècts with store of childish drops.	
	These eyes, which never shed remorseful tear,	160
	No, when my father York and Edward wept	
	To hear the piteous moan that Rutland made	
	When black-faced Clifford shook his sword at him,	
	Nor when thy warlike father, like a child,	
	Told the sad story of my father's death	165
	And twenty times made pause to sob and weep,	
	That all the standers-by had wet their cheeks	
	Like trees bedashed with rain. In that sad time	
	My manly eyes did scorn an humble tear.	
	And what these sorrows could not thence exhale	170
	Thy beauty hath, and made them blind with weeping.	
	I never sued to friend nor enemy.	
	My tongue could never learn sweet smoothing word.	
	But now thy beauty is proposed my fee,	
	My proud heart sues and prompts my tongue to speak.	175

         She looks scornfully at him

Teach not thy lip such scorn, for it was made
For kissing, lady, not for such contempt.

Richard offers Anne the opportunity to stab him. He admits he killed King Henry and Prince Edward. Anne refuses to use the dagger, so Richard offers to kill himself. He places his ring on Anne's finger.

1 Anne seduced? (in pairs)

Richard's delight in clever wordplay is revealed through the return to the language of stichomythia (see p. 20), but Anne's replies now seem less confident than earlier, and, unlike at the beginning of the scene, she is no longer abusive.

a Read lines 197–205 aloud, experimenting with the way Richard and Anne speak. For instance, is Anne:

- angry
- calmly confident
- scared or nervous
- humouring Richard just to get rid of him
- genuinely seduced by Richard's charms
- confused?

b Consider a range of ways to read Richard's part, then discuss which reading works best and why.

c Why do you think Anne does not take the opportunity to kill Richard?

▼ Choose a line from the script opposite that you think would work as a caption for this image.

lays his breast open opens his shirt to reveal his bare chest

offers at aims

dispatch kill me

falls lowers

dissembler hypocrite

àccessary guilty party, accomplice

figured represented

put up put away

Vouchsafe accept
Look how just as
encompasseth encircles, rings

	If thy revengeful heart cannot forgive,	
	Lo, here I lend thee this sharp-pointed sword,	
	Which if thou please to hide in this true breast	180
	And let the soul forth that adoreth thee,	
	I lay it naked to the deadly stroke	
	And humbly beg the death upon my knee.	

He lays his breast open[;] she offers at with his sword

Nay, do not pause, for I did kill King Henry,
But 'twas thy beauty that provokèd me.   185
Nay, now dispatch; 'twas I that stabbed young Edward,
But 'twas thy heavenly face that set me on.

She falls the sword

Take up the sword again, or take up me.

ANNE   Arise, dissembler; though I wish thy death,
I will not be thy executioner.   190

RICHARD   Then bid me kill myself, and I will do it.

ANNE   I have already.

RICHARD   That was in thy rage.
Speak it again, and even with the word,
This hand, which for thy love did kill thy love,
Shall for thy love kill a far truer love.   195
To both their deaths shalt thou be àccessary.

ANNE   I would I knew thy heart.

RICHARD   'Tis figured in my tongue.

ANNE   I fear me both are false.

RICHARD   Then never man was true.   200

ANNE   Well, well, put up your sword.

RICHARD   Say then my peace is made.

ANNE   That shalt thou know hereafter.

RICHARD   But shall I live in hope?

ANNE   All men, I hope, live so.   205

RICHARD   Vouchsafe to wear this ring.
Look how my ring encompasseth thy finger.
Even so thy breast encloseth my poor heart.
Wear both of them, for both of them are thine.
And if thy poor devoted servant may   210
But beg one favour at thy gracious hand,
Thou dost confirm his happiness forever.

ANNE   What is it?

Richard persuades Anne to stop mourning and allow him to take charge of King Henry's funeral. He exults at his success but predicts he will soon abandon Anne.

1 Richard the hypocrite (whole class)

As soon as Anne leaves the stage, Richard drops his public mask and becomes the schemer and master planner. In his soliloquy (which continues up to line 267), Richard revels in his triumph in successfully wooing the woman whose handsome husband, Edward, he has murdered. The rhythm and energy of the lines reveal his pleasure at having carried off such a coup.

a Form a large circle. Read Richard's soliloquy round the class, handing over to the next person at each punctuation mark. Then repeat the reading, but more quickly this time. Say aloud each phrase or line with as much energy and glee as you can. Add an appropriate gesture suggested by the words.

b Split into small groups and look more closely at the punctuation of this speech. Richard includes a number of questions and exclamations. What dramatic effect do these have? In your groups, suggest some ideas and then come back together as a class and share your thoughts.

Write about it

Advice to Anne

a Imagine that after the engagement of Anne and Richard has been announced at court, a shocked friend of Anne's writes to her pointing out all the reasons why she should not marry Richard. Write the letter. You might want to include:

- the circumstances surrounding her former husband's death
- the history of their families
- the timing of the engagement
- Anne's emotional state
- Richard's appearance
- Richard's reputation.

b As an additional challenge, you could write a second letter to Anne in the guise of another friend, this time persuading her that it is a shrewd diplomatic move to marry Richard. You might want to use the same prompts as above, but draw different conclusions from that information.

sad designs mourning (for Henry VI)

presently immediately

repair go to, withdraw

Crosby House (Richard's London residence)

interred buried

expedient swift

divers several

unknown secret

boon wish

Whitefriars another part of London

humour mood

bleeding witness bleeding body of Henry

by nearby

bars obstacles

suit wooing

all the world to nothing with nothing in my favour

Framed ... nature excessively gifted

right completely

RICHARD   That it may please you leave these sad designs
           To him that hath most cause to be a mourner   215
           And presently repair to Crosby House,
           Where, after I have solemnly interred
           At Chertsey monast'ry this noble king
           And wet his grave with my repentant tears,
           I will with all expedient duty see you.   220
           For divers unknown reasons, I beseech you,
           Grant me this boon.

ANNE   With all my heart, and much it joys me, too,
           To see you are become so penitent.
           Tressel and Berkeley, go along with me.   225

RICHARD   Bid me farewell.

ANNE   'Tis more than you deserve,
           But since you teach me how to flatter you,
           Imagine I have said farewell already.

                                        Exeunt two with Anne

GENTLEMAN Towards Chertsey, noble lord?

RICHARD   No, to Whitefriars; there attend my coming.   230

                  Exeunt [all but Richard with the] corpse

           Was ever woman in this humour wooed?
           Was ever woman in this humour won?
           I'll have her, but I will not keep her long.
           What, I that killed her husband and his father,
           To take her in her heart's extremest hate,   235
           With curses in her mouth, tears in her eyes,
           The bleeding witness of my hatred by,
           Having God, her conscience, and these bars against me,
           And I no friends to back my suit withal
           But the plain devil and dissembling looks?   240
           And yet to win her, all the world to nothing!
           Ha!
           Hath she forgot already that brave prince,
           Edward, her lord, whom I some three months since
           Stabbed in my angry mood at Tewkesbury?   245
           A sweeter and a lovelier gentleman,
           Framed in the prodigality of nature,
           Young, valiant, wise, and (no doubt) right royal,
           The spacious world cannot again afford.

Richard marvels at Anne's acceptance of him, in spite of his unattractive outward appearance. Elizabeth and her relatives discuss King Edward's illness.

1 The mask slips? (in pairs)

Imagine you are an actor and director in rehearsal. The actor playing Richard argues that in lines 250–8, Richard reveals genuine feelings of self-disgust and should speak the lines in such a way as to gain sympathy from the audience. The director disagrees, claiming that Richard is cynically mocking his own appearance, glorying in having seduced Anne in such an outrageous way. He believes that Richard should speak triumphantly.

a One person reads the lines as the actor suggests, the other as the director feels is right. Afterwards, talk together about which style seems the more successful.

b In your Director's Journal, write a paragraph outlining your ideas about the way this part of the speech should be played. Explain your conclusions, with reference to what you already know of Richard.

Characters

Richard in images

In the final couplet of the soliloquy, Richard picks up the contrasting images of sun and shadow once more, suggesting that he is made to cast a permanent shadow.

- Look back over Act 1 Scene 2 and pick out some of the most striking images Anne has used to describe Richard. Create a collage of these images, using pictures from newspapers, magazines and the Internet.

Stagecraft

A change of scene

Scene 3 offers a sharp change of scene and characters. There were no lights on Shakespeare's stage, nor were there the resources to build complicated sets. New characters were indicated by means of costumes and simple props.

- If you were directing a stage version of the play with limited resources at your disposal, how would you let your audience know that the scene has shifted to the royal palace? Consider music or other sounds, costumes, simple furniture, actions and gestures. Write your ideas in your Director's Journal.

abase lower, debase
cropped cut off

Edward's moiety a tiny fraction of his worth
denier worthless coin

proper handsome
be at charges for buy
entertain employ

turn yon fellow put that fellow (a disrespectful reference to the corpse of Henry VI)
glass mirror

betide on happen to

And will she yet abase her eyes on me,   250
That cropped the golden prime of this sweet prince
And made her widow to a woeful bed?
On me, whose all not equals Edward's moiety?
On me, that halts and am misshapen thus?
My dukedom to a beggarly denier,   255
I do mistake my person all this while.
Upon my life, she finds (although I cannot)
Myself to be a marv'lous proper man.
I'll be at charges for a looking-glass
And entertain a score or two of tailors   260
To study fashions to adorn my body.
Since I am crept in favour with myself,
I will maintain it with some little cost.
But first I'll turn yon fellow in his grave
And then return lamenting to my love.   265
Shine out, fair sun, till I have bought a glass,
That I may see my shadow as I pass.

Exit

Act 1 Scene 3
London: a room in King Edward's palace

Enter QUEEN ELIZABETH, LORD RIVERS, LORD GREY *and the*
MARQUESS OF DORSET

RIVERS	Have patience, madam. There's no doubt his majesty
	Will soon recover his accustomed health.
GREY	In that you brook it ill, it makes him worse.
	Therefore, for God's sake, entertain good comfort,
	And cheer his grace with quick and merry eyes. 5
ELIZABETH	If he were dead, what would betide on me?
GREY	No other harm but loss of such a lord.
ELIZABETH	The loss of such a lord includes all harms.
GREY	The heavens have blessed you with a goodly son
	To be your comforter when he is gone. 10

Elizabeth claims that Richard, soon to be Protector, hates her and her family. Buckingham says that the dying King Edward wants reconciliation between the factions. Richard condemns those who complain of him to the King.

1 Concerns for the future (in pairs)

All of the Woodville family faction hope the King will recover, as do Buckingham and Stanley. Elizabeth expresses her concerns for the future.

- Copy the diagram below and collect together all the troubles that are on Elizabeth's mind from line 6 to line 41 (add more circles if you need to).

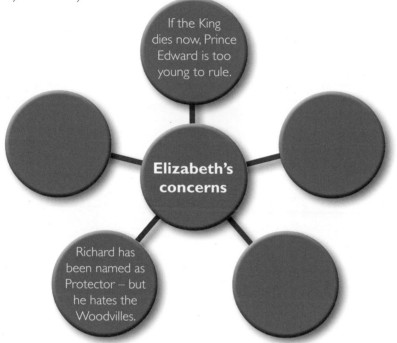

If the King dies now, Prince Edward is too young to rule.

Elizabeth's concerns

Richard has been named as Protector – but he hates the Woodvilles.

2 Enter Richard (in groups of six or seven)

Just as we learn that there is hope for reconciliation between the various warring factions, Richard suddenly makes an appearance and introduces a new note of conflict.

a Remind yourselves who is on stage at the moment of Richard's entrance, and share out the roles. Using the information you have gathered from the play so far, group the characters according to their allegiances. Freeze the action at line 42 ('They do me wrong and I will not endure it'). Decide how to show the delicate political situation from the way people stand or sit, the space between them and the direction of their gaze.

b Discuss who Richard might be addressing. For example, do you think line 42 is part of his ongoing conversation with Hastings? Or is he openly addressing the whole room?

c Look back over the concerns voiced by Elizabeth (see Activity 1 above), and discuss how she might react to Richard's surprise entrance.

his minority while he is too young to rule

Protector (guardian appointed to help a boy king to rule)
determined, not concluded yet agreed, but not finalised
miscarry die

envious malicious

wayward sickness depression

amendment recovery

atonement reconciliation

warn call

forsooth in truth, indeed
holy Paul St Paul
his grace Edward IV
dissentious contentious

ELIZABETH	Ah, he is young, and his minority
	Is put unto the trust of Richard Gloucester,
	A man that loves not me nor none of you.
RIVERS	Is it concluded he shall be Protector?
ELIZABETH	It is determined, not concluded yet,
	But so it must be if the king miscarry.

15

Enter BUCKINGHAM *and* [STANLEY EARL OF] DERBY

GREY	Here come the lords of Buckingham and Derby.
BUCKINGHAM	Good time of day unto your royal grace.
STANLEY	God make your majesty joyful, as you have been.
ELIZABETH	The Countess Richmond, good my lord of Derby,
	To your good prayer will scarcely say amen.
	Yet Derby, not withstanding she's your wife
	And loves not me, be you, good lord, assured
	I hate not you for her proud arrogance.
STANLEY	I do beseech you, either not believe
	The envious slanders of her false accusers,
	Or if she be accused on true report,
	Bear with her weakness, which I think proceeds
	From wayward sickness and no grounded malice.
ELIZABETH	Saw you the king today, my lord of Derby?
STANLEY	But now the Duke of Buckingham and I
	Are come from visiting his majesty.
ELIZABETH	What likelihood of his amendment, lords?
BUCKINGHAM	Madam, good hope. His grace speaks cheerfully.
ELIZABETH	God grant him health. Did you confer with him?
BUCKINGHAM	Ay, madam. He desires to make atonement
	Between the Duke of Gloucester and your brothers,
	And between them and my Lord Chamberlain,
	And sent to warn them to his royal presence.
ELIZABETH	Would all were well, but that will never be.
	I fear our happiness is at the height.

20

25

30

35

40

Enter RICHARD [*and* HASTINGS]

RICHARD	They do me wrong, and I will not endure it.
	Who is it that complains unto the king
	That I, forsooth, am stern and love them not?
	By holy Paul, they love his grace but lightly
	That fill his ears with such dissentious rumours.

45

Richard claims the Woodvilles report ill of him to the King. Elizabeth says the King sends for him to find the truth. Richard implies that the Woodvilles are commoners. Elizabeth denies responsibility for Clarence's imprisonment.

1 'I cannot flatter and look fair' (in pairs)

Richard complains that he is an honest man, unfairly accused of being untrustworthy because of his looks. This is another example of dramatic irony (see p. 8).

- Look closely at the way Richard describes himself in lines 47–53, then find examples from Scenes 1 or 2 that appear to prove the opposite. Record your ideas in a table similar to the one below.

Richard claims he cannot ...	But ...
'flatter and look fair'	In Scene 2, he uses charm and flattery to win over Anne, when he says …
'smile in men's faces'	He jokes and smiles when he bumps into Clarence, even though …
'smooth, deceive and cog'	

Write about it

Who is telling the truth?

In lines 58–86, Richard makes accusations against the Woodvilles that Elizabeth refutes.

a Identify the lines in which the following accusations and refutations are made:
- What wrongs have I ever done to your dishonest family?
- Your faction has complained against me to the dying King.
- It was the King's own wish to send for you to find the reason for the hatred you show to my family.
- Commoners are being ennobled.
- You're envious that my supporters have achieved higher social status.
- Clarence is imprisoned because of you, I'm in disgrace, nobles are scorned and people of no rank are becoming nobles.
- I swear by God I never provoked Edward against Clarence. I've argued against his imprisonment.

b Decide which statements are true, which false and which cannot be proved. Write two or three paragraphs outlining the claims and counterclaims. Give your opinion of who is most likely to be believed, based on your understanding of the characters so far.

look fair put on a charming appearance

smooth compliment

cog cheat

French nods falsely elegant manners

apish courtesy empty show of politeness

rancorous hateful

plain honest, down to earth

silken effeminate

jacks commoners, knaves

nor ... nor either ... or

injured harmed in any way

scarce a breathing while for hardly a short time

lewd vulgar

on his ... disposition of his own will as King

suitor person who lobbies, seeks favours

belike probably

Makes him to send makes him send (for you)

the ground the reason

I cannot tell I really don't know

wrens very small birds

advancement promotion

ennoble confer a title (e.g. make into a lord)

noble small coin

careful full of care

hap life

	Because I cannot flatter and look fair,	
	Smile in men's faces, smooth, deceive, and cog,	
	Duck with French nods and apish courtesy,	
	I must be held a rancorous enemy.	50
	Cannot a plain man live and think no harm,	
	But thus his simple truth must be abused	
	With silken, sly, insinuating jacks?	
GREY	To who in all this presence speaks your grace?	
RICHARD	To thee, that hast nor honesty nor grace.	55
	When have I injured thee? When done thee wrong?	
	Or thee? Or thee? Or any of your faction?	
	A plague upon you all. His royal grace,	
	Whom God preserve better than you would wish,	
	Cannot be quiet scarce a breathing while	60
	But you must trouble him with lewd complaints.	
ELIZABETH	Brother of Gloucester, you mistake the matter.	
	The king, on his own royal disposition,	
	And not provoked by any suitor else,	
	Aiming, belike, at your interior hatred,	65
	That in your outward action shows itself	
	Against my children, brothers, and myself,	
	Makes him to send, that he may learn the ground.	
RICHARD	I cannot tell. The world is grown so bad	
	That wrens make prey where eagles dare not perch.	70
	Since every jack became a gentleman,	
	There's many a gentle person made a jack.	
ELIZABETH	Come, come, we know your meaning, brother Gloucester.	
	You envy my advancement and my friends'.	
	God grant we never may have need of you.	75
RICHARD	Meantime, God grants that I have need of you.	
	Our brother is imprisoned by your means,	
	My self disgraced, and the nobility	
	Held in contempt, while great promotions	
	Are daily given to ennoble those	80
	That scarce some two days since were worth a noble.	
ELIZABETH	By Him that raised me to this careful height	
	From that contented hap which I enjoyed,	
	I never did incense his majesty	
	Against the Duke of Clarence, but have been	85
	An earnest advocate to plead for him.	

Richard continues to accuse and insult Elizabeth. She swears to inform the King of his scornful behaviour. Queen Margaret enters silently, and quietly rails against both Richard and Elizabeth.

1 The argument gains pace (in threes)

Richard's sustained taunting of Elizabeth is too much for Grey and Rivers to bear. But once they step into the argument, Richard just shifts into a new gear and throws their words back at them.

- To gain a sense of the bitter exchange of views here, take parts as Richard, Rivers and Elizabeth and read lines 89–109 aloud, emphasising Richard's repetitions and Elizabeth's indignant response. Try to avoid leaving a gap where one person finishes speaking and the other responds – in a real argument, people often start speaking before the first person has finished.

Stagecraft

The entrance of 'old QUEEN MARGARET' (in pairs)

Queen Margaret (the widow of Henry VI) enters unseen by the other characters. She proceeds to comment on the conversation between Richard and Elizabeth in a series of **asides** to the audience. An aside is a stage convention that allows a character to voice his or her thoughts to the audience without other characters overhearing.

a Read the script from Margaret's entrance at line 110 up to line 162. Imagine you are directing a new stage production of the play. How are you going to present Margaret? How will she enter so that she can talk to the audience while remaining unseen by the other characters, until line 155 when she fully reveals herself and begins to speak directly to them?

- How does she enter, and where does she stand at first? (For example, she could stand right at the front of the stage, or she might stand on a gallery above, then come down the stairs to join the other characters. Or she could emerge from the audience.)
- What does she look like? Is she finely dressed to denote her royal status? Or is she dressed in rags to show that she has lost everything?
- How does she behave? Is she calm and authoritative or on the edge of insanity? Realistic or slightly ghost-like?

b Once you have played around with some ideas, make notes in your Director's Journal about the way you would stage this part of the play and why you have made those decisions.

My lord, you do me shameful injury
Falsely to draw me in these vile suspècts.

RICHARD   You may deny that you were not the mean
Of my Lord Hastings' late imprisonment.   90

RIVERS   She may, my lord, for –

RICHARD   She may, Lord Rivers, why, who knows not so?
She may do more, sir, than denying that.
She may help you to many fair preferments,
And then deny her aiding hand therein,   95
And lay those honours on your high desert.
What may she not? She may, ay, marry, may she.

RIVERS   What, marry, may she?

RICHARD   What, marry, may she? Marry with a king,
A bachelor, and a handsome stripling too.   100
I wis your grandam had a worser match.

ELIZABETH   My lord of Gloucester, I have too long borne
Your blunt upbraidings and your bitter scoffs.
By heaven, I will acquaint his majesty
Of those gross taunts that oft I have endured.   105
I had rather be a country servant maid
Than a great queen with this condition,
To be so baited, scorned, and stormèd at.
Small joy have I in being England's queen.

Enter old QUEEN MARGARET

MARGARET   [*Aside*] And lessened be that small, God I beseech him.   110
Thy honour, state, and seat is due to me.

RICHARD   What? Threat you me with telling of the king?
I will avouch't in presence of the king.
I dare adventure to be sent to th'Tower.
'Tis time to speak. My pains are quite forgot.   115

MARGARET   [*Aside*] Out, devil. I do remember them too well.
Thou kill'dst my husband, Henry, in the Tower,
And Edward, my poor son, at Tewkesbury.

RICHARD   Ere you were queen, ay, or your husband king,
I was a pack-horse in his great affairs,   120
A weeder-out of his proud adversaries,
A liberal rewarder of his friends.
To royalise his blood I spent mine own.

1 Queen Margaret

Margaret eventually reveals herself to Richard and the Woodvilles. How is Margaret portrayed in the production pictured here? Consider her clothes, her hair, the look on her face, the way she stands. How do you imagine Queen Margaret? Do you think she could be portrayed in a different way?

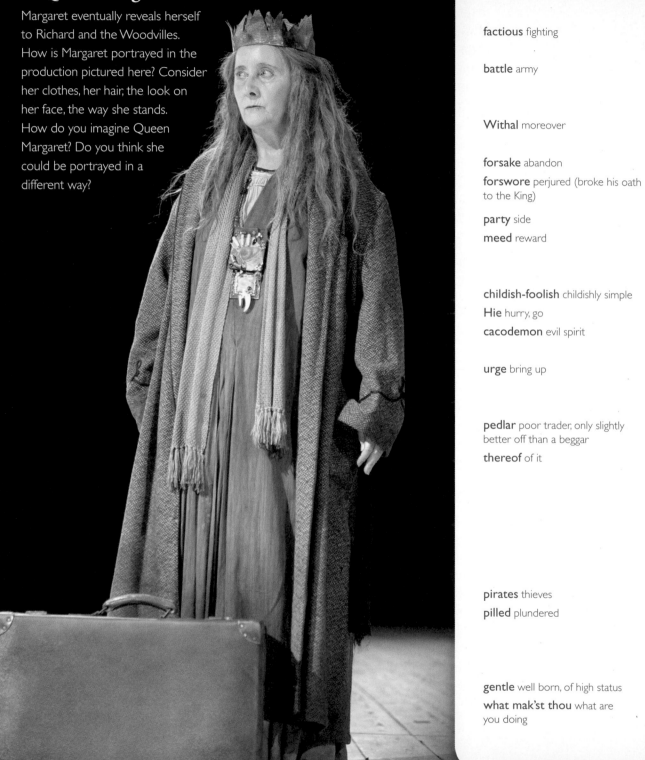

factious fighting

battle army

Withal moreover

forsake abandon
forswore perjured (broke his oath to the King)
party side
meed reward

childish-foolish childishly simple
Hie hurry, go
cacodemon evil spirit

urge bring up

pedlar poor trader, only slightly better off than a beggar
thereof of it

pirates thieves
pilled plundered

gentle well born, of high status
what mak'st thou what are you doing

MARGARET	[*Aside*] Ay, and much better blood than his or thine.	
RICHARD	In all which time, you and your husband Grey	125
	Were factious for the house of Lancaster,	
	And, Rivers, so were you. Was not your husband	
	In Margaret's battle at Saint Albans slain?	
	Let me put in your minds, if you forget,	
	What you have been ere this, and what you are;	130
	Withal, what I have been, and what I am.	
MARGARET	[*Aside*] A murderous villain, and so still thou art.	
RICHARD	Poor Clarence did forsake his father Warwick,	
	Ay, and forswore himself, which Jesu pardon.	
MARGARET	[*Aside*] Which God revenge.	135
RICHARD	To fight on Edward's party for the crown.	
	And for his meed, poor lord, he is mewed up.	
	I would to God my heart were flint, like Edward's,	
	Or Edward's soft and pitiful, like mine.	
	I am too childish-foolish for this world.	140
MARGARET	[*Aside*] Hie thee to hell for shame, and leave this world,	
	Thou cacodemon. There thy kingdom is.	
RIVERS	My lord of Gloucester, in those busy days	
	Which here you urge to prove us enemies,	
	We followed then our lord, our sovereign king.	145
	So should we you, if you should be our king.	
RICHARD	If I should be? I had rather be a pedlar.	
	Far be it from my heart, the thought thereof.	
ELIZABETH	As little joy, my lord, as you suppose	
	You should enjoy were you this country's king,	150
	As little joy you may suppose in me	
	That I enjoy, being the queen thereof.	
MARGARET	[*Aside*] A little joy enjoys the queen thereof,	
	For I am she, and altogether joyless.	
	I can no longer hold me patient –	155
	Hear me, you wrangling pirates, that fall out	
	In sharing that which you have pilled from me.	
	Which of you trembles not that looks on me?	
	If not that I am queen, you bow like subjects,	
	Yet that by you deposed, you quake like rebels.	160
	Ah, gentle villain, do not turn away.	
RICHARD	Foul wrinkled witch, what mak'st thou in my sight?	

Margaret demands the return of her throne. Richard tells how she pitilessly taunted his father. Everyone condemns that deed, but Margaret begins to curse them, prophesying deaths and sorrows ahead.

1 A complicated family feud (in large groups)

From lines 125 to 152, Richard, Elizabeth and the Woodvilles trade insults about their parts in their often violent recent history. Since various characters changed sides and switched loyalties more than once during the Wars of the Roses, Richard enjoys exposing his opponents' hypocrisies. However, once Margaret joins the argument (line 155), the relationship between those on stage shifts a little. Are there now three factions? Does Margaret have any allies? Who was loyal to whom and who behaved treacherously?

* You will need at least fifteen people for this activity, so clear a space in your classroom or drama studio. Check that you are allowed to use masking tape on the floor. Divide the floor space into three sections – one each for York, Lancaster and neutral/unknown. Turn to the family tree on page 266 and allocate parts for the people listed. First decide in which space you would place Henry VI, Queen Margaret and their son, Edward, when they ruled England. Then place Richard, Clarence and Rutland along with their father the Duke of York. Next, Elizabeth and her brothers take up a space. Where do you think Hastings, Rivers, Dorset and Buckingham might stand before Henry VI was defeated?

* Now read from line 125 (any members of the class who have not taken roles could read the script in turn) and follow the various accusations as they are made. For example, in lines 125–6, Richard accuses Elizabeth and her former husband of originally supporting the Lancastrians; they fought against Margaret and Henry (line 128), resulting in the death of Elizabeth's husband (line 127–8). As each accusation is made, or piece of history recounted, the identified person should decide whether they move, stay or die. Which characters switch allegiance?

Characters

Who hates whom most? (in eights)

* Consider Margaret's line 188, 'turn you all your hatred now on me?' and decide where loyalties lie at this moment. Freeze this moment on stage and show where each character is standing and what that reveals about their allegiance (or self interest).

* As an extra challenge, some of the characters in the tableaux could come alive and voice their thoughts at this moment.

repetition telling aloud
marred spoilt
That that repetition
Wert thou were you
on pain of death under a death sentence
abode staying there
thou (line 169) addressed to Elizabeth
usurp falsely claim

crown … with paper (Margaret had mocked the captured York by making him wear a paper crown)
clout cloth
faultless innocent

plagued punished

that babe the young Rutland

No man but everybody

catch each other by the throat quarrel viciously

but answer for only equal, match
peevish silly, irritable
quick sharp, lively
surfeit over-indulgence

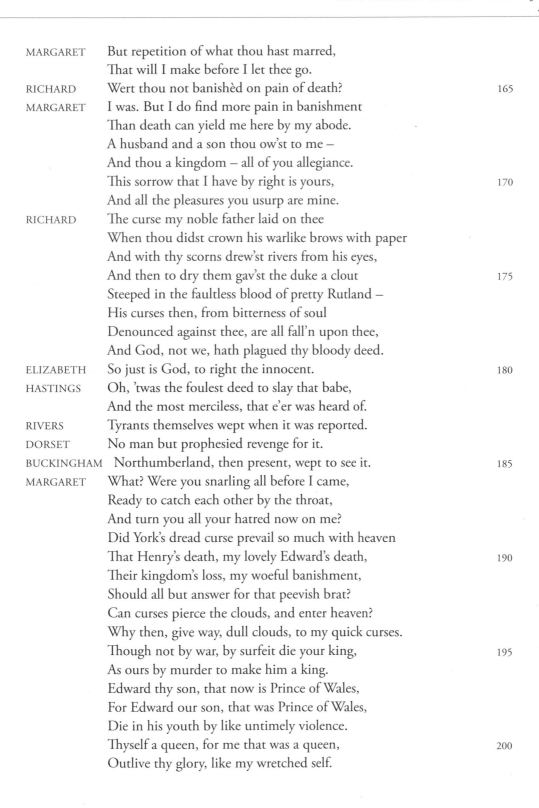

MARGARET	But repetition of what thou hast marred,
	That will I make before I let thee go.
RICHARD	Wert thou not banishèd on pain of death?	165
MARGARET	I was. But I do find more pain in banishment
	Than death can yield me here by my abode.
	A husband and a son thou ow'st to me –
	And thou a kingdom – all of you allegiance.
	This sorrow that I have by right is yours,	170
	And all the pleasures you usurp are mine.
RICHARD	The curse my noble father laid on thee
	When thou didst crown his warlike brows with paper
	And with thy scorns drew'st rivers from his eyes,
	And then to dry them gav'st the duke a clout	175
	Steeped in the faultless blood of pretty Rutland –
	His curses then, from bitterness of soul
	Denounced against thee, are all fall'n upon thee,
	And God, not we, hath plagued thy bloody deed.
ELIZABETH	So just is God, to right the innocent.	180
HASTINGS	Oh, 'twas the foulest deed to slay that babe,
	And the most merciless, that e'er was heard of.
RIVERS	Tyrants themselves wept when it was reported.
DORSET	No man but prophesied revenge for it.
BUCKINGHAM	Northumberland, then present, wept to see it.	185
MARGARET	What? Were you snarling all before I came,
	Ready to catch each other by the throat,
	And turn you all your hatred now on me?
	Did York's dread curse prevail so much with heaven
	That Henry's death, my lovely Edward's death,	190
	Their kingdom's loss, my woeful banishment,
	Should all but answer for that peevish brat?
	Can curses pierce the clouds, and enter heaven?
	Why then, give way, dull clouds, to my quick curses.
	Though not by war, by surfeit die your king,	195
	As ours by murder to make him a king.
	Edward thy son, that now is Prince of Wales,
	For Edward our son, that was Prince of Wales,
	Die in his youth by like untimely violence.
	Thyself a queen, for me that was a queen,	200
	Outlive thy glory, like my wretched self.

Margaret continues her prophetic cursing, wishing grief on Elizabeth and early deaths on Rivers, Dorset and Hastings. Her most powerful curse is on Richard. He turns her words against her.

Write about it

Awards and censures

A committee of disabled people is awarding prizes to the films, plays and TV programmes that have portrayed disabled people most accurately. The awards also censure those that have portrayed the handicapped badly or ignored the problem of physical disability. Margaret's lines (226–31) are 'politically incorrect' in that they equate Richard's disability with his evil nature.

- Write a letter to the awarding committee, in which you complain about the offensive nature of the lines. Consider whether you agree with Queen Margaret's opinion that Richard's disability is a reflection of his evil character.
- Write the reply that the committee might make.

Decked dressed
stalled installed

charm spell, cursing

1 Curses and prophecies

Some of Queen Margaret's curses are colourful and vindictive, especially when directed towards Richard. Other curses are mixed with realistic prophecies.

- Read through the lines in which she curses some of the other characters (lines 195 to 231). Make a list of each person she curses and what she curses them with. Copy the following table and, in the final column, make notes on how likely you think it is that this curse will be fulfilled in the course of the play.

elvish-marked disfigured by evil fairies
abortive disfigured
rooting hog earth-eating pig
sealed branded
nativity birth
rag worthless fragment

The person addressed	Queen Margaret's curse	How likely is it that this curse will be fulfilled?
King Edward		
Prince Edward		
Queen Elizabeth		
Rivers and Dorset		
Richard		

I cry thee mercy I beg your pardon

period end, full stop

	Long mayst thou live to wail thy children's death	
	And see another, as I see thee now,	
	Decked in the rights, as thou art stalled in mine.	
	Long die thy happy days before thy death,	205
	And after many lengthened hours of grief,	
	Die neither mother, wife, nor England's queen.	
	Rivers and Dorset, you were standers-by,	
	And so wast thou, Lord Hastings, when my son	
	Was stabbed with bloody daggers. God I pray him,	210
	That none of you may live his natural age,	
	But by some unlooked accident cut off.	
RICHARD	Have done thy charm, thou hateful, withered hag.	
MARGARET	And leave out thee? Stay, dog, for thou shalt hear me.	
	If heaven have any grievous plague in store	215
	Exceeding those that I can wish upon thee,	
	Oh, let them keep it till thy sins be ripe	
	And then hurl down their indignation	
	On thee, the troubler of the poor world's peace.	
	The worm of conscience still begnaw thy soul.	220
	Thy friends suspect for traitors while thou liv'st,	
	And take deep traitors for thy dearest friends.	
	No sleep close up that deadly eye of thine,	
	Unless it be while some tormenting dream	
	Affrights thee with a hell of ugly devils.	225
	Thou elvish-marked, abortive, rooting hog,	
	Thou that wast sealed in thy nativity	
	The slave of nature and the son of hell.	
	Thou slander of thy heavy mother's womb,	
	Thou loathèd issue of thy father's loins,	230
	Thou rag of honour, thou detested –	
RICHARD	Margaret.	
MARGARET	Richard.	
RICHARD	Ha?	
MARGARET	I call thee not.	
RICHARD	I cry thee mercy then, for I did think	235
	That thou hadst called me all these bitter names.	
MARGARET	Why so I did, but looked for no reply.	
	Oh, let me make the period to my curse.	
RICHARD	'Tis done by me, and ends in 'Margaret'.	

Margaret predicts that Elizabeth will come to curse Richard. She rebukes Hastings, Rivers and Dorset, and sorrows for her dead son. She calls on God to punish the house of York.

1 Who's who? (in large groups)

a Work out who is mentioned in this section by taking parts as Margaret, Hastings, Rivers, Dorset and Richard. Speak lines 240–63 slowly. As each person (or persons) is mentioned, point to them.

b How would you want to group the characters on stage to show their relationships to each other and to reveal where their loyalties lie? For example, in lines 259–60, Margaret observes that the higher the rank, the greater the consequences of a fall as she talks to Dorset (Queen Elizabeth's son, who has only recently been raised to high status). Where would you place Dorset to reflect his recent change of rank?

Language in the play
Imagery of authority and nobility

In lines 263–5, Richard compares the house of York's position at the top of the tree to that of an eagle. It was believed to be a sign of the eagle's noble nature that it could gaze into the sun unblinded. Richard claims that, like the eagle, the house of York 'scorns the sun'.

a Look back at the 'Language' box on page 12. Now consider further how imagery can enhance the audience's understanding of Richard's character and add to the tension of a scene. Add another paragraph to your earlier one, in which you outline your responses to the imagery in the script opposite.

b What other animal imagery might be appropriate for Richard (and any other characters of your choice) at this point in the play?

Themes
Lancaster or York: the right to rule?

Margaret accuses Richard of causing the death of her son – 'turns the sun to shade' (line 266) – and accuses the house of York of unjustly stealing Lancaster's high status: 'Your aerie buildeth in our aerie's nest' (line 270).

• Write out in your own words how the crown has passed from the house of Lancaster to the house of York and back again since the time of Richard II. Who do you think really has the right to rule England?

painted unreal imitation
vain flourish of my fortune empty show or worthless decoration in a life that properly belongs to me
bottled shaped like a bottle
bunch-backed hunch-backed
False-boding false prophesying

Were you well served if you got what you deserved

Teach me to be show me that I am

master (a title for a young boy and therefore an insult to the adult Dorset)
malapert impudent
Your fire-new stamp of honour your new title is like a coin fresh from the mint, hardly legal yet
young newly acquired
blasts winds
born so high noble by birth
aerie an eagle's nest or the young eagles in the nest
cedar (a tall tree noted for its long life and seen as a symbol of nobility)
dallies plays with

Peace be quiet

ELIZABETH	Thus have you breathed your curse against yourself.	240
MARGARET	Poor painted queen, vain flourish of my fortune,	
	Why strew'st thou sugar on that bottled spider	
	Whose deadly web ensnareth thee about?	
	Fool, fool, thou whet'st a knife to kill thyself.	
	The day will come that thou shalt wish for me	245
	To help thee curse this poisonous bunch-backed toad.	
HASTINGS	False-boding woman, end thy frantic curse,	
	Lest to thy harm thou move our patience.	
MARGARET	Foul shame upon you. You have all moved mine.	
RIVERS	Were you well served, you would be taught your duty.	250
MARGARET	To serve me well, you all should do me duty,	
	Teach me to be your queen, and you my subjects;	
	Oh, serve me well and teach yourselves that duty.	
DORSET	Dispute not with her. She is lunatic.	
MARGARET	Peace, master marquess, you are malapert.	255
	Your fire-new stamp of honour is scarce current.	
	Oh, that your young nobility could judge	
	What 'twere to lose it and be miserable.	
	They that stand high have many blasts to shake them,	
	And if they fall, they dash themselves to pieces.	260
RICHARD	Good counsel, marry. Learn it, learn it, marquess.	
DORSET	It touches you, my lord, as much as me.	
RICHARD	Ay, and much more. But I was born so high.	
	Our aerie buildeth in the cedar's top,	
	And dallies with the wind and scorns the sun.	265
MARGARET	And turns the sun to shade, alas, alas.	
	Witness my son, now in the shade of death,	
	Whose bright out-shining beams thy cloudy wrath	
	Hath in eternal darkness folded up.	
	Your aerie buildeth in our aerie's nest.	270
	O God that seest it, do not suffer it;	
	As it is won with blood, lost be it so.	
BUCKINGHAM	Peace, peace, for shame, if not for charity.	
MARGARET	Urge neither charity nor shame to me.	
	Uncharitably with me have you dealt,	275
	And shamefully my hopes by you are butchered.	
	My charity is outrage, life my shame,	
	And in that shame still live my sorrow's rage.	

Margaret extends friendship to Buckingham and warns him against Richard. He rejects her and she prophesies his downfall. Richard expresses sympathy for Margaret and those who imprisoned Clarence.

1 Buckingham disappoints Margaret (in pairs)

Margaret, having accused everyone of responsibility for the bloody deeds of the civil war, now turns to Buckingham. She says he had no part in harming her family and therefore he is the only one she does not curse.

- Take parts as Buckingham and Margaret, and speak lines 279–94, indicating how Margaret pleads with Buckingham in her first two speeches.
- Then speak their lines 296–304, exploring how Margaret's tone might change as Buckingham does not respond in the way she hopes.
- What does Buckingham's reply in line 296 reveal about his character?

Stagecraft

Margaret's stage business

In line 295, Richard says: 'What does she say, my lord of Buckingham?' But what does this mean? Is Margaret whispering to Buckingham, or is Richard simply suggesting that people who matter (such as himself) have stopped listening to her?

- In your Director's Journal, write your own stage direction to describe what would be going on at this point if you were directing the play.

princely Buckingham (Buckingham was a descendant of Thomas, Duke of Gloucester, the youngest son of King Edward III)

league allegiance, bonding

amity friendship

fair befall good fortune come to

compass range

pass get any further than

will not think but will only believe that

Look expect that

venom envenomed, poisonous

rankle infect, fester

ministers devils

counsel advice

soothe conciliate, flatter

muse wonder

God's holy mother (Richard swears by the Virgin Mary)

vantage benefits

hot eager

somebody King Edward

franked up styed like a pig

scathe injury

BUCKINGHAM	Have done, have done.	
MARGARET	O princely Buckingham, I'll kiss thy hand	280
	In sign of league and amity with thee.	
	Now fair befall thee and thy noble house.	
	Thy garments are not spotted with our blood,	
	Nor thou within the compass of my curse.	
BUCKINGHAM	Nor no one here, for curses never pass	285
	The lips of those that breathe them in the air.	
MARGARET	I will not think but they ascend the sky	
	And there awake God's gentle sleeping peace.	
	O Buckingham, take heed of yonder dog.	
	Look when he fawns, he bites; and when he bites,	290
	His venom tooth will rankle to the death.	
	Have not to do with him; beware of him.	
	Sin, death, and hell have set their marks on him,	
	And all their ministers attend on him.	
RICHARD	What doth she say, my lord of Buckingham?	295
BUCKINGHAM	Nothing that I respect, my gracious lord.	
MARGARET	What, dost thou scorn me for my gentle counsel	
	And soothe the devil that I warn thee from?	
	Oh, but remember this another day,	
	When he shall split thy very heart with sorrow,	300
	And say poor Margaret was a prophetess.	
	Live each of you the subjects to his hate,	
	And he to yours, and all of you to God's.	*Exit*
BUCKINGHAM	My hair doth stand on end to hear her curses.	
RIVERS	And so doth mine. I muse why she's at liberty.	305
RICHARD	I cannot blame her, by God's holy mother,	
	She hath had too much wrong, and I repent	
	My part thereof that I have done to her.	
ELIZABETH	I never did her any to my knowledge.	
RICHARD	Yet you have all the vantage of her wrong.	310
	I was too hot to do somebody good	
	That is too cold in thinking of it now.	
	Marry, as for Clarence, he is well repaid;	
	He is franked up to fatting for his pains.	
	God pardon them that are the cause thereof.	315
RIVERS	A virtuous and a Christian-like conclusion,	
	To pray for them that have done scathe to us.	

Catesby informs the Queen and courtiers that King Edward has sent for them. Alone on stage, Richard discloses his techniques for deceiving others. He instructs the Murderers to kill Clarence quickly, without pity.

1 Mock innocence and false piety (in pairs)

In lines 324–38, Richard tells the audience how he uses Derby, Hastings and Buckingham and persuades them that the Queen has caused Clarence's imprisonment. When his 'gulls' urge him to take revenge on the Woodvilles, he uses the Bible ('scripture', 'holy writ') to pretend he pardons his enemies. Part of Richard's style is mock innocence and false piety (pretending to be very religious), often tinged with menace.

- In modern English, improvise a conversation between Richard and one of these gullible courtiers to imitate his style of saintly innocence and forgiveness. Remember that actors playing Richard often try to bring out his humorous delight in clever play-acting, unnoticed by those on stage.

Stagecraft

Murder and manipulation (in small groups)

a Prepare a dramatic reading of Richard's conversation with the Murderers (lines 339–55). Use the following questions to help you:

- Would Richard be seated while the Murderers stand, or would all stand?
- Would Richard remain hidden in shadows or would he tower above the Murderers?
- Would he have freedom of movement and a wide vocal range to show his power over the Murderers, who fearfully stay in one place on the stage?
- Would the Murderers be restless, wild and violent men, or would they be cold and calculating?
- What stage business might be created around the warrant (line 344) to make the audience smile, and to remind them of Richard's duplicity?

b Make notes about the reasons for your performance choices in your Director's Journal. Use these notes to script a conversation between the director and the actor playing Richard or one of the Murderers. Explain their motives and actions to the actor. Imagine how the actor might respond – would he agree or have alternative suggestions?

---

well advised cautious

brawl quarrel

The secret mischiefs … others
I will lay the blame on others for the secret plots I have set in motion

cast in darkness thrown into prison or sentenced to death

beweep weep for him

gulls gullible fools, dupes

whet encourage, incite

do good for evil repay with good deeds instead of taking revenge (this is one of Richard's stock arguments)

ends scraps

soft quiet

resolvèd resolute, determined

sudden quick

obdurate unbending

mark listen to

| RICHARD | So do I ever, being well advised. |
| | (*Speaks to himself*) For had I cursed now, I had cursed myself. |

Enter CATESBY

CATESBY	Madam, his majesty doth call for you,	320
	And for your grace, and you, my gracious lord.	
ELIZABETH	Catesby, I come. Lords, will you go with me?	
RIVERS	We wait upon your grace.	

Exeunt all but Gloucester

RICHARD	I do the wrong, and first begin to brawl.	
	The secret mischiefs that I set abroach	325
	I lay unto the grievous charge of others.	
	Clarence, who I indeed have cast in darkness,	
	I do beweep to many simple gulls,	
	Namely to Derby, Hastings, Buckingham,	
	And tell them 'tis the queen and her allies	330
	That stir the king against the duke my brother.	
	Now they believe it, and withal whet me	
	To be revenged on Rivers, Dorset, Grey.	
	But then I sigh, and with a piece of scripture	
	Tell them that God bids us do good for evil.	335
	And thus I clothe my naked villainy	
	With odd old ends stol'n forth of holy writ,	
	And seem a saint when most I play the devil.	

Enter two MURDERERS

	But soft, here come my executioners –	
	How now, my hardy, stout, resolvèd mates,	340
	Are you now going to dispatch this thing?	
FIRST MURDERER	We are, my lord, and come to have the warrant	
	That we may be admitted where he is.	
RICHARD	Well thought upon, I have it here about me.	
	When you have done, repair to Crosby Place.	345
	But, sirs, be sudden in the execution,	
	Withal obdurate. Do not hear him plead,	
	For Clarence is well spoken and perhaps	
	May move your hearts to pity if you mark him.	

Richard dismisses the Murderers to kill Clarence. In the Tower, Clarence recounts his dream of escaping to Burgundy by boat, from which he was pushed overboard by Richard.

1 'Go, go, dispatch'

The word 'dispatch' is a **pun** – a play on words that have more than one meaning or that look or sound the same (see p. 250). Here, 'dispatch' could mean either 'kill' or 'go quickly'.

- Invent gestures that Richard might use to accompany his words in the shared line 355. Then write a detailed stage direction to advise the actors playing Richard and the Murderers at this point.

2 Symbolising the Tower

Three of the four scenes in Act 1 are set outside, near or in the Tower of London. Some directors of the play use this famous building as a symbol of Richard's cruel regime. Elizabethan staging would have indicated the play's location through dialogue. Modern stage productions, however, often use sophisticated scenery, props or set design.

- Imagine you are the set designer for a modern stage production. Look for clues about location and other stage properties in the dialogue.
- Sketch how you would present the Tower to symbolise its atmosphere and gruesome associations. You might like to make use of some of the imagery in this scene (for example, line 353, where Richard suggests that the Murderers are so hard that if they wept, they would weep stones rather than tears).

3 Clarence's nightmare

In lines 9–63 of Scene 4, Clarence recounts a dream in which he escaped from the Tower and, while sailing to Burgundy, was pushed into the sea by Richard. Drowning, he experiences the terrors of death as he goes to hell. There, he is accused of perjury and murder, and is taken to be tortured. He wakes, thinking he is in hell.

- Find a copy of the image of 'Doom' in the Guild Chapel in Stratford-upon-Avon, which Shakespeare would have seen often as a child. List the similarities between Clarence's nightmare and this scene.
- Describe in your own words why Shakespeare's visual imagery is more frightening or alarming. Identify some of the vivid images of death, torture and hell as you do so.

prate chat

millstones blocks of granite (falling millstones would kill anyone in the way, so they are dangerous whether they weep or not)
fall drip
straight straight away, speedily

heavily sadly

Christian faithful man devout and religious man

Burgundy the Low Countries, a Yorkist sanctuary

tempted persuaded
hatches deck
cited up recalled
heavy difficult, trying

giddy unsteady

stay steady, save
main ocean

SECOND MURDERER   Tut, tut, my lord, we will not stand to prate;   350
                    Talkers are no good doers. Be assured
                    We go to use our hands and not our tongues.
RICHARD   Your eyes drop millstones when fools' eyes fall tears.
                    I like you, lads. About your business straight.
                    Go, go, dispatch.
MURDERERS   We will, my noble lord.   355

Exeunt

Act 1 Scene 4
A room in the Tower of London

Enter CLARENCE *and* KEEPER

KEEPER   Why looks your grace so heavily today?
CLARENCE   Oh, I have passed a miserable night,
                    So full of fearful dreams, of ugly sights,
                    That as I am a Christian faithful man,
                    I would not spend another such a night   5
                    Though 'twere to buy a world of happy days,
                    So full of dismal terror was the time.
KEEPER   What was your dream, my lord? I pray you, tell me.
CLARENCE   Methoughts that I had broken from the Tower,
                    And was embarked to cross to Burgundy,   10
                    And in my company my brother Gloucester,
                    Who from my cabin tempted me to walk
                    Upon the hatches. There we looked toward England
                    And cited up a thousand heavy times
                    During the wars of York and Lancaster   15
                    That had befall'n us. As we paced along
                    Upon the giddy footing of the hatches,
                    Methought that Gloucester stumbled, and in falling
                    Struck me, that thought to stay him, overboard
                    Into the tumbling billows of the main.   20

Clarence tells the Keeper of the agony of drowning. He recounts how his soul goes to hell, where Warwick accuses him of betrayal. Prince Edward, whom he killed, adds another accusation.

1 Dreams of drowning (in pairs)

Clarence's dream of drowning can be divided into four sections. Lines 21–5 tell of the physical pain of drowning; lines 26–8 describe the wealth on the sea bed; lines 29–33 mock the worthlessness of that wealth; and lines 36–41 return to the pain Clarence feels as he wishes to die but cannot.

- One person speaks the lines while the other echoes the key words for each section – for example, words signifying pain in the first section, wealth in the second and so on. Swap roles between sections.

2 Dreams of hell (in pairs or small groups)

Hell was a real and terrifying place for the Elizabethans, and the shrieking of the 'foul fiends' convinces Clarence he is still in hell even after he awakes. The series of vivid images provides one of the most poetic moments in the play.

a Collect images from magazines or the Internet to create a collage that illustrates Clarence's fearful journey through hell. You might get some ideas by looking at paintings by Hieronymus Bosch and Pieter Bruegel.

b In writing, describe your own imagined nightmare in which you journey to hell. Start with the same words:

Oh, I have passed a miserable night,
So full of fearful dreams, of ugly sights …

Write about it

Self-realisation (by yourself)

The dream sequence captures a moment of self-revelation as Clarence begins to realise the terrifying consequences of his actions. While in hell, Clarence is first accused of perjury by his father-in-law Warwick (Clarence betrayed Warwick when he switched allegiance in the Wars of the Roses). His second accuser is Edward, Prince of Wales. This ghostly figure, murdered by Richard and Clarence after the Battle of Tewkesbury, is still covered in his own blood.

- Imagine that Clarence had time between his nightmare and his death to write to his family. What might he confess or explain to them? Write two or three paragraphs in a letter to capture his thoughts and emotions as he feels death drawing closer.

fearful inspiring fear
wracks wrecks
Wedges bars
Inestimable unable to be counted
unvalued priceless

in scorn of in imitation of, mocking
wooed addressed, sought intimacy with

yield the ghost die, release the soul from the body
envious flood spiteful water
Stopped held
panting bulk gasping body

melancholy flood River Styx (in classical mythology, the Styx led to Hades, the underworld)
sour ferryman Charon (who ferried souls across the Styx to Hades)
perpetual night the afterlife
stranger-soul soul newly arrived in the afterlife
scourge punishment
perjury oath breaking
afford provide
shadow shade (the ghost of Prince Edward)
Dabbled daubed, smeared
fleeting inconstant, fickle
furies avenging goddesses
torment hell

O Lord, methought what pain it was to drown,
What dreadful noise of water in mine ears,
What sights of ugly death within mine eyes.
Methoughts I saw a thousand fearful wracks,
A thousand men that fishes gnawed upon, 25
Wedges of gold, great anchors, heaps of pearl,
Inestimable stones, unvalued jewels,
All scattered in the bottom of the sea.
Some lay in dead men's skulls, and in the holes
Where eyes did once inhabit there were crept, 30
As 'twere in scorn of eyes, reflecting gems,
That wooed the slimy bottom of the deep
And mocked the dead bones that lay scattered by.

KEEPER   Had you such leisure in the time of death
To gaze upon these secrets of the deep? 35

CLARENCE   Methought I had, and often did I strive
To yield the ghost; but still the envious flood
Stopped in my soul and would not let it forth
To find the empty, vast, and wandering air,
But smothered it within my panting bulk, 40
Who almost burst to belch it in the sea.

KEEPER   Awaked you not in this sore agony?

CLARENCE   No, no, my dream was lengthened after life.
Oh, then began the tempest to my soul.
I passed, methought, the melancholy flood, 45
With that sour ferryman which poets write of,
Unto the kingdom of perpetual night.
The first that there did greet my stranger-soul
Was my great father-in-law, renownèd Warwick,
Who spake aloud, 'What scourge for perjury 50
Can this dark monarchy afford false Clarence?'
And so he vanished. Then came wandering by
A shadow like an angel, with bright hair
Dabbled in blood, and he shrieked out aloud,
'Clarence is come: false, fleeting, perjured Clarence, 55
That stabbed me in the field by Tewkesbury.
Seize on him, furies, take him unto torment.'

Clarence, recalling his dream, confesses his misdeeds. He prays for mercy from God for his family, then sleeps. Brakenbury reflects on how outward appearance often hides inner turmoil. The Murderers bring Richard's warrant.

1 After the dream (in threes)

Clarence admits committing horrific acts during the civil war, and his conversation with the Keeper reveals his troubled state of mind.

a Talk together about how far (if at all) Clarence's dream journey of self-exploration and confession has changed your opinion of him.

b Take parts as Clarence and the Keeper to prepare a dramatic reading of lines 64–75. The third person, in role as director, advises on the tone and the actions to express:

- the fear both men feel
- Clarence's confessional and religious tone
- the Keeper's sympathy for Clarence.

Stagecraft

The cares of high office (in pairs)

The actor playing Brakenbury asks you for help. He finds some of lines 76–83 unclear and is unsure what he should do as he speaks. He points out that 'unfelt imaginations' could mean 'things imagined but not experienced', or 'ordinary people imagine a happiness that princes have never felt'. He is confident in his interpretation of the first four lines (that sorrow destroys the borders between the seasons, sleep, day and night; and that even the title 'prince' cannot prevent the consequences of sorrow).

- In role as the director of a new production of the play, consider how to advise the actor. What help would you give him and what is your understanding of these lines?
- Write notes for the actor, giving your interpretation of the meaning of the second part of Brakenbury's speech (lines 80–3), and suggesting how this will affect his behaviour towards the sleeping Clarence. Remember to make reference to your interpretation of specific words and phrases from the speech in the script opposite.
- Add to your notes to describe how Brakenbury should react when his thoughts are interrupted at the stage direction 'Enter two MURDERERS'.

legion battalion
Environed imprisoned

season time

impression image in my mind
though that

requites rewards
appease pacify

fain gladly

breaks seasons disrupts normal schedules
reposing hours hours for sleeping
inward toil unrest of mind
unfelt imaginations illusory honours, glories imagined but not experienced
restless unsettling, worrying
low name the status (title) of ordinary citizens
fame report, public estimation

brief abrupt, rude

commission warrant

With that, methought, a legion of foul fiends
Environed me, and howlèd in mine ears
Such hideous cries that with the very noise 60
I trembling waked, and for a season after
Could not believe but that I was in hell,
Such terrible impression made my dream.
KEEPER   No marvel, lord, though it affrighted you.
I am afraid, methinks, to hear you tell it. 65
CLARENCE   Ah keeper, keeper, I have done these things
That now give evidence against my soul
For Edward's sake, and see how he requites me.
O God, if my deep prayers cannot appease thee,
But thou wilt be avenged on my misdeeds, 70
Yet execute thy wrath in me alone.
Oh, spare my guiltless wife and my poor children.
Keeper, I prithee sit by me awhile.
My soul is heavy, and I fain would sleep.
KEEPER   I will, my lord. God give your grace good rest. 75

Enter BRAKENBURY, *the Lieutenant*

BRAKENBURY   Sorrow breaks seasons and reposing hours,
Makes the night morning and the noontide night.
Princes have but their titles for their glories,
An outward honour for an inward toil,
And for unfelt imaginations 80
They often feel a world of restless cares;
So that between their titles and low name
There's nothing differs but the outward fame.

Enter two MURDERERS

FIRST MURDERER   Ho, who's here?
BRAKENBURY   What wouldst thou, fellow? And how cam'st thou 85
hither?
SECOND MURDERER   I would speak with Clarence, and I came hither on
my legs.
BRAKENBURY   What, so brief?
FIRST MURDERER   'Tis better, sir, than to be tedious. 90
Let him see our commission, and talk no more.

Brakenbury leaves the Murderers alone with Clarence. They discuss whether to kill Clarence immediately. The Second Murderer fears that he will be damned for killing Clarence, but is tempted by the thought of reward.

Write about it

Brakenbury's motives (in pairs)

Brakenbury has received Richard's warrant. In contrast to the ambiguity of his first speech, he is now very clear about what he must do to protect himself from blame.

a In preparation for the writing activity, take turns to speak lines 92–8. Afterwards, talk together about Brakenbury's reaction to the warrant. Why might he want to tell King Edward how he has acted? What would *you* do?

b Write Brakenbury's diary entry at the end of the day to show his motives for behaving the way he did and his responses to the events that have taken place.

Themes

The pangs of conscience (1) (in pairs)

Conscience is a major theme of the play. Characters delight in, or are tortured by, thoughts of their misdeeds. Both Clarence and Brakenbury have listened anxiously to their consciences, and now Shakespeare presents the Murderers wrestling with their sense of right and wrong in a witty and clever way, as they balance conscience and payment. The Second Murderer is worried that Clarence's murder could damn his soul, but is persuaded by the reward Richard will give him. Even the First Murderer seems to feel the pangs of conscience briefly.

a To gain a first impression of this 'wrestling with conscience' episode, take parts as the two Murderers. Stand opposite each other as you read through lines 100–44. Take steps forward or backward according to how forceful or persuasive your Murderer is at any given line. Which Murderer is most dominant by the end of this section?

b Create a table with two columns. In one column list what stops the Murderers from killing Clarence, and in the second column list the advantages of murdering him.

[*Brakenbury*] *reads*

BRAKENBURY I am in this commanded to deliver
The noble Duke of Clarence to your hands.
I will not reason what is meant hereby,
Because I will be guiltless from the meaning.   95
There lies the duke asleep, and there the keys.
I'll to the king and signify to him
That thus I have resigned to you my charge.

Exeunt [*Brakenbury and Keeper*]

FIRST MURDERER You may, sir, 'tis a point of wisdom. Fare you well.

SECOND MURDERER What, shall we stab him as he sleeps?   100

FIRST MURDERER No. He'll say 'twas done cowardly, when he wakes.

SECOND MURDERER Why, he shall never wake until the great judgement day.

FIRST MURDERER Why, then he'll say we stabbed him sleeping.

SECOND MURDERER The urging of that word judgement hath bred a   105
kind of remorse in me.

FIRST MURDERER What? Art thou afraid?

SECOND MURDERER Not to kill him, having a warrant,
But to be damned for killing him, from the which
No warrant can defend me.   110

FIRST MURDERER I thought thou hadst been resolute.

SECOND MURDERER So I am, to let him live.

FIRST MURDERER I'll back to the Duke of Gloucester and tell him so.

SECOND MURDERER Nay, I prithee stay a little.
I hope this passionate humour of mine will change.   115
It was wont to hold me but while one tells twenty.

FIRST MURDERER How dost thou feel thyself now?

SECOND MURDERER Some certain dregs of conscience are yet within
me.

FIRST MURDERER Remember our reward when the deed's done.   120

SECOND MURDERER Come, he dies. I had forgot the reward.

FIRST MURDERER Where's thy conscience now?

SECOND MURDERER Oh, in the Duke of Gloucester's purse.

FIRST MURDERER When he opens his purse to give us our reward, thy
conscience flies out.   125

SECOND MURDERER 'Tis no matter; let it go. There's few or none will
entertain it.

FIRST MURDERER What if it come to thee again?

The Murderers reject the claims of conscience. They decide to strike Clarence on the head and throw his body in a barrel of wine. Clarence wakes and guesses correctly that they have come to murder him.

Themes

The pangs of conscience (II) (in pairs)

Lines 129–37 are the Second Murderer's catalogue of how conscience constrains human behaviour. Stealing, swearing and adultery are three of the fundamental sins prohibited in the Bible.

a One person speaks the lines and pauses at the end of each sentence. The other person explains in their own words what conscience makes humans do.

b What else does conscience make people do? List the ideas given in the script opposite. Then come up with some ideas and add them to the list. Try to capture the same kind of comic tone by describing why conscience is such a hindrance to someone who has evil intentions.

it conscience

checks stops
detects notices, catches
shamefaced bashful, ashamed
bosom heart
beggars impoverishes

1 Get on with it! (in threes)

Some critics argue that the Murderers' lines 100–44 are irrelevant to the plot. Imagine the director wants to cut the lines to reduce the play's running time. The actors playing the Murderers disagree, arguing that the episode expresses major themes of the play.

• Make notes from both perspectives, then improvise the discussion that takes place, developing each argument as you do so. Remember to quote directly from the play to illustrate your points.

Take the devil resist or stop the devil
insinuate with thee be friendly with you
tall brave

Take him on the costard hit him on the head
malmsey butt keg of malmsey, (a sweet wine)
sop piece of bread soaked in wine before being eaten
reason talk

anon shortly

Stagecraft

On stage or off stage? (in pairs)

Some stage designers have wanted to cut the words 'in the next room' from line 146 because they want 'the malmsey butt' to be visible to the audience as a symbol of Clarence's fear of drowning.

• In role as stage designer, write out the advice you would give to the director about the set design, props and lighting for this scene. Then give the director's response to the stage designer's ideas in the form of footnotes at the bottom of the page in your Director's Journal.

darkly threateningly or obscurely, with a hidden meaning

SECOND MURDERER   I'll not meddle with it; it makes a man a coward.
A man cannot steal but it accuseth him. A man cannot swear but it   130
checks him. A man cannot lie with his neighbour's wife, but it
detects him. 'Tis a blushing, shamefaced spirit that mutinies in a
man's bosom. It fills a man full of obstacles. It made me once restore
a purse of gold that by chance I found. It beggars any man that
keeps it. It is turned out of towns and cities for a dangerous   135
thing, and every man that means to live well endeavours to trust to
himself and live without it.

FIRST MURDERER   'Tis even now at my elbow, persuading me not to
kill the duke.

SECOND MURDERER   Take the devil in thy mind, and believe him not.   140
He would insinuate with thee but to make thee sigh.

FIRST MURDERER   I am strong framed, he cannot prevail with me.

SECOND MURDERER   Spoke like a tall man that respects thy reputation. Come, shall we fall to work?

FIRST MURDERER   Take him on the costard with the hilts of thy sword,   145
and then throw him into the malmsey butt in the next room.

SECOND MURDERER   Oh, excellent device. And make a sop of him.

FIRST MURDERER   Soft, he wakes.

SECOND MURDERER   Strike!

FIRST MURDERER   No, we'll reason with him.   150

CLARENCE   Where art thou, keeper? Give me a cup of wine.

SECOND MURDERER   You shall have wine enough, my lord, anon.

CLARENCE   In God's name, what art thou?

FIRST MURDERER   A man, as you are.

CLARENCE   But not, as I am, royal.   155

FIRST MURDERER   Nor you, as we are, loyal.

CLARENCE   Thy voice is thunder, but thy looks are humble.

FIRST MURDERER   My voice is now the king's, my looks mine own.

CLARENCE   How darkly and how deadly dost thou speak!
Your eyes do menace me. Why look you pale?   160
Who sent you hither? Wherefore do you come?

SECOND MURDERER   To, to, to –

CLARENCE   To murder me?

BOTH   Ay, ay.

CLARENCE   You scarcely have the hearts to tell me so,   165
And therefore cannot have the hearts to do it.
Wherein, my friends, have I offended you?

FIRST MURDERER   Offended us you have not, but the king.

Clarence argues that he has not been convicted of any crime, and that only God has the right to punish him. He claims that he murdered Prince Edward for the sake of his brother, King Edward.

Themes

A damnable deed

To save his life, Clarence cites the supreme authority of God's law against murder. He argues that the law of God ('The great King of kings') is above the secular power of the earthly king. In response, the Murderers remind Clarence of the murders he himself has committed in battle and tell him he has no right to tell them to keep God's law.

a Read through the script opposite. Then condense the conversation into main points so that you capture the essence of the argument (try to limit yourself to fewer than seven points).

b In groups, share your main points and discuss which you think carries the most weight. List them in order to show how convincing each point is, with the most convincing point at the top of the list.

c In a paragraph, explain why you think Shakespeare extended this murder scene with such detailed discussion about God's authority versus kingly authority.

quest jury

convìct convicted

as you hope for any goodness as you hope to achieve salvation

is damnable condemns you to hell

Erroneous vassals mistaken servants, underlings
King of kings God
table of his law the Ten Commandments
Spurn at his edict reject his law

receive the sacrament religiously vow

thy sovereign's son Edward, son of Henry VI

dear important, costly

yet still
he doth it publicly he does that himself, openly
indirect devious, secret

CLARENCE   I shall be reconciled to him again.

SECOND MURDERER   Never, my lord. Therefore prepare to die.   170

CLARENCE   Are you drawn forth among a world of men
                To slay the innocent? What is my offence?
                Where is the evidence that doth accuse me?
                What lawful quest have given their verdict up
                Unto the frowning judge? Or who pronounced   175
                The bitter sentence of poor Clarence' death
                Before I be convìct by course of law?
                To threaten me with death is most unlawful.
                I charge you, as you hope for any goodness,
                That you depart and lay no hands on me.   180
                The deed you undertake is damnable.

FIRST MURDERER   What we will do, we do upon command.

SECOND MURDERER   And he that hath commanded is our king.

CLARENCE   Erroneous vassals! The great King of kings
                Hath in the table of his law commanded   185
                That thou shalt do no murder. Will you then
                Spurn at his edict and fulfil a man's?
                Take heed, for he holds vengeance in his hand
                To hurl upon their heads that break his law.

SECOND MURDERER   And that same vengeance doth he hurl on thee   190
                For false forswearing and for murder, too.
                Thou didst receive the sacrament to fight
                In quarrel of the house of Lancaster.

FIRST MURDERER   And, like a traitor to the name of God,
                Didst break that vow, and with thy treacherous blade   195
                Unripped'st the bowels of thy sovereign's son.

SECOND MURDERER   Whom thou wast sworn to cherish and defend.

FIRST MURDERER   How canst thou urge God's dreadful law to us
                When thou hast broke it in such dear degree?

CLARENCE   Alas! For whose sake did I that ill deed?   200
                For Edward, for my brother, for his sake.
                He sends you not to murder me for this,
                For in that sin he is as deep as I.
                If God will be avengèd for the deed,
                Oh, know you yet, he doth it publicly.   205
                Take not the quarrel from his powerful arm.
                He needs no indirect or lawless course
                To cut off those that have offended him.

Clarence, believing King Edward seeks his death, claims Richard will reward the Murderers for letting him live. Refusing to believe Richard has ordered his murder, he argues that the Murderers will be damned for killing him.

1 The Plantagenets (in sixes)

Lines 209–28 are filled with references to the Plantagenet family: Prince Edward (son of Henry VI), King Edward, Richard (Duke of Gloucester), the Duke of York.

- Take parts as Clarence (himself a Plantagenet) and these four characters. The sixth person speaks all the lines slowly, and each person raises their hand as their character is mentioned. The others should point to the character they believe is referred to.

2 Two Murderers (in pairs)

In lines 224–38, the First Murderer's play on words is at once comic and cruel. His attitude towards Clarence is contrasted with that of the Second Murderer and reveals much about his character.

a Identify each instance of sarcasm or punning in which the First Murderer contradicts Clarence, and consider how Clarence might respond to him.

b How would you describe the difference between the two Murderers? Write a paragraph comparing them and explaining how you would like to see them represented on stage.

Stagecraft

A brother's love – or hate? (in threes)

Clarence cannot believe that his brother Richard wants him dead, but the two Murderers know the truth: Richard is scheming and duplicitous. Somewhere between lines 236 and 240, Clarence abandons his belief that Richard loves him. Shakespeare leaves it up to the actor to work out what triggers Clarence's realisation of the truth and how he responds to the news that his brother seeks his death.

a In small groups, step into the roles of Clarence and the Murderers. Discuss what each man might do to show the audience what brings about Clarence's sudden realisation that his brother has ordered his death.

b Write notes in your Director's Journal to describe how you would want this scene to be portrayed in a modern stage production.

gallant-springing courageous and young

Plantagenet Prince Edward

novice beginner

tidings news

holds me dear loves me; thinks I am worth a high price

lessoned taught

labour my delivery work for my release

thraldom slavery

set you on instructed you

FIRST MURDERER   Who made thee, then, a bloody minister

When gallant-springing brave Plantagenet, 210

That princely novice, was struck dead by thee?

CLARENCE   My brother's love, the devil, and my rage.

FIRST MURDERER   Thy brother's love, our duty, and thy faults

Provoke us hither now to slaughter thee.

CLARENCE   If you do love my brother, hate not me. 215

I am his brother, and I love him well.

If you are hired for meed, go back again,

And I will send you to my brother Gloucester,

Who shall reward you better for my life

Than Edward will for tidings of my death. 220

SECOND MURDERER   You are deceived. Your brother Gloucester hates you.

CLARENCE   Oh, no, he loves me, and he holds me dear.

Go you to him from me.

FIRST MURDERER   Ay, so we will.

CLARENCE   Tell him, when that our princely father York 225

Blessed his three sons with his victorious arm,

He little thought of this divided friendship.

Bid Gloucester think on this, and he will weep.

FIRST MURDERER   Ay, millstones, as he lessoned us to weep.

CLARENCE   Oh, do not slander him, for he is kind. 230

FIRST MURDERER   Right, as snow in harvest.

Come, you deceive yourself,

'Tis he that sends us to destroy you here.

CLARENCE   It cannot be, for he bewept my fortune,

And hugged me in his arms, and swore with sobs 235

That he would labour my delivery.

FIRST MURDERER   Why, so he doth, when he delivers you

From this earth's thraldom to the joys of heaven.

SECOND MURDERER   Make peace with God, for you must die, my lord.

CLARENCE   Have you that holy feeling in your souls 240

To counsel me to make my peace with God,

And are you yet to your own souls so blind

That you will war with God by murdering me?

O sirs, consider, they that set you on

To do this deed will hate you for the deed. 245

SECOND MURDERER   What shall we do?

Clarence begs the murderers to have pity, but he is stabbed by the First Murderer, who drags off the body and throws it in the malmsey butt. The Second Murderer wishes he had saved Clarence.

Stagecraft

Staging Clarence's murder (in small groups)

a The murder of Clarence is the dramatic climax of Act 1. Work out how to stage the episode for greatest dramatic effect. Some hints and suggestions are given below.

- Clarence's words 'My friend, I spy some pity in thy looks' and the following 'Look behind you, my lord' suggest that the Second Murderer tries to prevent the killing (lines 254 and 258).

- One person speaks lines 253–9; the others mime Clarence and the two Murderers. In very slow motion, devise the most dramatically effective method for the stabbing of Clarence.

- The actor playing the First Murderer wants Clarence alive after the stabbing so he can be drowned in the malmsey butt. He argues that this will make the scene even more horrific. The actor playing the Second Murderer disagrees, saying that if Clarence were still alive, his remorse would make him intervene to save Clarence from drowning. Talk together about which actor's suggestion you find the more convincing.

- The First Murderer plans to find a temporary hiding place for Clarence's body, then escape before the deed is discovered. The Second Murderer distances himself from the killing (lines 266–8), wishing he had tried to save Clarence and refusing his share of the reward.

- Work out how to stage the exits of the two Murderers, emphasising their contrasting characters. Does the First Murderer exit with Clarence's body? Or does he leave the body on stage and expect the Second Murderer to do the heavy lifting, returning to tell him off when he does not?

b When you have worked through these ideas, experiment with different ways of performing this exciting climax. Remember to include some of the main points of the discussions between Clarence and the Murderers in the lead-up to the murder.

pent from liberty imprisoned

entreat beg

as you would beg as if you were begging

womanish (Shakespeare's villains often associate pity or compassion with women)

if thine … flatterer if your appearance is not false

malmsey butt within wine barrel in the next room

desperately recklessly

Pilate Pontius Pilate (the Roman governor who washed his hands publicly to show that he took no responsibility for the death of Jesus)

will out will become common knowledge

CLARENCE   Relent, and save your souls.
                    Which of you, if you were a prince's son,
                    Being pent from liberty, as I am now,
                    If two such murderers as yourselves came to you,
                    Would not entreat for life as you would beg,   250
                    Were you in my distress?
FIRST MURDERER   Relent? No. 'Tis cowardly and womanish.
CLARENCE   Not to relent is beastly, savage, devilish.
                    My friend, I spy some pity in thy looks.
                    Oh, if thine eye be not a flatterer,   255
                    Come thou on my side and entreat for me;
                    A begging prince, what beggar pities not?
SECOND MURDERER   Look behind you, my lord.
FIRST MURDERER   Take that, and that.
                              (*Stabs him*)
                                    If all this will not do,
                    I'll drown you in the malmsey butt within.   260
                                        Exit [*with Clarence's body*]
SECOND MURDERER   A bloody deed, and desperately dispatched.
                    How fain, like Pilate, would I wash my hands
                    Of this most grievous murder.

                        Enter FIRST MURDERER

FIRST MURDERER   How now? What mean'st thou that thou help'st me not?
                    By heaven, the duke shall know how slack you have been.   265
SECOND MURDERER   I would he knew that I had saved his brother.
                    Take thou the fee, and tell him what I say,
                    For I repent me that the duke is slain.   *Exit*
FIRST MURDERER   So do not I. Go, coward as thou art.
                    Well, I'll go hide the body in some hole   270
                    Till that the duke give order for his burial;
                    And when I have my meed, I will away,
                    For this will out, and then I must not stay.   *Exit*

Looking back at Act 1
Activities for groups or individuals

1 Setting the scene

Many productions try to establish the play's atmosphere and concerns in its opening moments through a striking dramatic image. The 1996 movie version begins with an eight-minute sequence that includes a battle followed by Yorkist celebrations. Laurence Olivier's film (made in 1955) has a five-minute portrayal of King Edward's coronation before Richard's opening soliloquy.

- Before Richard speaks, what dramatic image or brief sequence would you use to suggest an important theme of the play? Discuss with a partner, then make some notes or sketches in your Director's Journal.

2 Richard insulted

In Scenes 2 and 3, many characters insult and direct abuse at Richard.

- List as many insults directed at Richard as you can. (One example is 'hedgehog' in Scene 2, line 105, which could refer to Richard's emblem of the hog or boar, or to his hunchback, or it could simply be a general term for a person without feelings.)
- Suggest what each of the insults you have found might mean, and identify what common themes they reveal about how others regard Richard.

3 Richard's secret agenda

Richard makes clear his secret thoughts and intentions through soliloquies or apparently innocuous remarks addressed to characters on stage. For example, in Scene 1, he openly reveals his plot against Clarence and finds ways to insult and arouse suspicions about Queen Elizabeth, the Woodville family and Jane Shore.

- Quickly read through Scenes 1, 2 and 3 and identify where Richard reveals his secret thoughts.
- Jot down the objectives he has for the future at these moments. Which of these have been achieved by the end of the act?

4 Richard's appearance

Richard's physical appearance is vital to the play. Shakespeare relied on Sir Thomas More's *History of King Richard the Third* (published in 1513) for a description of what Richard was like. More described Richard as:

> *Little of stature, ill featured of limbs, crook-backed, his left shoulder much higher than his right, hard favoured of visage.*

In Shakespeare's play, Richard tells us that he was born 'deformed, unfinished' and so 'rudely stamped' that dogs bark at him as he limps past them. In Shakespeare's day, many people believed that Richard's 'deformity' was an outward sign of his wickedness, although in his opening speech Richard claims that he has turned to evil because he looks different and feels unloved.

Directors might choose to represent Richard as completely evil and grotesque in appearance, or realistically as someone with a physical disability that makes him different from other people.

a   In pairs, study the picture of Richard opposite and those elsewhere in this edition. Then step into role as director and the actor playing Richard and discuss some possible ways of presenting him physically.

b   On your own, write a paragraph or two outlining your ideas and giving a detailed description of how you would portray Richard on stage in a new production.

King Edward attempts to reconcile the quarrelling nobles. Queen Elizabeth, Rivers and Dorset (the Woodvilles) swear love and friendship with Hastings. The King asks Buckingham to join the peace pact.

1 Do actions speak louder than words?
(in small groups)

King Edward attempts to reconcile the Woodville family (Queen Elizabeth, her son Dorset and her brother Rivers) with those who oppose them (Hastings and Buckingham).

a As one person speaks lines 1–40, the rest of the group echoes all the words and phrases about friendship and religion.

b Draw a simple representation (such as a stick figure) of each character and write down their intentions in a thought bubble.

2 How genuine is the reconciliation? (in sixes)

Take parts as King Edward, Rivers, Hastings, Queen Elizabeth, Dorset and Buckingham. Act out lines 1–40, using all the actions that are mentioned or suggested – for example: 'Rivers and Hastings, take each other's hand' (line 7), 'So thrive I, as I truly swear the like' (line 11), 'There, Hastings, I will never more remember / Our former hatred, so thrive I and mine' (line 23), 'Dorset, embrace him' (line 25).

• First perform the lines so that an audience would see a sincere agreement of friendship.

• Then perform the lines so that an audience would see a display of friendship that conceals hatred and suggests a lack of forgiveness.

Stagecraft

Dramatic irony (in pairs)

King Edward warns Rivers and Hastings not to be insincere in front of him, because God will see through their deceit and their hypocrisy will be revealed. He is unaware that Clarence has just been murdered, and he uses the language of piety, love and peace.

• As the director of a modern performance, how would you use sound effects, lighting, stage space and actors' gestures to increase the dramatic tension in the script opposite? Remember, the dramatic irony is that the audience understands the King's request for peace and his threats of divine justice in the light of Clarence's murder. Discuss this with your partner, then write notes in your Director's Journal.

peers lords

united league friendship, alliance

embassage message

my redeemer … hence Christ to save me (Edward expects to die)

Dissemble not do not pretend

purged cleansed

So thrive … swear the like may I flourish according to the truth of the oath I swear

dally pretend

Confound overthrow

award ensure

factious divided by forming different factions or parties

unfeignedly genuinely, without pretence

protest swear

inviolable permanent, unbreakable

Act 2 Scene 1

London: a room in King Edward's palace

Flourish. Enter KING EDWARD (*sick*), QUEEN ELIZABETH,
LORD MARQUESS DORSET, RIVERS, HASTINGS, CATESBY,
BUCKINGHAM *and others*

KING EDWARD	Why, so. Now have I done a good day's work.
	You peers, continue this united league.
	I every day expect an embassage
	From my redeemer to redeem me hence.
	And more to peace my soul shall part to heaven,
	Since I have made my friends at peace on earth.
	Rivers and Hastings, take each other's hand.
	Dissemble not your hatred; swear your love.
RIVERS	By heaven, my soul is purged from grudging hate,
	And with my hand I seal my true heart's love.
HASTINGS	So thrive I, as I truly swear the like.
KING EDWARD	Take heed you dally not before your king,
	Lest he that is the supreme King of kings
	Confound your hidden falsehood and award
	Either of you to be the other's end.
HASTINGS	So prosper I, as I swear perfect love.
RIVERS	And I, as I love Hastings with my heart.
KING EDWARD	Madam, yourself is not exempt from this,
	Nor you, son Dorset, Buckingham, nor you;
	You have been factious one against the other.
	Wife, love Lord Hastings, let him kiss your hand,
	And what you do, do it unfeignedly.
ELIZABETH	There, Hastings, I will never more remember
	Our former hatred, so thrive I and mine.
KING EDWARD	Dorset, embrace him. Hastings, love lord marquess.
DORSET	This interchange of love, I here protest,
	Upon my part shall be inviolable.
HASTINGS	And so swear I.
KING EDWARD	Now, princely Buckingham, seal thou this league
	With thy embracements to my wife's allies,
	And make me happy in your unity.

5

10

15

20

25

30

Buckingham pledges his love and loyalty to King Edward. The King wishes for Richard to arrive to complete the peace process. Richard enters and expresses peace and goodwill to everyone present.

1 Enter Ratcliffe and Richard (in pairs)

In some productions, Richard and Ratcliffe are already on stage and hear King Edward's wish that his brother Richard was present (line 43).

- Suggest what dramatic effects might be achieved by having Richard and Ratcliffe enter unobserved by the others before this point in the scene.

Characters

Sincere friendship? (in pairs)

Richard asks to be reconciled with those he might have offended. But he suggests that people's hostility arises from wrong information ('fasle intelligence') and incorrect conclusions ('wrong surmise'). He suggests that if he did anything to cause resentment, it was done 'unwillingly, or in my rage'.

a How might an actor playing Richard make it clear to an audience that his words are not sincere?

b 'Lord Woodville' and 'Lord Scales' (line 68) are other titles of Lord Rivers. How might Richard make a joke of line 68?

c Suggest how each character reacts to Richard's offer of friendship.

but except

Deep mysterious, secretive

cordial medicine

wanteth is only missing
period conclusion

charity love, reconciliation

swelling hostile
wrong-incensèd wrongly angered
princely heap high-born company

aught committed committed anything
is hardly borne causes hurt
at enmity in a state of hatred

cousin (term used to address both close and distant relatives)
lodged established

all without desert entirely without cause

BUCKINGHAM   Whenever Buckingham doth turn his hate
              Upon your grace, but with all duteous love
              Doth cherish you and yours, God punish me
              With hate in those where I expect most love.   35
              When I have most need to employ a friend,
              And most assurèd that he is a friend,
              Deep, hollow, treacherous, and full of guile
              Be he unto me. This do I beg of heaven,
              When I am cold in love to you or yours.   40

                          Embrace

KING EDWARD   A pleasing cordial, princely Buckingham,
              Is this thy vow unto my sickly heart.
              There wanteth now our brother Gloucester here
              To make the blessèd period of this peace.

BUCKINGHAM   And in good time,   45
              Here comes Sir Richard Ratcliffe and the duke.

                  Enter RATCLIFFE *and* RICHARD

RICHARD   Good morrow to my sovereign king and queen;
              And princely peers, a happy time of day.

KING EDWARD   Happy indeed, as we have spent the day.
              Gloucester, we have done deeds of charity,   50
              Made peace of enmity, fair love of hate,
              Between these swelling wrong-incensèd peers.

RICHARD   A blessèd labour, my most sovereign lord.
              Among this princely heap, if any here
              By false intelligence or wrong surmise   55
              Hold me a foe; if I unwillingly or in my rage
              Have aught committed that is hardly borne
              To any in this presence, I desire
              To reconcile me to his friendly peace.
              'Tis death to me to be at enmity;   60
              I hate it and desire all good men's love.
              First, madam, I entreat true peace of you,
              Which I will purchase with my duteous service;
              Of you, my noble cousin Buckingham,
              If ever any grudge were lodged between us;   65
              Of you and you, Lord Rivers, and of Dorset,
              That all without desert have frowned on me;
              Of you, Lord Woodville, and Lord Scales, of you;
              Dukes, earls, lords, gentlemen, indeed of all.

Stagecraft

'They all start' (in pairs)

Amid words of peace and reconciliation – and as Queen Elizabeth anticipates future celebrations of this new unity in the court – Richard suddenly announces the shocking news that his brother Clarence is dead.

a Discuss how you would stage lines 70–88 to make the shift in mood as dramatic as possible. How would you heighten the impact of the series of questions that follows?

b After this revelation, Richard seizes the opportunity to cast suspicion on the Woodvilles. One person speaks lines 89–96 very slowly, pausing at the end of each line. In the pause, the other suggests how Richard can use actions and expressions to throw suspicion on others.

1 Shakespeare's stage

Shakespeare's stage was bare, with none of the lavish sets, stage mechanics or special lighting and sound effects that we are familiar with today. As a result, Shakespeare included many verbal cues so that the audience could imagine rather than actually see what was happening on stage. Buckingham's line 85 ('Look I so pale, Lord Dorset, as the rest?') is an example of one of these visual clues.

• What might be the significance of Buckingham's comment, if Shakespeare is drawing the audience's attention to it in this way?

Write about it

Stanley's awkward moment (by yourself)

Stanley, Earl of Derby, makes an unfortunate entrance at a tense and emotional moment. He asks for his servant's life to be spared as a favour, in return for the services he has rendered to his lord. Stanley does not realise that he is intruding on the King's grief and shock at the discovery of Clarence's death. Stanley is in the wrong place at the wrong time, and his request prompts an emotional outburst from the King from line 104.

• Write Stanley's diary entry, describing the treatment he receives and noting his observations of the scene he walks into. (You might like to read ahead to the end of the scene before you start writing).

---

jot small portion
at odds in conflict

kept hereafter remembered by people
compounded resolved

grace favour

flouted outraged, insulted
in this royal presence in the presence of the King

wingèd Mercury (in classical mythology, a messenger of the gods who wore a winged helmet)
tardy cripple slow and incapacitated person
lag late
Nearer … not in blood not of royal blood, but having murder in their minds
go current from escape
boon favour

forfeit sparing

	I do not know that Englishman alive	70
	With whom my soul is any jot at odds	
	More than the infant that is born tonight.	
	I thank my God for my humility.	
ELIZABETH	A holy day shall this be kept hereafter.	
	I would to God all strifes were well compounded.	75
	My sovereign lord, I do beseech your highness	
	To take our brother Clarence to your grace.	
RICHARD	Why, madam, have I offered love for this,	
	To be so flouted in this royal presence?	
	Who knows not that the gentle duke is dead?	80

They all start

	You do him injury to scorn his corpse.	
KING EDWARD	Who knows not he is dead?	
	Who knows he is?	
ELIZABETH	All-seeing heaven, what a world is this?	
BUCKINGHAM	Look I so pale, Lord Dorset, as the rest?	85
DORSET	Ay, my good lord, and no man in the presence	
	But his red colour hath forsook his cheeks.	
KING EDWARD	Is Clarence dead? The order was reversed.	
RICHARD	But he (poor man) by your first order died,	
	And that a wingèd Mercury did bear;	90
	Some tardy cripple bare the countermand,	
	That came too lag to see him burièd.	
	God grant that some, less noble and less loyal,	
	Nearer in bloody thoughts and not in blood,	
	Deserve not worse than wretched Clarence did,	95
	And yet go current from suspicion.	

Enter [STANLEY] EARL OF DERBY

STANLEY	A boon, my sovereign, for my service done.	
KING EDWARD	I prithee, peace, my soul is full of sorrow.	
STANLEY	I will not rise unless your highness hear me.	
KING EDWARD	Then say at once what is it thou requests.	100
STANLEY	The forfeit, sovereign, of my servant's life,	
	Who slew today a riotous gentleman	
	Lately attendant on the Duke of Norfolk.	

King Edward contrasts Stanley's plea with the lack of pleas for mercy for Clarence. Edward remembers Clarence's many favours to him. He grants pardon, but fears God's revenge. Richard blames the Woodvilles for Clarence's death.

1 Why didn't you all plead for Clarence? (in pairs)

a Put the following summary in order and match it to the King's lines in the script opposite.

1 Why should I pardon a slave, when I ordered my own brother's death?

2 Clarence killed no one, yet he was killed.

3 Why didn't anyone plead for him or remind me of all he did for me?

4 In my anger, I forgot Clarence's good deeds and none of you reminded me.

5 But when one of your servants offends, you immediately plead for mercy for them.

6 I have to grant the plea for a servant though neither I nor you pleaded for Clarence.

7 We and our children will be punished for his death.

b How convinced are you by Edward's explanation of his behaviour? Take it in turns to read his lines 104–35 aloud as meaningfully and sincerely as you can.

Stagecraft

Richard's friends?

Look back through this scene and note the characters who appear on stage. Then look at the stage direction at line 136: '*Exeunt some with K[ing] and Queen*'.

- Write a list of characters who you think are left on stage after the exit of the King and Queen. Sketch a bird's-eye view of the stage and mark on it where you would place these characters (blocking) to show their relationships.

Themes

Manipulation and insinuations (in pairs)

Richard's half-truths and insinuations allow him to manipulate the people around him. In the script opposite, Richard points out that the Queen's family looked guilty and pale (lines 138–9).

- What is the truth in his comment and what is only a half-truth? Write out what you think Richard's intentions are at this point in the play.

to doom to be responsible for
slave servant
killed no man (Clarence killed no man except during war in support of Edward)
his fault was thought (Edward believes that Clarence plotted against him but did not act against him)

Oxford (an enemy nobleman)

lap wrap

thin thinly covered

carters heavy labourers
waiting vassals table servants
defaced ... dear redeemer killed a man (since people were made in the image of God)
straight immediately

ungracious lacking grace

beholding indebted

closet private room

the fruits of rashness the result of his poor judgement

still always

74

KING EDWARD   Have I a tongue to doom my brother's death,
                And shall that tongue give pardon to a slave?   105
                My brother killed no man; his fault was thought,
                And yet his punishment was bitter death.
                Who sued to me for him? Who (in my wrath)
                Kneeled at my feet and bid me be advised?
                Who spoke of brotherhood? Who spoke of love?   110
                Who told me how the poor soul did forsake
                The mighty Warwick and did fight for me?
                Who told me, in the field at Tewkesbury,
                When Oxford had me down, he rescued me
                And said 'Dear brother, live, and be a king'?   115
                Who told me, when we both lay in the field,
                Frozen almost to death, how he did lap me
                Even in his garments and did give himself
                (All thin and naked) to the numb cold night?
                All this from my remembrance brutish wrath   120
                Sinfully plucked, and not a man of you
                Had so much grace to put it in my mind.
                But when your carters or your waiting vassals
                Have done a drunken slaughter and defaced
                The precious image of our dear redeemer,   125
                You straight are on your knees for pardon, pardon,
                And I, unjustly too, must grant it you.
                But for my brother not a man would speak,
                Nor I, ungracious, speak unto myself
                For him, poor soul. The proudest of you all   130
                Have been beholding to him in his life,
                Yet none of you would once beg for his life.
                O God, I fear thy justice will take hold
                On me and you, and mine and yours, for this.
                Come, Hastings, help me to my closet.   135
                Ah, poor Clarence!
                                        Exeunt some with K[ing] and Queen

RICHARD   This is the fruits of rashness. Marked you not
                How that the guilty kindred of the queen
                Looked pale when they did hear of Clarence' death?
                Oh, they did urge it still unto the king.   140
                God will revenge it. Come, lords, will you go
                To comfort Edward with our company?

BUCKINGHAM   We wait upon your grace.   *Exeunt*

Clarence's children suspect their father is dead, but the Duchess of York, their grandmother, says she grieves for King Edward's illness. She admits that Clarence is dead and warns the children not to be fooled by Richard.

1 The language of deceit (in threes)

The Duchess of York begins with a lie, and Clarence's son has difficulty in working out what she really means.

- Take parts as the Duchess, the Boy and the Girl. Speak lines 1–33, pausing at the end of each sentence. In each pause, talk together about whether the sentence is true, false or unproven (impossible to judge).

Write about it

The dissembling uncle (by yourself)

The Duchess of York is in no doubt about Richard's ability to 'dissemble' and deceive (demonstrated by the way he behaved towards Clarence's son).

- Read lines 20–6 and imagine how this brief scene might have occurred from Richard's perspective. Then write Richard's diary entry for that day, describing his meeting with Clarence's son (Edward Plantagenet) and revealing his motives and future intentions. Try to capture Richard's witty yet outrageous tone and the extent of his cunning manipulation.

Themes

Richard's vice (in pairs)

In lines 27–30, Richard's mother, the Duchess of York, gives her unflattering view of her son's character. The word 'vice' is significant. Not only does it refer to the way Richard hides his sins under a mask of goodness, it also reminds the audience that he is related to the Vice figure in medieval religious drama. Vice was a personification of evil and represented the devil's temptations and manipulation as he schemed against humanity.

- Talk together about the deep vices that you know Richard is hiding under his mask of goodness.
- Prepare two tableaux – one representing Richard's mask of goodness and the other depicting his hidden evil intentions.

Clarence's two children
(Margaret, 12, and Edward, 10)

cousins grandchildren

lament weep for

loath unwilling

lost sorrow … lost futile grief because they are dead and there is nothing to be done

importune beg

Incapable … innocents young children lacking knowledge

impeachments accusations of treason

kindly benevolently or as a relative would

gentle shape kindly actions

visor outward appearance or disguise

vice vicious evil, or the Vice figure in medieval drama

dugs breasts

dissemble pretend, act a part, lie

Act 2 Scene 2

London: a room in King Edward's palace

Enter the old DUCHESS OF YORK *with Clarence's two children*
[BOY *and* GIRL]

BOY	Good grandam, tell us, is our father dead?
DUCHESS	No, boy.
GIRL	Why do you weep so oft, and beat your breast,
	And cry, 'O Clarence, my unhappy son'?
BOY	Why do you look on us, and shake your head, 5
	And call us orphans, wretches, castaways,
	If that our noble father were alive?
DUCHESS	My pretty cousins, you mistake me both.
	I do lament the sickness of the king,
	As loath to lose him, not your father's death. 10
	It were lost sorrow to wail one that's lost.
BOY	Then you conclude, my grandam, he is dead.
	The king mine uncle is to blame for it.
	God will revenge it, whom I will importune
	With earnest prayers all to that effect. 15
GIRL	And so will I.
DUCHESS	Peace, children, peace. The king doth love you well.
	Incapable and shallow innocents,
	You cannot guess who caused your father's death.
BOY	Grandam, we can, for my good uncle Gloucester 20
	Told me the king, provoked to it by the queen,
	Devised impeachments to imprison him.
	And when my uncle told me so, he wept,
	And pitied me, and kindly kissed my cheek;
	Bade me rely on him as on my father, 25
	And he would love me dearly as a child.
DUCHESS	Ah, that deceit should steal such gentle shape
	And with a virtuous visor hide deep vice.
	He is my son, ay, and therein my shame,
	Yet from my dugs he drew not this deceit. 30
BOY	Think you my uncle did dissemble, grandam?
DUCHESS	Ay, boy.

The grieving Queen Elizabeth brings news of King Edward's death. The Duchess laments the loss of two sons and Richard's false character. She and Clarence's children seem to lack sympathy for Elizabeth.

1 Elizabeth's grief (in pairs)

Queen Elizabeth enters, knowing her husband, King Edward, is dead. Her grief is emphasised by the stage direction: '*with her hair about her ears*'. Loose and dishevelled hair was a conventional sign of distress in women.

a How would you advise the actor playing Elizabeth to make a dramatic and emotional entrance? One of you take the role of director, and instruct the other in how to read lines 35–40. Afterwards, swap roles so the other person performs Elizabeth's lines.

b List the ways in which the death of Elizabeth's husband has made her vulnerable.

Language in the play
Imagery of grief and loss (in pairs)

Lines 1–88 are full of references to death, loss and grief. Two children are left fatherless, Queen Elizabeth is widowed and the Duchess of York has lost two sons. Elizabeth and the Duchess use a great deal of imagery.

- The 'branches' and 'root' (line 41) are images of the family tree of King Edward – a tree that will now die.
- In lines 50–4, the 'two mirrors' are the Duchess of York's sons, Edward and Clarence, and the 'false glass' is Richard.
- In lines 66–70, Queen Elizabeth asks for her eyes to be like the ocean so she can flood the world with her tears.

a Create a visual representation of the imagery of grief and loss, using images from magazines or the Internet. Annotate your representation with words and phrases from the script opposite.

b Write a paragraph to explore how this imagery adds to your understanding of the characters' grief and the dramatic tension of the scene.

chide reprimand, rebuke

to myself ... enemy seek to destroy myself

rude rough, uncivilised

act action (suicide) or theatrical act, display

want lack

brief quick

ne'er-changing night death

interest personal concern

title right (as a mother)

his images his sons

semblance appearance, form

false glass distorted mirror or reflection (Richard)

my shame in him I am ashamed of him

two crutches the support of her two sons (Edward and Clarence)

moiety small portion

moan grief

overgo exceed, outdo

kindred tears tears that come from being in the same family, similar tears

widow-dolour widow's sadness

reduce bring

BOY I cannot think it. Hark, what noise is this?

Enter the QUEEN [ELIZABETH] *with her hair about her ears,*
RIVERS *and* DORSET *after her*

ELIZABETH Ah, who shall hinder me to wail and weep,
To chide my fortune and torment myself? 35
I'll join with black despair against my soul,
And to myself become an enemy.

DUCHESS What means this scene of rude impatience?

ELIZABETH To make an act of tragic violence.
Edward, my lord, thy son, our king, is dead. 40
Why grow the branches when the root is gone?
Why wither not the leaves that want their sap?
If you will live, lament; if die, be brief,
That our swift-wingèd souls may catch the king's,
Or, like obedient subjects, follow him 45
To his new kingdom of ne'er-changing night.

DUCHESS Ah, so much interest have I in thy sorrow
As I had title in thy noble husband.
I have bewept a worthy husband's death
And lived with looking on his images, 50
But now two mirrors of his princely semblance
Are cracked in pieces by malignant death,
And I for comfort have but one false glass,
That grieves me when I see my shame in him.
Thou art a widow, yet thou art a mother 55
And hast the comfort of thy children left.
But death hath snatched my husband from mine arms
And plucked two crutches from my feeble hands,
Clarence and Edward. Oh, what cause have I,
Thine being but a moiety of my moan, 60
To overgo thy woes and drown thy cries.

BOY Ah, aunt, you wept not for our father's death.
How can we aid you with our kindred tears?

GIRL Our fatherless distress was left unmoaned.
Your widow-dolour likewise be unwept. 65

ELIZABETH Give me no help in lamentation.
I am not barren to bring forth complaints.
All springs reduce their currents to mine eyes,

Language in the play
The rhetoric of grief and loss (in small groups)

The use of rhetorical figures and patterns in the language of the script opposite can focus attention on two aspects of grief and loss:

- the formality of the public grief of the solemn and noble royal family
- the emotional intensity of their personal sorrow and their pitiful vulnerability.

a Take parts as the children, the Duchess of York and Queen Elizabeth. Speak lines 71–85, emphasising the exact repetition and pattern of the words.

b Identify the following rhetorical figures from the script opposite:
- **Anaphora** – the repetition of the same word at the beginning of successive sentences.
- **Epistrophe** – the repetition of a word or phrase at the end of a series of sentences or clauses.
- Rhetorical questions.

c Write a detailed stage direction at line 71 to help the actors. What tone of voice, gestures and movement would you want them to use to highlight different aspects of their grief and loss? How would you want them to emphasise the repetition and language patterns?

1 Criticism or comfort? (in pairs)

a Read what Dorset and Rivers say to Elizabeth in lines 89–95 and 96–100. Whose advice is most fitting for this moment? Discuss the following questions, then explain why their advice is helpful or not, well timed or not.

- How does Dorset's advice affect the Queen? Is he rebuking or comforting his mother?
- How is Rivers' practical advice and understanding of political implications received by the Queen?

b What comfort or advice would you give the Queen at this point? Write your own lines of verse in **iambic pentameter** (see p. 249), using similarly striking words as Dorset and Rivers.

governed controlled

stay support

dear costly

parcelled individual, partial
general complete

threefold distressed (she grieves for her husband and two sons)
pamper care for

opposite with contrary or hostile towards
For because
requires calls in, wants return of
royal debt (the King)

plant place
living Edward the prince of Wales, (Edward IV's son)

Sister sister-in-law

cry you mercy beg your pardon

That I, being governed by the watery moon,
May send forth plenteous tears to drown the world. 70
Ah, for my husband, for my dear lord Edward.

CHILDREN Ah, for our father, for our dear lord Clarence.

DUCHESS Alas for both, both mine Edward and Clarence.

ELIZABETH What stay had I but Edward? And he's gone.

CHILDREN What stay had we but Clarence? And he's gone. 75

DUCHESS What stays had I but they? And they are gone.

ELIZABETH Was never widow had so dear a loss.

CHILDREN Were never orphans had so dear a loss.

DUCHESS Was never mother had so dear a loss.
Alas, I am the mother of these griefs; 80
Their woes are parcelled, mine is general.
She for an Edward weeps, and so do I;
I for a Clarence weep, so doth not she.
These babes for Clarence weep, and so do I;
I for an Edward weep, so do not they. 85
Alas, you three, on me, threefold distressed,
Pour all your tears; I am your sorrow's nurse,
And I will pamper it with lamentation.

DORSET Comfort, dear mother. God is much displeased
That you take with unthankfulness his doing. 90
In common worldly things 'tis called ungrateful
With dull unwillingness to repay a debt
Which with a bounteous hand was kindly lent;
Much more to be thus opposite with heaven,
For it requires the royal debt it lent you. 95

RIVERS Madam, bethink you like a careful mother
Of the young prince your son. Send straight for him.
Let him be crowned. In him your comfort lives.
Drown desperate sorrow in dead Edward's grave
And plant your joys in living Edward's throne. 100

Enter RICHARD, BUCKINGHAM, [STANLEY EARL OF]
DERBY, HASTINGS, *and* RATCLIFFE

RICHARD Sister, have comfort. All of us have cause
To wail the dimming of our shining star,
But none can help our harms by wailing them.
Madam, my mother, I do cry you mercy;

1 Mother and son

The Duchess blesses Richard, but his aside shows that he does not take her words seriously. He says that the 'butt-end' (110) of her blessing would be that he would die naturally in old age, a reformed character.

- Invent an aside for the Duchess to speak to the audience before line 107. Remember that her earlier comments, including her description of Richard as a 'false glass', demonstrate what she really thinks of him (see lines 27–8 and 53).

Language in the play

Buckingham's imagery (in pairs)

Buckingham takes the initiative and puts forward a plan of action. To strengthen his argument, he uses a series of **metaphors** (see p. 250) to describe the fragility of the power structure in the kingdom:

- reaping a future harvest (lines 115–16)
- healing fractured bones (lines 117–19)
- training a horse to submit to its rider (lines 129–30).

a Talk together about how these metaphors add to Buckingham's persuasive powers and how his imagery increases the strength of his argument.

b In writing, describe each metaphor in your own words. Explore what Buckingham means by each one and the effect it might have on each of the characters present.

2 A small escort

Buckingham's proposal is accepted: only a small escort will fetch Prince Edward from Ludlow and accompany him on the journey to London for his coronation. At first Dorset questions the wisdom of this, but he is soon persuaded to change his mind.

- Write a sentence for each character that reveals either their suspicions or their true intentions regarding this 'small escort'. This should take the form of an aside that each character could deliver to the audience without any of the other characters hearing.

---

crave beg
meekness humility, gentleness

butt-end unpleasant dregs left in a barrel of wine
cloudy gloomy, depressed

spent lost

broken rancour interrupted hostility

Me seemeth it seems to me
train escort
Ludlow (a castle on the Welsh border)
fet fetched
multitude large escort

green weak, new

compact pact of friendship

apparent likelihood obvious possibility
breach break, rupture
haply perhaps
urged incited
meet right, appropriate

straight shall post immediately ride

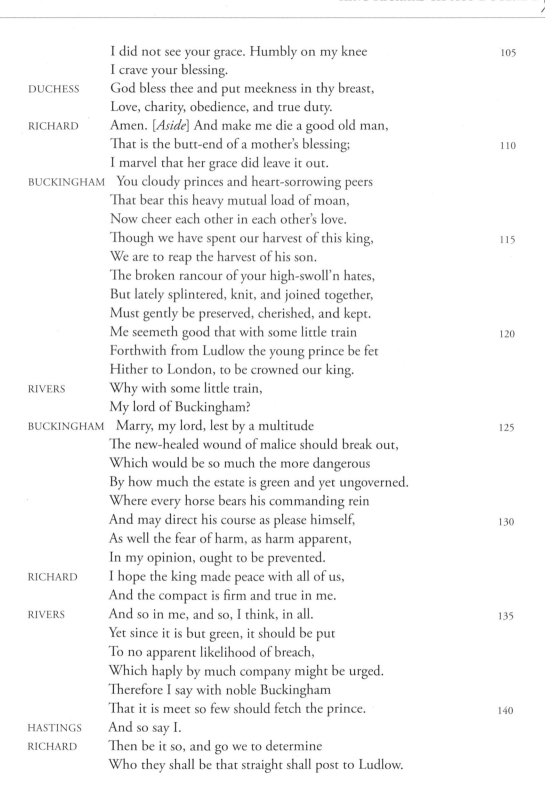

	I did not see your grace. Humbly on my knee	105
	I crave your blessing.
DUCHESS	God bless thee and put meekness in thy breast,
	Love, charity, obedience, and true duty.
RICHARD	Amen. [*Aside*] And make me die a good old man,
	That is the butt-end of a mother's blessing;	110
	I marvel that her grace did leave it out.
BUCKINGHAM	You cloudy princes and heart-sorrowing peers
	That bear this heavy mutual load of moan,
	Now cheer each other in each other's love.
	Though we have spent our harvest of this king,	115
	We are to reap the harvest of his son.
	The broken rancour of your high-swoll'n hates,
	But lately splintered, knit, and joined together,
	Must gently be preserved, cherished, and kept.
	Me seemeth good that with some little train	120
	Forthwith from Ludlow the young prince be fet
	Hither to London, to be crowned our king.
RIVERS	Why with some little train,
	My lord of Buckingham?
BUCKINGHAM	Marry, my lord, lest by a multitude	125
	The new-healed wound of malice should break out,
	Which would be so much the more dangerous
	By how much the estate is green and yet ungoverned.
	Where every horse bears his commanding rein
	And may direct his course as please himself,	130
	As well the fear of harm, as harm apparent,
	In my opinion, ought to be prevented.
RICHARD	I hope the king made peace with all of us,
	And the compact is firm and true in me.
RIVERS	And so in me, and so, I think, in all.	135
	Yet since it is but green, it should be put
	To no apparent likelihood of breach,
	Which haply by much company might be urged.
	Therefore I say with noble Buckingham
	That it is meet so few should fetch the prince.	140
HASTINGS	And so say I.
RICHARD	Then be it so, and go we to determine
	Who they shall be that straight shall post to Ludlow.

1 Showing the power struggle

Richard appears to be empowering Queen Elizabeth and the Duchess of York by asking them to give their opinions on who should escort Edward, Prince of Wales, to London for his coronation. Lines 151–4 reveal that he has quite different plans in mind. The exit of the Queen's 'proud kindred', leaving Richard and Buckingham alone on stage, is a great opportunity for actors to show the struggle for power between the Woodvilles and Richard and Buckingham.

• Write notes on how to perform the stage direction at line 145, so that the audience can appreciate this power struggle.

Characters

'My other self' (in pairs)

In lines 151–3, Richard's flattering description of Buckingham would be recognised by an Elizabethan audience as characteristic language of the Vice figure, who would flatter people in order to deceive them. Take parts as Buckingham and Richard, and enact the lines in the ways listed below. In each case, show Buckingham's response.

• Richard really means what he says.
• Richard is quite insincere.
• Richard speaks the lines as an aside to the audience as Buckingham strides away.

Themes

'a giddy world' (in threes)

The social insecurity and political instability of England on the death of King Edward is the focus of this scene's discussion between three citizens of London. Their concern is that, with no strong leadership, the country and its people will be troubled and fearful.

a Assign parts and read through Scene 3 to bring out the differing viewpoints of the citizens.

b Pick out all the adjectives and descriptive phrases used to describe England and the world after the death of King Edward.

c What is it exactly that makes the three citizens so fearful? Discuss this in your groups.

---

censures opinions

by the way on the way to Ludlow
sort occasion make an opportunity
index introduction
story plan
my counsel's consistory my mind's council chamber (the exact representation of my thoughts)
oracle someone who foretells the future
as a child as obedient as a child

promise assure
abroad being spread

by'r Lady by the Virgin Mary (a mild oath)
seldom comes the better seldom comes good news
giddy crazy, unstable
God speed God give you good speed (usually a farewell rather than a greeting)
Give you God give you
while present time
masters sirs, gentlemen
troublous troubled

Madam, and you my sister, will you go
To give your censures in this business?   145

Exeunt [all but] Buckingham and Richard

BUCKINGHAM   My lord, whoever journeys to the prince,
For God's sake let not us two stay at home,
For by the way I'll sort occasion,
As index to the story we late talked of,
To part the queen's proud kindred from the prince.   150

RICHARD   My other self, my counsel's consistory,
My oracle, my prophet, my dear cousin,
I, as a child, will go by thy direction.
Toward Ludlow then, for we'll not stay behind.

Exeunt

Act 2 Scene 3
London: a street

Enter FIRST CITIZEN *and* SECOND CITIZEN

FIRST CITIZEN   Good morrow, neighbour. Whither away so fast?
SECOND CITIZEN   I promise you, I scarcely know myself.
Hear you the news abroad?
FIRST CITIZEN   Yes, that the king is dead.
SECOND CITIZEN   Ill news, by'r Lady; seldom comes the better.   5
I fear, I fear, 'twill prove a giddy world.

Enter another [THIRD] CITIZEN

THIRD CITIZEN   Neighbours, God speed.
FIRST CITIZEN   Give you good morrow, sir.
THIRD CITIZEN   Doth the news hold of good King Edward's death?
SECOND CITIZEN   Ay, sir, it is too true, God help the while.   10
THIRD CITIZEN   Then, masters, look to see a troublous world.
FIRST CITIZEN   No, no, by God's good grace his son shall reign.
THIRD CITIZEN   Woe to that land that's governed by a child.

The citizens hope for a peaceful future under the new young King. The Third Citizen fears that rivalry between Richard and the Woodvilles will bring harsh and dangerous times.

1 The voice of the people (in threes)

The Second and Third Citizens have a very pessimistic view of a future England under the rule of the young Prince Edward ('Woe to that land that's governed by a child', line 13). This is the only scene in the play in which the ordinary people of England – unattended by the aristocracy – express their hopes and fears for England's future.

- Take roles as the citizens and write an aside for each of them at a suitable point in the script opposite. Your aim is to allow the characters to think aloud and to express their concerns and anxieties more fully This scene only hints at some of the problems they may face and their expectations for the future. This is your chance to express their thoughts in more detail.

2 Formal verse (in pairs)

The citizens speak in stylised and formal language. The Third Citizen uses a lot of imagery in lines 34–7 and 44–6, and foresees dangerous rivalry between Prince Edward's uncles.

a Identify these images and discuss how effective you find them in conveying the Third Citizen's meaning.

b If you were directing a new production, how would you present the Citizens on stage? Write a set of director's notes, giving your reasons for how the Citizens dress and speak. Would you want to signal to an audience that their words are prophetic (as Shakespeare seems to do through his use of verse)?

Themes

National instability

The three citizens have been called to the justices and it is unclear whether they will be fined or reprimanded. They are more concerned about their own immediate future than that of the kingdom.

- What can you decipher (or discover through research) about beliefs in Shakespeare's day about personal distress, national chaos and unlawful kingship? Use resources in your library or the Internet, and summarise your findings as a poster, using images as well as writing.

nonage minority (a child)
council the King's council of ministers, who are normally under his control, but govern in his place if the King is a child

wot knows

politic grave counsel wise, solemn advice

emulation competition, rivalry
touch us all too near seriously harm everyone

queen's sons Dorset and Grey
haught haughty
solace have comfort

dearth famine
sort orders

heavily worriedly, mournful
still always

Ensuing danger forthcoming disasters
proof experience

SECOND CITIZEN   In him there is a hope of government,
Which in his nonage, council under him,   15
And in his full and ripened years, himself
No doubt shall then, and till then, govern well.

FIRST CITIZEN   So stood the state when Henry the Sixth
Was crowned in Paris but at nine months old.

THIRD CITIZEN   Stood the state so? No, no, good friends, God wot,   20
For then this land was famously enriched
With politic grave counsel. Then the king
Had virtuous uncles to protect his grace.

FIRST CITIZEN   Why, so hath this, both by his father and mother.

THIRD CITIZEN   Better it were they all came by his father,   25
Or by his father there were none at all.
For emulation who shall now be nearest
Will touch us all too near, if God prevent not.
Oh, full of danger is the Duke of Gloucester,
And the queen's sons and brothers haught and proud.   30
And were they to be ruled, and not to rule,
This sickly land might solace as before.

FIRST CITIZEN   Come, come, we fear the worst; all will be well.

THIRD CITIZEN   When clouds are seen, wise men put on their cloaks;
When great leaves fall, then winter is at hand;   35
When the sun sets, who doth not look for night?
Untimely storms makes men expect a dearth.
All may be well, but if God sort it so,
'Tis more than we deserve or I expect.

SECOND CITIZEN   Truly, the hearts of men are full of fear.   40
You cannot reason almost with a man
That looks not heavily and full of dread.

THIRD CITIZEN   Before the days of change, still is it so.
By a divine instinct, men's minds mistrust
Ensuing danger, as by proof, we see   45
The water swell before a boisterous storm.
But leave it all to God. Whither away?

SECOND CITIZEN   Marry, we were sent for to the justices.

THIRD CITIZEN   And so was I. I'll bear you company.

Exeunt

1 Waiting for the new king (in pairs)

This scene opens with the new young King's family waiting for his arrival from Ludlow. Some productions start with a reminder of the death of his father and focus on the grief of the two royal widows. Others emphasise the youthful liveliness of the Duke of York.

a How would you want to stage this scene to contrast the grief of Queen Elizabeth and the Duchess of York with the liveliness of the young Duke of York?

b Write notes to advise the young actor on how to understand his role in this scene. Include some analysis of his character as well as considerations of how to move and speak on stage. Remember, the Duke of York is insightful, lively and observant. He understands what his uncle Richard means in line 13, but does he notice the effect of his own words on his mother and grandmother?

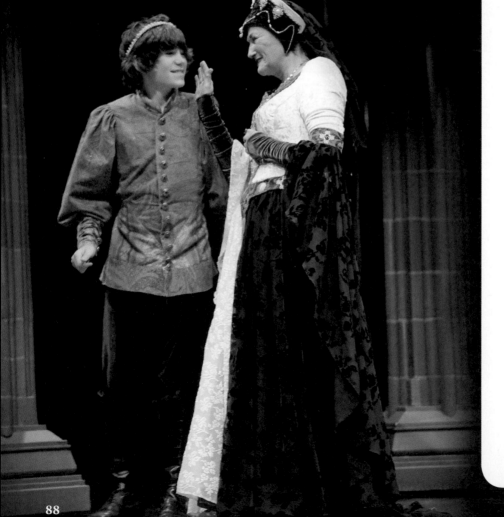

Stony Stratford (a village in Buckinghamshire)

My son of York the young prince, brother to the new King

overta'en overtaken

quoth said

my uncle Gloucester (Richard)

herbs plants

grace good qualities

apace quickly

methinks it seems to me

did not hold was not true

object say, assert

leisurely slowly

gracious virtuous

troth faith, truth

had been remembered had remembered

my uncle's grace the grace my uncle supposedly gained by slow growth

flout rebuff, mocking reply

touch strike at, criticise

Act 2 Scene 4
London: a room in King Edward's palace

Enter the ARCHBISHOP OF YORK, *the young* DUKE OF YORK,
QUEEN ELIZABETH, *and the* DUCHESS OF YORK

ARCHBISHOP	Last night, I heard, they lay at Stony Stratford,	
	And at Northampton they do rest tonight.	
	Tomorrow, or next day, they will be here.	
DUCHESS	I long with all my heart to see the prince.	
	I hope he is much grown since last I saw him.	5
ELIZABETH	But I hear no. They say my son of York	
	Has almost overta'en him in his growth.	
YORK	Ay, mother, but I would not have it so.	
DUCHESS	Why, my good cousin? It is good to grow.	
YORK	Grandam, one night as we did sit at supper,	10
	My uncle Rivers talked how I did grow	
	More than my brother. 'Ay', quoth my uncle Gloucester,	
	'Small herbs have grace; great weeds do grow apace.'	
	And since, methinks, I would not grow so fast,	
	Because sweet flowers are slow, and weeds make haste.	15
DUCHESS	Good faith, good faith, the saying did not hold	
	In him that did object the same to thee.	
	He was the wretched'st thing when he was young,	
	So long a-growing, and so leisurely,	
	That if his rule were true, he should be gracious.	20
YORK	And so no doubt he is, my gracious madam.	
DUCHESS	I hope he is, but yet let mothers doubt.	
YORK	Now, by my troth, if I had been remembered,	
	I could have given my uncle's grace a flout	
	To touch his growth nearer than he touched mine.	25
DUCHESS	How, my young York? I prithee, let me hear it.	

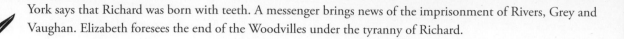

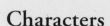 York says that Richard was born with teeth. A messenger brings news of the imprisonment of Rivers, Grey and Vaughan. Elizabeth foresees the end of the Woodvilles under the tyranny of Richard.

Characters

An unnatural childhood (in pairs)

Many rumours were spread about Richard of Gloucester's growth and development in childhood. In this scene, Richard's mother does not deny that he grew unusually quickly as a child or that he was born with teeth.

a When the Duke of York repeats some of these stories, his mother rebukes him and says he is mischievous and sharp-tongued. Where do you think he heard this gossip about his uncle (line 37 gives you a clue)?

b What other details of Richard's childhood have you picked up from the play so far? Do you think these stories are true or are they meant to reflect his evil nature?

c Prepare a character growth chart for Richard to describe what he was like from birth to the age of twenty. Include as many details about his character and physical appearance as you can gather from the script. You can include your own ideas, but make sure they are in keeping with the portrayal of Richard in the play.

1 Bad news (in fours)

a Take parts as the Archbishop, the Messenger, Queen Elizabeth and the Duchess of York and prepare a dramatic reading of lines 38–51. As you do so, consider the effect of the sharp, short phrases and volley of questions on the way you speak the lines.

b Write a stage direction at line 38 to describe how you would want the actors to perform these lines. Give them detailed advice about the mood of this part of the script. Include some reflection on the implications of the news for each character.

2 The hunter and the prey

Elizabeth foresees the destruction of the Woodvilles.

a Identify who is the 'tiger' and who 'the gentle hind' in line 53.

b Read again both Elizabeth's sudden vision of the 'end of all' and Clarence's nightmare in Act 1 Scene 4. Compare and contrast these two visions of destruction and chaos. What do you think the future holds for the Woodvilles?

---

gnaw chew

biting jest effective joke

ere before
thou wast you were
parlous dangerously mischievous
shrewd sharp-tongued, biting
Pitchers jugs (proverb: children overhear what they are not supposed to)

Pomfret (a castle in Yorkshire, known as a place of political executions, like the Tower of London)

sum total
disclosed told

house family
gentle hind defenceless deer
Insulting abusive
jut encroach
aweless throne vulnerable young king
map diagram

YORK	Marry, they say my uncle grew so fast
	That he could gnaw a crust at two hours old.
	'Twas full two years ere I could get a tooth.
	Grandam, this would have been a biting jest.
DUCHESS	I prithee, pretty York, who told thee this?
YORK	Grandam, his nurse.
DUCHESS	His nurse? Why, she was dead ere thou wast born.
YORK	If 'twere not she, I cannot tell who told me.
ELIZABETH	A parlous boy; go to, you are too shrewd.
DUCHESS	Good madam, be not angry with the child.
ELIZABETH	Pitchers have ears.

30

35

Enter a MESSENGER

ARCHBISHOP	Here comes a messenger. What news?
MESSENGER	Such news, my lord, as grieves me to report.
ELIZABETH	How doth the prince?
MESSENGER	Well, madam, and in health.
DUCHESS	What is thy news?
MESSENGER	Lord Rivers and Lord Grey
	Are sent to Pomfret, and with them
	Sir Thomas Vaughan, prisoners.
DUCHESS	Who hath committed them?
MESSENGER	The mighty dukes, Gloucester and Buckingham.
ARCHBISHOP	For what offence?
MESSENGER	The sum of all I can, I have disclosed.
	Why or for what the nobles were committed
	Is all unknown to me, my gracious lord.
ELIZABETH	Aye me! I see the ruin of my house.
	The tiger now hath seized the gentle hind;
	Insulting tyranny begins to jut
	Upon the innocent and aweless throne.
	Welcome, destruction, blood, and massacre.
	I see, as in a map, the end of all.

40

45

50

55

1 The Wars of the Roses: a woman's view (in pairs, then whole class)

The Duchess of York bemoans the constant fighting she has witnessed in the battle for the throne (see p. 1). She describes her conflicting emotions at her husband's death and her sons' defeats and victories. Even after their success, when enthroned ('being seated') and the civil war over, they continue to fight within the family.

- Compose between three and five questions that you would want to ask the Duchess about her experience of the Wars of the Roses and her prediction of future events.
- Then, as a whole class, take turns to sit in the hot-seat and answer questions from everyone while in role as the Duchess.

Write about it

Sanctuary – a safe place

Queen Elizabeth wants to go with the Duke of York to the safety of Westminster Abbey. In medieval times, Church law guaranteed that a fugitive from justice or debt was immune from arrest if they sought sanctuary in a church or other sacred place.

- Script the conversation between Queen Elizabeth and the Duke of York when they leave, as she explains why they have to seek sanctuary in the church. Try to include some of the insightful observations and witty comments that Shakespeare gives to the young prince, as well as some sense of the hopes and fears that both characters have for the future.

2 The Archbishop (in pairs)

The Archbishop's lines 73–8 are open to a range of interpretations. Whom is he addressing as 'gracious lady' and 'your grace'? Does he, the keeper of the 'seal' of England – the symbol of sovereignty (line 76) – actually hand it over?

- Step into role as director and advise the actor playing the Archbishop how he should deliver his speech, line by line.

wrangling quarrelling

being seated when on the throne
domestic broils the civil war
Clean over-blown completely over
Make war upon themselves fight amongst the family
preposterous ridiculous, unnatural
spleen anger

sanctuary (by old English custom, churches and churchyards served as refuges from the law)

seal (the great seal of England was used by the King and kept by the Archbishop in his office as chancellor of England)
so betide to me may similar fortune befall me
tender have high regard for

DUCHESS Accursèd and unquiet wrangling days,
How many of you have mine eyes beheld?
My husband lost his life to get the crown, 60
And often up and down my sons were tossed
For me to joy and weep their gain and loss.
And being seated, and domestic broils
Clean over-blown, themselves the conquerors
Make war upon themselves, brother to brother, 65
Blood to blood, self against self. Oh, preposterous
And frantic outrage, end thy damnèd spleen,
Or let me die, to look on earth no more.

ELIZABETH Come, come, my boy, we will to sanctuary.
Madam, farewell. 70

DUCHESS Stay, I will go with you.

ELIZABETH You have no cause.

ARCHBISHOP My gracious lady, go,
And thither bear your treasure and your goods.
For my part, I'll resign unto your grace 75
The seal I keep, and so betide to me
As well I tender you and all of yours.
Go, I'll conduct you to the sanctuary.

          Exeunt

Looking back at Act 2
Activities for groups or individuals

1 Two scenes with children

Look again at the two scenes in which children play an important role. In Scene 2, the Duchess of York unsuccessfully attempts to hide from Clarence's children their father's murder. In Scene 4, the young Duke of York makes witty comments about his uncle, Richard.

a How would you cast the children? Make notes on their age and appearance, and find images from magazines or the Internet that suit your ideas about how they should be portrayed.

b Do they talk and act like children? Make notes on their effect on the adults around them. Are they cute and humorous, sharp and intelligent, or uncanny and unnerving?

c Suggest how the children affect the mood and atmosphere of the play, and how they might be played to create different moods.

2 Women in danger

In this act, there are two women who have changed from queens to widows: the Duchess lost her husband before the play started and has now lost two of her sons (Clarence and Edward). Elizabeth has just lost her husband, the King, and now fears for the life of her two young sons. Elizabeth resolves to escape danger, but comments that the Duchess of York has 'no cause' (Scene 4, line 72) to join her in seeking sanctuary.

a Step into role as the Duchess of York. Describe your feelings as you begin to understand the significance of your present situation and then give your reply to Elizabeth's comment.

b Consider how the memory of Margaret (the Lancastrian queen whose husband and sons were killed by the Duchess of York's sons before this play started) might haunt the Duchess. Do you think she would be a reminder of how these two queens might end their lives?

3 Increasing tyranny

Buckingham's decision to assist Richard begins a relationship that brings with it increasing tyranny and menace for all those who oppose them.

• Look back at the exchanges between Richard and Buckingham. Chart the growth of their relationship during the act by writing down how their affinity is established and how it develops. List the characters who seem to be or feel threatened by this alliance.

4 Appearance and reality

An important theme in the play is whether outside appearance is a true guide to a person's inner nature. Some characters see Richard's true nature and others are fooled by him.

• List those characters who see Richard for what he is, and make a second list of those who are fooled by him. When you have completed your lists, write down a quotation from the play for each of these characters that encompasses their thoughts about Richard.

5 Revenge

In Scene 2, line 14, Clarence's son says 'God will revenge it' and echoes Richard's words three lines from the end of the previous scene.

a Look back through Act 2 and record the motivations of different characters. Who is motivated by revenge, and who lives by the belief that God will avenge the innocent who suffer at the hands of evil people?

b Write a few paragraphs discussing how revenge becomes an increasingly important theme in the play. How does it link with other themes that have been explored so far? Use quotations and examples from the play to back up your points.

95

Arriving in London, Prince Edward is saddened by the arrest of Rivers and Grey, disagreeing with Richard that they were disloyal. He seems puzzled that his mother and brother have not yet arrived.

1 Royal entrance (in large groups)

Richard has plotted with Buckingham and intends to proclaim himself King. There is no hint of this intention as Richard and Buckingham welcome Prince Edward, the heir to the throne, to London.

- Try out ways in which the entrance could be staged to show Edward's importance. (The stage directions list the others who enter with the Prince.) He is now, in all but name, King of England.

- Work out a running commentary from Richard, in which he reveals his thoughts about the young heir and the other characters. Present your version of the royal entrance to the rest of the class as a mime, with Richard's running commentary as a voiceover.

Characters

More duplicity (in pairs)

Richard welcomes Prince Edward with superficial courtesy, but once again his words have sinister double meanings. 'My thoughts' sovereign' could mean both 'king of my thoughts' and 'my overriding thought of your death'. Richard adopts the tactics he accuses Rivers and Grey of using on Edward: he tells the young Prince they are untrustworthy.

a Talk together about ways in which Richard's tone and actions could bring out the dramatic irony of his own 'sugared words'.

b Write down ways in which the young Prince Edward's unease – and consequently his vulnerability – could be made obvious on stage.

2 Prince Edward's troubles (in pairs)

Prince Edward blames problems he encountered on his journey ('crosses on the way') as the reason for his sadness. He is also unhappy at the arrest of his uncles and does not believe they are traitors. He seems further troubled by the absence of his mother and brother, and by Hastings's late arrival. The Prince does not speak between lines 26 and 59.

- Write his diary entry at the end of this eventful day. Who does he trust and who does he not trust? How does he feel about his new role and responsibilities?

chamber royal residence

crosses troubles

want lack

more uncles (Rivers was Edward's uncle and Grey was his half-brother)

untainted pure

jumpeth agrees

heart character

sugared sweet

slug slow person, slacker

Act 3 Scene 1
London: a street

The Trumpets sound. Enter young PRINCE EDWARD, RICHARD
DUKE OF GLOUCESTER, BUCKINGHAM, LORD CARDINAL
BOURCHIER, CATESBY, *with others*

BUCKINGHAM	Welcome, sweet prince, to London, to your chamber.	
RICHARD	Welcome, dear cousin, my thoughts' sovereign.	
	The weary way hath made you melancholy.	
PRINCE EDWARD	No, uncle, but our crosses on the way	
	Have made it tedious, wearisome, and heavy.	5
	I want more uncles here to welcome me.	
RICHARD	Sweet prince, the untainted virtue of your years	
	Hath not yet dived into the world's deceit.	
	No more can you distinguish of a man	
	Than of his outward show, which God he knows,	10
	Seldom or never jumpeth with the heart.	
	Those uncles which you want were dangerous.	
	Your grace attended to their sugared words	
	But looked not on the poison of their hearts.	
	God keep you from them and from such false friends.	15
PRINCE EDWARD	God keep me from false friends, but they were none.	
RICHARD	My lord, the Mayor of London comes to greet you.	

Enter LORD MAYOR

MAYOR	God bless your grace with health and happy days.	
PRINCE EDWARD	I thank you, good my lord, and thank you all.	
	I thought my mother and my brother York	20
	Would long ere this have met us on the way.	
	Fie, what a slug is Hastings, that he comes not	
	To tell us whether they will come or no.	

Enter LORD HASTINGS

BUCKINGHAM	And in good time, here comes the sweating lord.	
PRINCE EDWARD	Welcome, my lord. What, will our mother come?	25

Hastings explains that the Queen has taken sanctuary, so preventing the Duke of York from meeting his brother. Buckingham recommends bringing the boy by force. The Cardinal disagrees, but is persuaded to fetch the Prince.

Themes

Church and state (in pairs)

Act 3 emphasises the conflict between Church and state, and this theme is obvious in the script opposite. The Cardinal, a man of the Church, says he will try to persuade the Queen to come out of hiding, but he refuses to break the 'holy privilege / Of blessèd sanctuary'. But Buckingham is a statesman and a man of action, whose humour (such as in lines 55–6) sometimes disguises his determined persuasiveness. Buckingham accuses the Cardinal of being old-fashioned, and asserts that the Duke of York neither deserved nor claimed sanctuary – he was forced into it by his mother.

a Take parts as Buckingham and the Cardinal and speak lines 31–57 to express their different attitudes. How would you advise actors playing these two men to portray their disagreement?

b Write a paragraph exploring how the conflict between Church and state in the script opposite is used by Richard and Buckingham for their own ends. Who wins the argument – the Cardinal or Buckingham? Why is this significant? Use embedded quotations and examples from the script in your writing.

1 Can York claim sanctuary? (in pairs)

The argument between the Cardinal and Buckingham is prompted by Hastings's statement that the Duke of York wanted to meet his brother but was prevented by his mother. Buckingham's reaction to Hastings's message is to say that either the Queen must be persuaded to send the Duke of York, or Hastings must take him by force. The Cardinal finally agrees to carry out Buckingham's instructions.

• Script the scene that might have occurred when the Cardinal and Hastings arrived at Westminster Abbey to take the Duke of York away from his mother and bring him to his brother.

On what occasion for what reason

tender young
Would fain have wished to

peevish perverse, contrary

oratory pleading, persuasion

Anon at once

senseless foolishly, unreasonably

Weigh it but with judge it only according to
grossness coarseness, lack of moral refinement

charter warrant of immunity

sojourn stay

HASTINGS   On what occasion God he knows, not I,
               The queen your mother and your brother York
               Have taken sanctuary. The tender prince
               Would fain have come with me to meet your grace,
               But by his mother was perforce withheld.   30

BUCKINGHAM   Fie, what an indirect and peevish course
               Is this of hers. Lord Cardinal, will your grace
               Persuade the queen to send the Duke of York
               Unto his princely brother presently?
               If she deny, Lord Hastings, go with him,   35
               And from her jealous arms pluck him perforce.

CARDINAL   My lord of Buckingham, if my weak oratory
               Can from his mother win the Duke of York,
               Anon expect him here; but if she be obdurate
               To mild entreaties, God forbid   40
               We should infringe the holy privilege
               Of blessèd sanctuary. Not for all this land
               Would I be guilty of so great a sin.

BUCKINGHAM   You are too senseless obstinate, my lord,
               Too ceremonious and traditional.   45
               Weigh it but with the grossness of this age:
               You break not sanctuary in seizing him.
               The benefit thereof is always granted
               To those whose dealings have deserved the place
               And those who have the wit to claim the place.   50
               This prince hath neither claimed it nor deserved it,
               And therefore, in mine opinion, cannot have it.
               Then taking him from thence that is not there,
               You break no privilege nor charter there.
               Oft have I heard of sanctuary men,   55
               But sanctuary children ne'er till now.

CARDINAL   My lord, you shall o'er-rule my mind for once.
               Come on, Lord Hastings, will you go with me?

HASTINGS   I go, my lord.
                                        [*Exeunt*] *Cardinal and Hastings*

PRINCE EDWARD   Good lords, make all the speedy haste you may.   60
               Say, uncle Gloucester, if our brother come,
               Where shall we sojourn till our coronation?

Richard's suggestion that Prince Edward should stay in the Tower dismays the Prince. As Edward reflects on the nature of fame and reputation, Richard hints that the young Prince has not long to live.

1 Richard's asides: to whom? (in small groups)

Prince Edward's words in line 68 may remind a modern audience of the Tower's sinister reputation: it was both a royal castle and a state prison. The sense of impending tragedy and the vulnerability of the young Prince are reinforced by Richard's three asides (lines 79, 81–3 and 94), which remind the audience that he intends Prince Edward's death.

- The theatrical convention of asides is that they are made to the audience, and not heard by the other characters on stage. Might Richard speak all three asides to Buckingham? Or are they directed at the audience? Experiment with different ways of performing these asides.
- Afterwards, talk together about the dramatic consequences of delivering them in each way. Which do you think might be most effective on stage?

2 History repeats itself

Buckingham tells Prince Edward two untruths about the Tower of London (it was not built by Julius Caesar and there is no written record that it was). Edward's reflection on Julius Caesar heightens the sense of irony in the episode, as it unwittingly forecasts his own fate. Julius Caesar was a brave man, but was murdered by the men he trusted.

- What do you think are Shakespeare's dramatic purposes in this episode? Give your reply in a written paragraph with justified reasons for your thoughts.

Stagecraft

The two young princes

How do the two brothers greet each other at lines 96–7? Do they embrace in an emotional reunion, or do they meet with great formality and solemnity? Take note of their formal language and the fact that the two brothers are observed by the rest of the court. Then write a stage direction at line 96 to show how you would stage the meeting of the royal brothers.

fit apt

Julius Caesar (the oldest part of the Tower of London was begun by William the Conqueror, but there is a tradition that a fort was also built by Caesar on the same site)
re-edified repaired
reported by word of mouth
registered written down

retailed repeated
the general ending day Judgement Day

characters written records
formal Vice stock villain from English religious dramas (who often had the name of a particular sin such as Iniquity or Vanity)
moralise explain, interpret
wit wisdom

lightly often, probably
forward early, precocious

my dear lord my dear King

Too late too recently

RICHARD	Where it think'st best unto your royal self.
	If I may counsel you, some day or two
	Your highness shall repose you at the Tower,
	Then where you please and shall be thought most fit
	For your best health and recreation.
PRINCE EDWARD	I do not like the Tower, of any place.
	Did Julius Caesar build that place, my lord?
BUCKINGHAM	He did, my gracious lord, begin that place,
	Which since, succeeding ages have re-edified.
PRINCE EDWARD	Is it upon recòrd, or else reported
	Successively from age to age, he built it?
BUCKINGHAM	Upon recòrd, my gracious lord.
PRINCE EDWARD	But say, my lord, it were not registered,
	Methinks the truth should live from age to age,
	As 'twere retailed to all posterity,
	Even to the general ending day.
RICHARD	[Aside] So wise so young, they say, do never live long.
PRINCE EDWARD	What say you, uncle?
RICHARD	I say, without characters fame lives long.
	[Aside] Thus, like the formal Vice, Iniquity,
	I moralise two meanings in one word.
PRINCE EDWARD	That Julius Caesar was a famous man.
	With what his valour did enrich his wit,
	His wit set down to make his valour live.
	Death makes no conquest of his conqueror,
	For now he lives in fame, though not in life.
	I'll tell you what, my cousin Buckingham.
BUCKINGHAM	What, my gracious lord?
PRINCE EDWARD	And if I live until I be a man,
	I'll win our ancient right in France again
	Or die a soldier, as I lived a king.
RICHARD	[Aside] Short summers lightly have a forward spring.

Enter young YORK, HASTINGS, *and* CARDINAL

BUCKINGHAM	Now in good time, here comes the Duke of York.
PRINCE EDWARD	Richard of York, how fares our noble brother?
YORK	Well, my dear lord, so must I call you now.
PRINCE EDWARD	Ay, brother, to our grief, as it is yours.
	Too late he died that might have kept that title,
	Which by his death hath lost much majesty.

65

70

75

80

85

90

95

100

The young Duke of York, in a witty conversation, taunts his uncle Richard, whose responses are filled with menacing double meanings. Richard invites his nephews to the Tower.

1 Innocence and menace (in small groups)

The Duke of York is reunited with his brother, Prince Edward. York seems a more exuberant child, and engages in witty exchanges with his uncle, Richard, based on punning and veiled (disguised) insults. Take parts and work out a performance of lines 95–151. Use the following to help you:

- Identify lines where Richard acts like a kindly uncle, hiding his sinister intentions.
- Find some of the puns in the script opposite and suggest how Richard reacts to a young boy outsmarting him at his own verbal game.
- Is Buckingham genuine in his admiration of York in lines 133–6? Explore ways of speaking the lines – for example, sincerely, sarcastically, menacingly, or in some other way.

▶ In many productions, York leaps on Richard's back at line 132. What do you think of the dramatic effect of this action? How might Richard react?

idle useless

beholding indebted

kinsman relation, relative

With all my heart (this could either mean that Richard agrees to let him have the dagger or that Richard really wants to 'let him have it', in the sense of stabbing him)

toy trifle

light valueless or lacking weight

still always

cross contradictory, annoying

bear tolerate or carry

sharp-provided ready, sharply alert

mitigate lessen

wonderful a cause of wonder

pass come

RICHARD	How fares our cousin, noble lord of York?
YORK	I thank you, gentle uncle. O my lord,
	You said that idle weeds are fast in growth;
	The prince my brother hath outgrown me far.
RICHARD	He hath, my lord.
YORK	And therefore is he idle?
RICHARD	O my fair cousin, I must not say so.
YORK	Then he is more beholding to you than I.
RICHARD	He may command me as my sovereign,
	But you have power in me as in a kinsman.
YORK	I pray you, uncle, give me this dagger.
RICHARD	My dagger, little cousin? With all my heart.
PRINCE EDWARD	A beggar, brother?
YORK	Of my kind uncle, that I know will give,
	And being but a toy, which is no grief to give.
RICHARD	A greater gift than that I'll give my cousin.
YORK	A greater gift? Oh, that's the sword to it.
RICHARD	Ay, gentle cousin, were it light enough.
YORK	Oh, then I see you will part but with light gifts.
	In weightier things you'll say a beggar nay.
RICHARD	It is too weighty for your grace to wear.
YORK	I weigh it lightly, were it heavier.
RICHARD	What, would you have my weapon, little lord?
YORK	I would, that I might thank you as you call me.
RICHARD	How?
YORK	Little.
PRINCE EDWARD	My lord of York will still be cross in talk.
	Uncle, your grace knows how to bear with him.
YORK	You mean to bear me, not to bear with me.
	Uncle, my brother mocks both you and me:
	Because that I am little, like an ape,
	He thinks that you should bear me on your shoulders.
BUCKINGHAM	With what a sharp-provided wit he reasons.
	To mitigate the scorn he gives his uncle,
	He prettily and aptly taunts himself.
	So cunning and so young is wonderful.
RICHARD	My lord, will't please you pass along?
	Myself and my good cousin Buckingham
	Will to your mother, to entreat of her
	To meet you at the Tower and welcome you.

Line numbers: 105, 110, 115, 120, 125, 130, 135, 140

1 Changes of mood (in pairs)

The mood of foreboding is heightened in the repeated references to the Tower (lines 140, 141, 143 and 151), York's fear of Clarence's ghost, and Edward's thoughts about the fate of Grey and Rivers.

a Talk together about whether Edward suspects his uncle's intentions at this point. Does he fear or respect his uncle?

b In your Director's Journal, write notes to advise the actor playing Edward how to speak all his lines opposite to reveal his true feelings about Richard.

Stagecraft

Stage the princes' exit (in small groups)

The departure of the princes for the Tower is the last time they appear alive in the play.

- Stage their exit with Hastings. In particular, think about what York might do to prompt Richard's descriptions of him in lines 155–6.

2 Queen Elizabeth's influence (in pairs)

Did Queen Elizabeth really incense her son against Richard, as Buckingham suggests? Or is this another of Buckingham's slanderous comments?

- Talk together about the influence the Queen may have had on how the Duke of York relates to his uncle. Then improvise an imaginary conversation between Queen Elizabeth and the young Duke of York prior to this scene.

Write about it

Instructions to Catesby

Catesby first appears in Act 1 Scene 3. He assumes a growing importance in the play as he becomes involved in Richard's plots. Buckingham has told him of the scheme to make Richard King. He now sends Catesby to discover what Hastings thinks of the plan.

- Imagine Buckingham has also written a letter of instructions for Catesby. Write the letter, basing it on lines 158–82, and provide more details about how to 'sound out' Lord Hastings.

in quiet peacefully

on them on his dead relatives
sennet (trumpet call played at the approach or departure of a procession)
prating talkative
incensèd incited
opprobriously scandalously
perilous dangerous
capable intelligent

deeply earnestly
effect do

of our mind agree with us

as it were far off casually, subtly

doth stand affected to feels about

sit about attend a meeting about
tractable to in agreement with

YORK	What, will you go unto the Tower, my lord?	
PRINCE EDWARD	My Lord Protector will have it so.	
YORK	I shall not sleep in quiet at the Tower.	
RICHARD	Why, what should you fear?	

YORK   Marry, my uncle Clarence' angry ghost.   145
              My grandam told me he was murdered there.

PRINCE EDWARD   I fear no uncles dead.

RICHARD   Nor none that live, I hope.

PRINCE EDWARD   And if they live, I hope I need not fear.
              But come, my lord, and with a heavy heart,   150
              Thinking on them, go I unto the Tower.

A sennet. Exeunt Prince, York, Hastings, [and others, except]
Richard, Buckingham, and Catesby

BUCKINGHAM   Think you, my lord, this little prating York
              Was not incensèd by his subtle mother
              To taunt and scorn you thus opprobriously?

RICHARD   No doubt, no doubt. Oh, 'tis a perilous boy,   155
              Bold, quick, ingenious, forward, capable.
              He is all the mother's, from the top to toe.

BUCKINGHAM   Well, let them rest. Come hither, Catesby.
              Thou art sworn as deeply to effect what we intend
              As closely to conceal what we impart.   160
              Thou know'st our reasons urged upon the way.
              What think'st thou? Is it not an easy matter
              To make William Lord Hastings of our mind
              For the instalment of this noble duke
              In the seat royal of this famous isle?   165

CATESBY   He for his father's sake so loves the prince
              That he will not be won to aught against him.

BUCKINGHAM   What think'st thou, then, of Stanley? Will not he?

CATESBY   He will do all in all as Hastings doth.

BUCKINGHAM   Well then, no more but this: 170
              Go, gentle Catesby, and as it were far off,
              Sound thou Lord Hastings
              How he doth stand affected to our purpose,
              And summon him tomorrow to the Tower
              To sit about the coronation.   175
              If thou dost find him tractable to us,
              Encourage him, and tell him all our reasons.

Buckingham tells Catesby to bring news of Hastings's intentions. Richard threatens to behead Hastings if he refuses his support. He promises Buckingham the earldom of Hereford. Hastings receives a messenger from Stanley.

1 'Divided councils'

The two 'divided councils' refer to the two councils that Richard will summon. The first will meet at Crosby Place (Richard's London home) to offer him the crown. The second council, mainly the supporters of Edward IV, will meet at the Tower to plan Prince Edward's coronation.

• In role as Richard, write a soliloquy for the end of this scene, in which you relate your thoughts, feelings and plans for what will happen at these two councils. Try to capture Richard's ability to engage the audience as well as to make outrageous plans that allow him to move closer to the throne. Remind yourself of Richard's other soliloquies (Act 1 Scene 1 and Act 1 Scene 2) to prompt your own writing.

2 Richard takes the initiative (in pairs)

Richard's greeting to Hastings ('Lord William') seems clear and favourable. But is there a threatening meaning behind the good news that his enemies are to be killed?

• Speak lines 183–7 in two ways: first, as a friendly greeting with 'good news'; and second, in a tone of menace that hints at future trouble for Hastings.

• Decide which one you prefer, or whether you would recommend a quite different delivery.

Characters
Richard's manipulations

What do we learn about Richard's character and schemes in lines 196–205?

• Compile a list of all the techniques he has used so far in the play to manipulate his way to the throne. You could start your list with bribery, murder and feigned friendship. Try to give a specific example of each technique by quoting or referring to the script as you add to this list.

---

divided councils two different meetings

highly in an important position

knot group

are let blood will be killed

Mistress Shore (Jane Shore became Hastings's mistress after the King died)

soundly effectively

heed speed

complots plots, conspiracies

determine arrange

movables personal property (not land and houses)

look expect

betimes early

digest arrange

form order

If he be leaden, icy, cold, unwilling,
Be thou so too, and so break off the talk,
And give us notice of his inclination. 180
For we tomorrow hold divided councils,
Wherein thyself shalt highly be employed.

RICHARD   Commend me to Lord William. Tell him, Catesby,
His ancient knot of dangerous adversaries
Tomorrow are let blood at Pomfret Castle; 185
And bid my lord, for joy of this good news,
Give Mistress Shore one gentle kiss the more.

BUCKINGHAM   Good Catesby, go, effect this business soundly.

CATESBY   My good lords both, with all the heed I can.

RICHARD   Shall we hear from you, Catesby, ere we sleep? 190

CATESBY   You shall, my lord.

RICHARD   At Crosby House, there shall you find us both.

Exit Catesby

BUCKINGHAM   Now, my lord,
What shall we do if we perceive
Lord Hastings will not yield to our complots? 195

RICHARD   Chop off his head.
Something we will determine.
And look when I am king, claim thou of me
The earldom of Hereford and all the movables
Whereof the king my brother was possessed. 200

BUCKINGHAM   I'll claim that promise at your grace's hand.

RICHARD   And look to have it yielded with all kindness.
Come, let us sup betimes, that afterwards
We may digest our complots in some form.

Exeunt

Act 3 Scene 2
Outside the house of Lord Hastings

Enter a MESSENGER *who knocks on the door of Hastings*

MESSENGER   My lord! My lord!

HASTINGS   [*Within*] Who knocks?

MESSENGER   One from the Lord Stanley.

▲ The boar was Richard's emblem, as seen in his crest at the Bosworth Battlefield Heritage Centre near Market Bosworth in Leicestershire. How could the actors make it clear that the 'boar' refers to Richard?

tedious wearisome

commends him sends his greetings

certifies swears
boar wild pig (Richard's emblem)
razed knocked, torn

rue regret

post ride quickly
the north (Stanley's power base)
divines foretells

toucheth affects
intelligence information
shallow unfounded
instance reason, cause
simple foolish
mockery counterfeit

kindly gently, after his own nature (i.e. the nature of a boar)

1 Naive Hastings (in pairs)

Shakespeare builds a good deal of dramatic irony into Hastings's lines 19–33. Only a few minutes earlier, the audience has heard Richard's intention towards Hastings: 'Chop off his head' (Scene 1, line 196). Now Shakespeare makes Hastings appear naive and trusting by giving him language that stands in ironic contrast to what the play has revealed.

a Hastings speaks of his 'good friend Catesby' (line 22) and his confidence that 'the boar will use us kindly' (line 33). How is this ironic?

b Stanley's dream reveals his fear that Richard will turn on Hastings and himself. Hastings dismisses Stanley's dream and the fear it has provoked in him. Given what you know of the significance of other dreams in the play so far, why is this foolish?

c Take parts as Hastings and the Messenger and speak lines 4–33 to bring out Hastings's confident but ill-founded trust.

HASTINGS	[*Within*] What is't o'clock?
MESSENGER	Upon the stroke of four.

5

Enter LORD HASTINGS

HASTINGS	Cannot my Lord Stanley sleep these tedious nights?
MESSENGER	So it appears by that I have to say.
	First, he commends him to your noble self.
HASTINGS	What then?
MESSENGER	Then certifies your lordship that this night

10

He dreamt the boar had razèd off his helm.
Besides, he says there are two councils kept,
And that may be determined at the one
Which may make you and him to rue at th'other.
Therefore he sends to know your lordship's pleasure,

15

If you will presently take horse with him
And with all speed post with him toward the north,
To shun the danger that his soul divines.

HASTINGS	Go, fellow, go, return unto thy lord;

Bid him not fear the separated council.

20

His honour and myself are at the one,
And at the other is my good friend Catesby,
Where nothing can proceed that toucheth us
Whereof I shall not have intelligence.
Tell him his fears are shallow, without instance.

25

And for his dreams, I wonder he's so simple
To trust the mockery of unquiet slumbers.
To fly the boar before the boar pursues
Were to incense the boar to follow us
And make pursuit where he did mean no chase.

30

Go, bid thy master rise and come to me,
And we will both together to the Tower,
Where he shall see the boar will use us kindly.

MESSENGER	I'll go, my lord, and tell him what you say.	*Exit*

Enter CATESBY

CATESBY	Many good morrows to my noble lord.	35
HASTINGS	Good morrow, Catesby. You are early stirring.	
	What news, what news, in this our tott'ring state?	

Hastings refuses to support Richard's bid for the crown, but welcomes news of the fate of Rivers, Grey and Vaughan. He feels confident of Richard's friendship, but Catesby's words have an ominous meaning.

1 Hastings's fatal mistakes (in pairs)

Catesby probes Hastings's intentions and Hastings is unaware that his words are sealing his own fate. Take parts as Hastings and Catesby and speak lines 35–71 to emphasise the menace and dramatic irony of the situation. Use the following points to help you:

- Hastings constantly refers to death, both his own and his enemies'. Emphasise these in your performance.
- Catesby's replies are full of double meanings. Explore ways of showing how Catesby's sinister implications are hidden from the self-confident Hastings, but not the audience.

Themes
False confidence (in pairs)

Because of his false confidence in his supposed friendship with Richard, Hastings fails to see that he has fallen on the wrong side of this ambitious man. He disagrees with Catesby's conclusion that Richard should be King, arguing that he would rather first lose his own head ('this crown').

- In line 70, Catesby's aside refers to the custom of displaying the heads of traitors on poles at London Bridge. If Catesby addresses line 70 directly to the audience, what gestures and expressions might he use to draw attention to Hastings's false confidence?

Language in the play
Personification

Catesby develops the metaphor of 'our tott'ring state' (line 37) to convey the impression of a country that is drunk and out of control, and to support the idea that the only solution is to crown Richard as King. This is an example of **personification** (giving human attributes to non-human things, see p. 250).

- What other images could be used to personify the political instability of England at this point in the play? Develop your ideas as an extended metaphor in writing, or assemble a collection of images from magazines to represent this instability and insecurity.

---

reeling tottering, spinning

crown of mine my head

forward / Upon supporting

still always
adversaries enemies
my master's ... descent King Edward's sons, the rightful successors to the crown
to the death at the risk of death

send some packing kill

The princes (Richard and Buckingham)
high account of regard highly
account count on, expect
the bridge London Bridge (where the severed heads of traitors were stuck up on poles as a warning to others)

CATESBY	It is a reeling world indeed, my lord,
	And I believe will never stand upright
	Till Richard wear the garland of the realm.
HASTINGS	How, wear the garland? Dost thou mean the crown?
CATESBY	Ay, my good lord.
HASTINGS	I'll have this crown of mine cut from my shoulders
	Before I'll see the crown so foul misplaced.
	But canst thou guess that he doth aim at it?
CATESBY	Ay, on my life, and hopes to find you forward
	Upon his party for the gain thereof.
	And thereupon he sends you this good news,
	That this same very day your enemies,
	The kindred of the queen, must die at Pomfret.
HASTINGS	Indeed, I am no mourner for that news,
	Because they have been still my adversaries.
	But that I'll give my voice on Richard's side
	To bar my master's heirs in true descent,
	God knows I will not do it, to the death.
CATESBY	God keep your lordship in that gracious mind.
HASTINGS	But I shall laugh at this a twelvemonth hence,
	That they which brought me in my master's hate,
	I live to look upon their tragedy.
	Well, Catesby, ere a fortnight make me older,
	I'll send some packing that yet think not on't.
CATESBY	'Tis a vile thing to die, my gracious lord,
	When men are unprepared and look not for it.
HASTINGS	Oh, monstrous, monstrous! And so falls it out
	With Rivers, Vaughan, Grey; and so 'twill do
	With some men else that think themselves as safe
	As thou and I, who, as thou know'st, are dear
	To princely Richard and to Buckingham.
CATESBY	The princes both make high account of you.
	[*Aside*] For they account his head upon the bridge.
HASTINGS	I know they do, and I have well deserved it.

Line numbers: 40, 45, 50, 55, 60, 65, 70

Enter LORD STANLEY [EARL OF DERBY]

Come on, come on, where is your boar spear, man?
Fear you the boar and go so unprovided?

Stanley is troubled by the separate meetings of the two councils and the executions at Pomfret. He agrees to go with Hastings to the Tower. Hastings recalls his own former imprisonment there.

1 Changing fortunes (in pairs)

Both Stanley and Hastings are aware of the dramatic changes in fortune experienced by those close to the throne. Hastings was himself imprisoned in the Tower. He now feels 'triumphant' (line 81) because he believes his future is secure. Stanley's warning that Rivers, Grey and Vaughan were happy when they rode to London to meet Prince Edward fails to shake Hastings's confidence.

a Take parts and speak lines 72–95. Work out how, in speech and action, you might express Hastings's feelings of triumph, in contrast to Stanley's concern about the rapid executions at Pomfret in line 86.

b Make a list of the contrasting views of Stanley and Hastings by copying and completing the table below.

Stanley	Hastings
Concerned that the councils are a bad sign	Certain that the councils pose no threat

Characters

Hastings's visitors

In this scene, Hastings receives visits from the Messenger, Catesby and Stanley. Each brings messages and news that Hastings ignores.

• Consider each 'visitor' in turn, suggesting how each adds to the dramatic effect of the scene (e.g. what they reveal of Hastings's character and how they deepen the dramatic irony).

rood cross
several separate

state position

jocund happy

o'ercast became dark
rancour ill-will

spent getting late
have with you come along

truth loyalty
wear their hats hold office

pursuivant (a royal messenger with the power to make arrests)

sirrah fellow

suggestion instigation

hold it keep it that way
Gramercy many thanks

STANLEY	My lord, good morrow. Good morrow, Catesby.
	You may jest on, but by the holy rood, 75
	I do not like these several councils, I.
HASTINGS	My lord, I hold my life as dear as yours,
	And never in my days, I do protest,
	Was it so precious to me as 'tis now.
	Think you, but that I know our state secure, 80
	I would be so triumphant as I am?
STANLEY	The lords at Pomfret, when they rode from London,
	Were jocund and supposed their states were sure,
	And they indeed had no cause to mistrust.
	But yet you see how soon the day o'ercast. 85
	This sudden stab of rancour I misdoubt.
	Pray God, I say, I prove a needless coward.
	What, shall we toward the Tower? The day is spent.
HASTINGS	Come, come, have with you.
	Wot you what, my lord? 90
	Today the lords you talk of are beheaded.
STANLEY	They, for their truth, might better wear their heads
	Than some that have accused them wear their hats.
	But come, my lord, let's away.

Enter a PURSUIVANT

HASTINGS	Go on before, I'll talk with this good fellow. 95

Exeunt Lord Stanley and Catesby

	How now, sirrah? How goes the world with thee?
PURSUIVANT	The better that your lordship please to ask.
HASTINGS	I tell thee, man, 'tis better with me now
	Than when thou met'st me last where now we meet.
	Then was I going prisoner to the Tower 100
	By the suggestion of the queen's allies.
	But now I tell thee (keep it to thyself)
	This day those enemies are put to death,
	And I in better state then e'er I was.
PURSUIVANT	God hold it to your honour's good content. 105
HASTINGS	Gramercy, fellow. There, drink that for me.

Throws him his purse

PURSUIVANT	I thank your honour. *Exit Pursuivant*

Hastings promises to pay the Priest on the following Sunday. Buckingham's aside reminds the audience that Hastings will die. Rivers, Grey and Vaughan show defiance as they face death.

1 Pursuivant and Priest

Hastings's meeting with the Pursuivant (line 94) and Priest (line 108) appear to be chance encounters.

- What do you think is Shakespeare's dramatic purpose in introducing them at this point in the play? When you have recorded your ideas, look at Act 3 Scene 4, lines 86–90 to see how Hastings reflects on this meeting.

2 More dramatic irony

The dramatic irony of Hastings's situation continues to the end of the scene. If Richard's plan succeeds, Hastings will not be alive to pay the Priest. The phrase 'no shriving work' is Buckingham's cruel joke and is dramatically ironic. 'Shriving', as Buckingham uses it, is the blessing for confessing his sins to a priest that a condemned person receives shortly before his execution. The confession and blessing signified that the executed person would not suffer in hell. Buckingham's surface meaning is that Hastings is in no need of shriving, but his aside at line 122 reminds the audience that Hastings is doomed (he will stay for 'supper', but he will be dead).

- Look back over Scene 2 to remind yourself of examples of irony and dramatic irony. Choose one example of each that you think is particularly effective on stage and write down how you would perform it.

Stagecraft

Executions at Pontefract Castle (by yourself)

The opening stage direction of Scene 3 describes the soldiers ('*Halberds*') taking the three men to their deaths. How would you stage an effective dramatic entrance for Rivers, Grey and Vaughan? Would they be treated as royal prisoners, with sympathy, cruelly, violently or with cold formality?

- Write notes in your Director's Journal outlining how you would stage their entrance and how you would want to influence the feelings of the audience towards the men as they face execution.

Sir (respectful address to a clergyman)

exercise sermon or prayer

content you give you money

no shriving work no need for confession

thence from there

Dispatch hurry up

The limit of your lives is out you have reached the end of your lives

Enter a PRIEST

PRIEST	Well met, my lord. I am glad to see your honour.
HASTINGS	I thank thee, good Sir John, with all my heart.
	I am in your debt for your last exercise. 110
	Come the next sabbath, and I will content you.
PRIEST	I'll wait upon your lordship.

Enter BUCKINGHAM

BUCKINGHAM	What, talking with a priest, Lord Chamberlain?
	Your friends at Pomfret, they do need the priest.
	Your honour hath no shriving work in hand. 115
HASTINGS	Good faith, and when I met this holy man,
	The men you talk of came into my mind.
	What, go you toward the Tower?
BUCKINGHAM	I do, my lord, but long I cannot stay there.
	I shall return before your lordship thence. 120
HASTINGS	Nay, like enough, for I stay dinner there.
BUCKINGHAM	[*Aside*] And supper too, although thou know'st it not. –
	Come, will you go?
HASTINGS	I'll wait upon your lordship.

Exeunt

Act 3 Scene 3
Yorkshire: Pontefract Castle

Enter SIR RICHARD RATCLIFFE *with Halberds, taking* RIVERS,
GREY, *and* VAUGHAN *to their deaths*

RIVERS	Sir Richard Ratcliffe, let me tell thee this:
	Today shalt thou behold a subject die
	For truth, for duty, and for loyalty.
GREY	God bless the prince from all the pack of you.
	A knot you are of damnèd bloodsuckers. 5
VAUGHAN	You live that shall cry woe for this hereafter.
RATCLIFFE	Dispatch. The limit of your lives is out.

1 Triple executions: on or off stage? (in pairs)

The stage direction clearly indicates that the Woodvilles are executed off stage. However, some productions show their deaths in front of the theatre audience.

a In your own production, would you show the executions or not? Explain your choice to your partner.

b How would you advise Rivers and Grey to speak their lines as they remember Margaret's curses? Vaughan has no lines. What might he be doing?

c Feed back your ideas to the rest of the class and discuss what is lost and gained by the different approaches to staging (or not staging) the execution.

slander disgrace
dismal seat sad place

exclaimed on cried out against

is expiate has come

determine of decide on

wants but nomination lacks only the naming of the day

Lord Protector (Richard)
inward intimate

RIVERS	O Pomfret, Pomfret! O thou bloody prison,
	Fatal and ominous to noble peers.
	Within the guilty closure of thy walls
	Richard the Second here was hacked to death,
	And, for more slander to thy dismal seat,
	We give to thee our guiltless blood to drink.
GREY	Now Margaret's curse is fall'n upon our heads,
	When she exclaimed on Hastings, you, and I
	For standing by when Richard stabbed her son.
RIVERS	Then cursed she Richard,
	Then cursed she Buckingham,
	Then cursed she Hastings. O remember God,
	To hear her prayer for them, as now for us.
	And for my sister and her princely sons,
	Be satisfied, dear God, with our true blood,
	Which, as thou know'st, unjustly must be spilt.
RATCLIFFE	Make haste. The hour of death is expiate.
RIVERS	Come, Grey, come, Vaughan, let us here embrace.
	Farewell, until we meet again in heaven.

Line numbers: 10, 15, 20, 25

Exeunt

Act 3 Scene 4
A room in the Tower of London

Enter BUCKINGHAM, STANLEY EARL OF DERBY, HASTINGS,
BISHOP OF ELY, NORFOLK, RATCLIFFE, LOVELL, *with others*

HASTINGS	Now, noble peers, the cause why we are met
	Is to determine of the coronation.
	In God's name, speak. When is the royal day?
BUCKINGHAM	Is all things ready for the royal time?
STANLEY	It is, and wants but nomination.
ELY	Tomorrow, then, I judge a happy day.
BUCKINGHAM	Who knows the Lord Protector's mind herein?
	Who is most inward with the noble duke?
ELY	Your grace, we think, should soonest know his mind.

Line number: 5

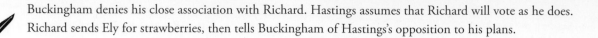

Buckingham denies his close association with Richard. Hastings assumes that Richard will vote as he does. Richard sends Ely for strawberries, then tells Buckingham of Hastings's opposition to his plans.

Write about it
Faces and hearts

Buckingham's lines 10–13 give dramatic force to the theme of appearance and reality and the ability to judge a person correctly by external signs. Buckingham says he knows Richard's outward appearance ('faces') but not his inward thoughts ('hearts').

In sharp contrast, Hastings claims a close relationship with Richard, and assumes that Richard will willingly accept Hastings's view as his own.

- The play has already shown many examples of the differences between 'faces' and 'hearts'. Write out a few of these and accompany each with a quotation. Then write two or three paragraphs describing the meaning and significance of these examples in relation to the general theme of appearance and reality.

1 Hastings's downfall (I) (in large groups)

Lines 21–78 trace the downfall of Hastings – a man who has proved unable to distinguish between 'faces' and 'hearts'. Take parts as Buckingham, Ely, Stanley, Hastings and Richard, and work out a performance of the lines. Use the following questions to help you:

- In what tone does Richard speak lines 22–5?
- How might you give special emphasis to Buckingham's use of theatrical metaphors (such as 'cue', 'pronounced', 'part', 'your voice' in lines 26–8)?
- In what style does Richard speak to Buckingham in lines 35–40?
- How do Richard and Buckingham make their exit? Are they obviously plotting or pretending normality?

purpose intention
sounded questioned

take in gentle part
accept willingly

neglect cause to be neglected
design plan

voice approval

strawberries (Richard's sudden request for strawberries shows him deliberately exhibiting a sunny mood)

testy irate
hot angry
His master's child
(Prince Edward)

sudden soon
provided convinced
prolonged postponed

BUCKINGHAM   We know each other's faces. For our hearts,   10
                    He knows no more of mine than I of yours,
                    Or I of his, my lord, than you of mine.
                    Lord Hastings, you and he are near in love.
HASTINGS   I thank his grace, I know he loves me well.
                    But for his purpose in the coronation,   15
                    I have not sounded him, nor he delivered
                    His gracious pleasure any way therein.
                    But you, my honourable lords, may name the time,
                    And in the duke's behalf I'll give my voice,
                    Which I presume he'll take in gentle part.   20

                    Enter [RICHARD DUKE OF] GLOUCESTER

ELY   In happy time, here comes the duke himself.
RICHARD   My noble lords and cousins all, good morrow.
                    I have been long a sleeper, but I trust
                    My absence doth neglect no great design
                    Which by my presence might have been concluded.   25
BUCKINGHAM   Had you not come upon your cue, my lord,
                    William Lord Hastings had pronounced your part,
                    I mean your voice for crowning of the king.
RICHARD   Than my Lord Hastings no man might be bolder.
                    His lordship knows me well and loves me well. –   30
                    My lord of Ely, when I was last in Holborn,
                    I saw good strawberries in your garden there.
                    I do beseech you, send for some of them.
ELY   Marry, and will, my lord, with all my heart.   *Exit Bishop*
RICHARD   Cousin of Buckingham, a word with you.   35
                    Catesby hath sounded Hastings in our business,
                    And finds the testy gentleman so hot
                    That he will lose his head ere give consent
                    His master's child, as worshipfully he terms it,
                    Shall lose the royalty of England's throne.   40
BUCKINGHAM   Withdraw yourself a while; I'll go with you.
                    Exeunt [*Richard and Buckingham*]
STANLEY   We have not yet set down this day of triumph.
                    Tomorrow, in my judgement, is too sudden,
                    For I myself am not so well provided
                    As else I would be, were the day prolonged.   45

Hastings claims that Richard's face is filled with good will. Richard accuses Queen Elizabeth and Jane Shore of using witchcraft to wither his arm. He condemns Hastings to death as Jane Shore's protector.

1 Hastings's downfall (II) (in large groups)

The dramatic irony intensifies as Hastings continues to assume that 'faces' equal 'hearts'. He claims that Richard is unable to conceal his feelings and intentions ('I think there's never a man in Christendom / Can lesser hide his love or hate, than he'). Continue to work on your performance by thinking about the following:

- How does Stanley speak lines 54–5? Does his tone reveal that he suspects Richard of false appearance?
- At what point does Hastings realise his faith in recognising 'hearts' and 'faces' is mistaken, and how does he react to his death sentence?
- How does Richard perform the internal stage direction in lines 66–8?
- Richard's command 'rise and follow me' (line 78) is an important part of his power-play. How do the nobles obey his order to desert Hastings and follow Richard? Identify how each character shows their allegiance to Richard.
- How do Lovell and Ratcliffe respond to Richard's order in line 77?

▼ Richard (on the table in the middle) accuses Hastings (far left) of treachery.

smooth at ease
conceit idea

Christendom Christian countries

livelihood liveliness

prevailed / Upon controlled

doom judge, condemn to death

blasted struck by lightning
sapling young tree
Consorted associated
strumpet prostitute

Enter the BISHOP OF ELY

ELY   Where is my lord the Duke of Gloucester?
     I have sent for these strawberries.

HASTINGS   His grace looks cheerfully and smooth this morning.
     There's some conceit or other likes him well
     When that he bids good morrow with such spirit.   50
     I think there's never a man in Christendom
     Can lesser hide his love or hate, than he,
     For by his face straight shall you know his heart.

STANLEY   What of his heart perceive you in his face
     By any livelihood he showed today?   55

HASTINGS   Marry, that with no man here he is offended,
     For were he, he had shown it in his looks.

Enter RICHARD *and* BUCKINGHAM

RICHARD   I pray you all, tell me what they deserve
     That do conspire my death with devilish plots
     Of damnèd witchcraft and that have prevailed   60
     Upon my body with their hellish charms.

HASTINGS   The tender love I bear your grace, my lord,
     Makes me most forward in this princely presence
     To doom th'offenders, whosoe'er they be.
     I say, my lord, they have deservèd death.   65

RICHARD   Then be your eyes the witness of their evil.
     Look how I am bewitched. Behold, mine arm
     Is like a blasted sapling, withered up.
     And this is Edward's wife, that monstrous witch,
     Consorted with that harlot, strumpet Shore,   70
     That by their witchcraft thus have markèd me.

HASTINGS   If they have done this deed, my noble lord –

RICHARD   If? Thou protector of this damnèd strumpet,
     Talk'st thou to me of ifs? Thou art a traitor.
     Off with his head! Now by Saint Paul I swear,   75
     I will not dine until I see the same.
     Lovell and Ratcliffe, look that it be done.
     The rest that love me, rise and follow me.

Exeunt [all but] Lovell and Ratcliffe, with the Lord Hastings

Hastings regrets ignoring Stanley's warning, the omen of his horse's stumbling and his earlier overconfidence. He recalls Margaret's curse, reflects on the nature of fame, and prophesies a bleak future for England under Richard.

1 What warnings did Hastings ignore? (in pairs)

As Hastings reflects on his actions and decisions, he blames his own foolishness for his fate. He now realises he has ignored or misinterpreted events and has failed to respond to ominous signs.

- Identify each event or sign he mentions in lines 79–92 (there are four of them). Copy and complete the table below to remind yourself of the particular moment when each occurred and how Hastings responded.

Event	Significance	Hastings's response
Stanley's dream of the violent boar.	It was a premonition of Richard's intent.	He joked about it and refused to take it seriously.

Characters

Does Hastings gain self-knowledge?

Hastings realises too late that in pursuing earthly fame ('momentary grace of mortal men') he has ignored the blessing of God. In an extended **simile** (see p. 250), he compares the fragility of human success to a drunken sailor on the mast of a sailing ship.

- How convincing do you find Hastings's discovery of self-knowledge as he is about to be executed?
- How would you advise the actor playing Hastings to deliver his final rhyming couplet?

2 Who? Us?

Lovell and Ratcliffe take Hastings away for execution.

- How would you direct the actors playing Lovell and Ratcliffe? Should they be brutal, mechanical, officious, embarrassed, or display some other emotion? How do they react to Hastings's final line (which appears to be directed at them)?

whit portion
fond foolish
rouse our helms raise our helmets

footcloth horse elaborately clothed horse (a symbol of wealth)

lighted landed
dispatch hurry up
short shrift brief confession
grace good fortune

in air of on the airy foundation of

the deep the sea
bootless useless
exclaim cry out

block execution block used for a beheading

HASTINGS	Woe, woe for England, not a whit for me,
	For I, too fond, might have prevented this. 80
	Stanley did dream the boar did rouse our helms,
	And I did scorn it and disdain to fly.
	Three times today my footcloth horse did stumble,
	And started when he looked upon the Tower,
	As loath to bear me to the slaughterhouse. 85
	Oh, now I need the priest that spake to me.
	I now repent I told the pursuivant,
	As too triumphing, how mine enemies
	Today at Pomfret bloodily were butchered,
	And I myself secure in grace and favour. 90
	O Margaret, Margaret, now thy heavy curse
	Is lighted on poor Hastings' wretched head.
RATCLIFFE	Come, come, dispatch. The duke would be at dinner.
	Make a short shrift; he longs to see your head.
HASTINGS	O momentary grace of mortal men, 95
	Which we more hunt for than the grace of God,
	Who builds his hope in air of your good looks
	Lives like a drunken sailor on a mast,
	Ready with every nod to tumble down
	Into the fatal bowels of the deep. 100
LOVELL	Come, come, dispatch; 'tis bootless to exclaim.
HASTINGS	O bloody Richard, miserable England,
	I prophesy the fearful'st time to thee
	That ever wretched age hath looked upon.
	Come, lead me to the block; bear him my head. 105
	They smile at me who shortly shall be dead.

Exeunt

Buckingham claims that he can act terror convincingly. He and Richard pretend an attack is imminent. Richard pretends to mourn Hastings's death, saying he loved him and thought him a great friend.

1 Enjoying the performance (in pairs)

Richard and Buckingham reveal the techniques they will use to act convincingly in front of the Mayor of London, then begin to put them into action.

a Lines 1–9 describe the techniques and methods of delivering lines used by actors of the great tragedies in Shakespeare's time. Practise each technique they describe, such as 'quake', 'change thy colour' and so on – there are at least twelve actions.

b Richard is a consummate actor who delights in playing roles that deceive or manipulate people. Buckingham clearly relishes the same type of deception. Discuss how effective you think their performance will be and whether you think their techniques will deceive the Mayor.

Stagecraft

Stage-managing an enemy attack (in large groups)

In the script opposite, Richard and Buckingham stage-manage a crisis for the benefit of the Mayor. They pretend they are being attacked by enemies.

a Take parts as Richard, Buckingham, Lovell, Ratcliffe, Catesby and the Mayor. Rehearse and perform lines 1–24, playing up Richard and Buckingham's malicious sense of fun and the panic they generate.

b The two men appear in rusty armour which is extremely ugly ('*marvellous ill-favoured*'). How might you achieve an impression of their appearance if you have no armour or costume?

c Identify the internal stage directions in the script opposite, and use them to work out your own performance to convince the Mayor that an attack is taking place. What is the Mayor doing and how is he reacting to this crisis?

d How and when might Hastings's head be revealed for greatest dramatic effect?

rotten rusty
marvellous ill-favoured extremely ugly

counterfeit the deep tragedian imitate the greatest tragic actor
pry look around suspiciously
Intending pretending

in their offices to function
stratagems tricks

o'erlook inspect

defend thee guard

plainest most honest

my book my diary, keeper of my secrets

Act 3 Scene 5
The courtyard of the Tower of London

Enter RICHARD *and* BUCKINGHAM *in rotten armour,*
marvellous ill-favoured

RICHARD	Come, cousin, canst thou quake and change thy colour,
	Murder thy breath in middle of a word,
	And then again begin, and stop again,
	As if thou were distraught and mad with terror?
BUCKINGHAM	Tut, I can counterfeit the deep tragedian,
	Speak and look back, and pry on every side,
	Tremble and start at wagging of a straw.
	Intending deep suspicion, ghastly looks
	Are at my service, like enforcèd smiles.
	And both are ready in their offices
	At any time to grace my stratagems.
	But what, is Catesby gone?
RICHARD	He is, and see, he brings the Mayor along.

Enter the MAYOR *and* CATESBY

BUCKINGHAM	Lord Mayor –
RICHARD	Look to the drawbridge there!
BUCKINGHAM	Hark, a drum!
RICHARD	Catesby, o'erlook the walls!
BUCKINGHAM	Lord Mayor, the reason we have sent –
RICHARD	Look back, defend thee, here are enemies!
BUCKINGHAM	God and our innocency defend and guard us!

Enter LOVELL *and* RATCLIFFE *with Hastings's head*

RICHARD	Be patient; they are friends, Ratcliffe and Lovell.
LOVELL	Here is the head of that ignoble traitor,
	The dangerous and unsuspected Hastings.
RICHARD	So dear I loved the man that I must weep.
	I took him for the plainest harmless creature
	That breathed upon the earth a Christian,
	Made him my book, wherein my soul recorded
	The history of all her secret thoughts.

5

10

15

20

25

Richard says that Hastings, apart from his affair with Jane Shore, was never suspected of evil. Buckingham claims Hastings plotted to kill him and Richard. He pretends to regret the Lord Mayor did not hear Hastings's confession.

1 Convincing the Lord Mayor (in threes)

Richard and Buckingham must convince the Lord Mayor that the seemingly innocent Hastings was a clever traitor who plotted their deaths and deserved to die. Take parts as Richard, Buckingham and the Lord Mayor and perform lines 24–71. Consider the following:

- The Lord Mayor's response (line 40) to Buckingham's lie that Hastings intended to murder both Richard and him could be spoken in different ways. How might you speak the line to express doubt, shock, disbelief, suspicion, amazement, or another emotion?
- Richard answers the Mayor with rhetorical questions (lines 41–6) invoking Christian ethics, the law, the country and the importance of his own and Buckingham's security. Speak the lines, giving each item different emphasis. What convinces the Lord Mayor? Is it one particular item or the collective argument? Or is it Richard's tone, gestures or physical movements that persuade him?

daubed plastered over
omitted excepted
conversation sexual affair
from all attainder of suspects free of all taint of suspicion
covert'st sheltered most secret and concealed

subtle clever

our persons' safety our personal safety

fair befall you good fortune come to you
determined intended

meanings intentions
prevented forestalled
timorously fearfully

haply perhaps
Misconster misinterpret

carping critical

So smooth he daubed his vice with show of virtue
That his apparent open guilt omitted, 30
I mean his conversation with Shore's wife,
He lived from all attainder of suspects.

BUCKINGHAM   Well, well, he was the covert'st sheltered traitor
That ever lived.
Would you imagine, or almost believe, 35
Were't not that by great preservation
We live to tell it, that the subtle traitor
This day had plotted, in the Council House,
To murder me and my good lord of Gloucester?

MAYOR   Had he done so? 40

RICHARD   What? Think you we are Turks or infidels?
Or that we would, against the form of law,
Proceed thus rashly in the villain's death,
But that the extreme peril of the case,
The peace of England, and our persons' safety, 45
Enforced us to this execution?

MAYOR   Now fair befall you, he deserved his death,
And your good graces both have well proceeded
To warn false traitors from the like attempts.

BUCKINGHAM   I never looked for better at his hands 50
After he once fell in with Mistress Shore.
Yet had we not determined he should die
Until your lordship came to see his end,
Which now the loving haste of these our friends,
Something against our meanings, have prevented; 55
Because, my lord, I would have had you heard
The traitor speak and timorously confess
The manner and the purpose of his treasons,
That you might well have signified the same
Unto the citizens, who haply may 60
Misconster us in him and wail his death.

MAYOR   But, my good lord, your graces' words shall serve
As well as I had seen and heard him speak.
And do not doubt, right noble princes both,
But I'll acquaint our duteous citizens 65
With all your just proceedings in this case.

RICHARD   And to that end we wished your lordship here,
T'avoid the censures of the carping world.

Richard sends Buckingham to spread rumours about Edward IV: the illegitimacy of his children, his uncontrolled lust, his injustice and his bastardy. If believed, Buckingham must bring the Lord Mayor and citizens to Baynard Castle.

1 Four rumours

Richard instructs Buckingham to spread rumours about Edward IV and his children, raising questions about their legal right to the throne. Buckingham is to make four allegations to the Lord Mayor and leading citizens at Guildhall:

- **Line 75** The illegitimacy of Edward IV's children.
- **Lines 76–9** Edward ordered the unjust execution of a merchant who had told his son he would inherit his house, named 'The Crown'. Edward misinterpreted the merchant's wishes, believing he referred to his 'crown', meaning kingdom.
- **Lines 80–4** Edward's lustful nature.
- **Lines 85–92** Edward is illegitimate because the Duchess of York conceived him while her husband was fighting in France, and there was no physical resemblance between father and son.

In Richard's time, the equivalent of a press release was a poster nailed up in public places. Use the rumours above to create the poster that Buckingham issues, casting doubt on Prince Edward's right to the throne.

Language in the play
Slander and suspicion (in pairs)

Explore Richard's use of language as he tells Buckingham what to say at Guildhall.

- Pick out all the words in the script opposite that are emotive and persuasive. Write brief notes on how you think Richard would say these words or use gestures on stage.
- What contrast does he develop between his brother 'that insatiate Edward' and his father 'the noble duke'? Note the language he uses to describe both. Explain how effective his words would be in creating suspicion among the crowd at Guildhall.

witness testify to

Go after follow
hies him in all post goes at top speed
meetest vantage of the time most opportune moment
Infer imply

house (the man's house, also his place of business was called 'The Crown')
by the sign thereof by the sign hanging in front of the shop
luxury lust

prey sexual conquest

went with child / Of was pregnant with

computation calculation
issue child
his begot fathered by him (York)
lineaments features

golden fee crown, payment

Baynard's Castle (one of Richard's London homes)

BUCKINGHAM   Which, since you come too late of our intent,
             Yet witness what you hear we did intend.   70
             And so, my good Lord Mayor, we bid farewell.

Exit Mayor

RICHARD   Go after, after, cousin Buckingham.
             The Mayor towards Guildhall hies him in all post.
             There, at your meetest vantage of the time,
             Infer the bastardy of Edward's children.   75
             Tell them how Edward put to death a citizen
             Only for saying he would make his son
             Heir to the crown, meaning indeed his house,
             Which, by the sign thereof, was termèd so.
             Moreover, urge his hateful luxury   80
             And bestial appetite in change of lust,
             Which stretched unto their servants, daughters, wives,
             Even where his raging eye or savage heart,
             Without control, lusted to make a prey.
             Nay, for a need, thus far come near my person: 85
             Tell them, when that my mother went with child
             Of that insatiate Edward, noble York,
             My princely father, then had wars in France,
             And by true computation of the time
             Found that the issue was not his begot,   90
             Which well appearèd in his lineaments,
             Being nothing like the noble duke, my father.
             Yet touch this sparingly, as 'twere far off,
             Because, my lord, you know my mother lives.

BUCKINGHAM   Doubt not, my lord, I'll play the orator   95
             As if the golden fee for which I plead
             Were for myself. And so, my lord, adieu.

RICHARD   If you thrive well, bring them to Baynard's Castle,
             Where you shall find me well accompanied
             With reverend fathers and well-learnèd bishops.   100

BUCKINGHAM   I go, and towards three or four o'clock
             Look for the news that the Guildhall affords.

Exit Buckingham

Richard sends for two churchmen, then plans to isolate Clarence's and Edward's children. The Scrivener reflects on the deceit involved in Hastings's execution. Buckingham reports the citizens' lack of reaction to his speech.

1 The next steps to the throne (in pairs)

Richard sends Lovell to fetch two influential churchmen, Dr Shaw and Friar Penker, to help win the citizens' support for his plan to become King.

a How do you think Richard intends to use the two churchmen? Write down your guess and then see what he actually does in Scene 7, lines 94–6.

b Richard intends to make secret arrangements ('some privy order') to ensure Clarence's children are kept out of the public eye. He will ensure King Edward's rightful heirs, the princes in the Tower, receive no visitors. Talk together about why Richard feels these moves are necessary to his plotting.

c Add to your list of techniques that Richard uses to manipulate and manoeuvre his way to the throne.

Stagecraft

Tampering with justice (in pairs)

The Scrivener, a professional writer who drafts legal documents, estimates eleven hours of work have gone into the original draft. He has worked on the draft for another eleven hours – yet only five hours previously, Hastings was a free man. The Scrivener questions whether anyone is so stupid that they cannot see such injustice. His thoughts reveal the world Richard is creating, in which people are afraid to criticise obvious injustice.

a This brief scene is often cut in performance. Write reasons for or against its inclusion, then script a conversation between the director who wants to cut it and an actor playing the Scrivener who thinks it is important.

b How else might a director demonstrate that this is a society full of oppression and repression? Write down some ideas for how to show this in a modern performance. For example, you might choose to have offstage sounds of torture, or silhouettes showing at the back of the stage.

Doctor Shaw (historically, Shaw was the Mayor's brother and a chaplain who preached in favour of Richard)

no manner person nobody
recourse access

indictment legal accusation
in a set … engrossed in the final, appropriate legal form
Paul's St Paul's (a meeting place for lawyers)
the sequel the sequence of events

precedent original draft

Untainted without accusation
unexamined unquestioned
the while at present
gross stupid, slow
palpable device obvious trickery
seen in thought only thought about, not spoken

Touched you did you mention

RICHARD   Go, Lovell, with all speed to Doctor Shaw.
Go thou to Friar Penker. Bid them both
Meet me within this hour at Baynard's Castle.   105

Exit [Lovell]

Now will I go to take some privy order
To draw the brats of Clarence out of sight,
And to give order that no manner person
Have any time recourse unto the princes.

Exeunt

Act 3 Scene 6
London: the scrivener's house

Enter a SCRIVENER

SCRIVENER   Here is the indictment of the good Lord Hastings,
Which in a set hand fairly is engrossed
That it may be today read o'er in Paul's.
And mark how well the sequel hangs together:
Eleven hours I have spent to write it over,   5
For yesternight by Catesby was it sent me;
The precedent was full as long a-doing.
And yet within these five hours Hastings lived,
Untainted, unexamined, free, at liberty.
Here's a good world the while.   10
Who is so gross that cannot see this palpable device?
Yet who so bold but says he sees it not?
Bad is the world, and all will come to naught
When such ill dealing must be seen in thought.

Exit

Act 3 Scene 7
London: the courtyard of Baynard's Castle

Enter RICHARD *and* BUCKINGHAM

RICHARD   How now, how now, what say the citizens?
BUCKINGHAM   Now, by the holy mother of our Lord,
The citizens are mum, say not a word.
RICHARD   Touched you the bastardy of Edward's children?

Buckingham reports that the citizens remained silent as he slandered Edward and praised Richard. He explains how he used the cheers of a few of his own men to claim that all the citizens supported Richard.

1 Buckingham's evidence (in pairs)

Buckingham plays an increasingly important role as Richard's chief henchman and mouthpiece, and he reveals a strong understanding of political double-dealing. He uses the four allegations suggested by Richard (see p. 128) and adds more ideas of his own in lines 5–6 and 15–17 in the script opposite.

- Identify the evidence Buckingham presents in favour of Richard and against the former King and his family. Then discuss how effective each example is in tarnishing the reputation of the dead King Edward and in presenting Richard in a more favourable light.

Write about it

Buckingham: an unsuccessful orator?

Buckingham has said that he will 'play the orator' (Act 3 Scene 5, line 95), but he does not seem to have been very successful.

- Imagine you are a newspaper reporter who observes Buckingham's attempts to get the citizens to support Richard. Write a report for your newspaper, describing what you heard and the citizens' reaction to it. Use quotations from the script opposite and make up some of your own from imagined interviews with the people who were there.

Lady Lucy (in some historical accounts, Edward was betrothed to Lady Elizabeth Lucy at the time he wooed Elizabeth Woodville)

enforcement violation

got conceived

right idea accurate image

Laid open plainly described
discipline in war skill in military affairs
bounty generosity

handled dealt with
discourse speech

reprehended rebuked
wilful silence lack of response

the Recorder a legal officer

nothing spoke ... himself refused to commit himself to Richard's cause

vantage advantage

Argues proves

BUCKINGHAM   I did, with his contràct with Lady Lucy   5
             And his contràct by deputy in France;
             Th'insatiate greediness of his desire
             And his enforcement of the city wives;
             His tyranny for trifles; his own bastardy,
             As being got, your father then in France,   10
             And his resemblance being not like the duke.
             Withal, I did infer your lineaments,
             Being the right idea of your father
             Both in your form and nobleness of mind;
             Laid open all your victories in Scotland,   15
             Your discipline in war, wisdom in peace,
             Your bounty, virtue, fair humility;
             Indeed, left nothing fitting for your purpose
             Untouched or slightly handled in discourse.
             And when my oratory drew toward end,   20
             I bid them that did love their country's good
             Cry 'God save Richard, England's royal king!'
RICHARD   And did they so?
BUCKINGHAM   No, so God help me, they spake not a word,
             But like dumb statuès or breathing stones   25
             Stared each on other and looked deadly pale.
             Which when I saw, I reprehended them,
             And asked the Mayor what meant this wilful silence.
             His answer was, the people were not used
             To be spoke to but by the Recorder.   30
             Then he was urged to tell my tale again:
             'Thus saith the duke, thus hath the duke inferred',
             But nothing spoke in warrant from himself.
             When he had done, some followers of mine own
             At lower end of the hall hurled up their caps,   35
             And some ten voices cried 'God save King Richard!'
             And thus I took the vantage of those few:
             'Thanks, gentle citizens and friends', quoth I,
             'This general applause and cheerful shout
             Argues your wisdom and your love to Richard.'   40
             And even here broke off and came away.
RICHARD   What tongueless blocks were they! Would they not speak?
             Will not the Mayor, then, and his brethren, come?

1 Sexism?

To fool the Lord Mayor and the citizens, Buckingham urges Richard to pretend fear and to be interrupted only by very important entreaties ('mighty suit'). The two men agree that Richard will 'Play the maid's part' and make jokes about women who say 'no' when they mean 'yes'. Richard hopes his 'nay' will bring a successful outcome.

- Imagine that someone says to you: 'I think lines 50–3 should be cut in performance. They are sexist and add nothing to the play.' Write your reply.

Themes

'a holy descant' (in threes)

Using a musical metaphor, Buckingham describes how he will play a variety of ingenious variations on Richard's repeated theme of pretended piety. He intends to present Richard as a religious man, and both hide their ambitious intentions beneath a display of piety and gentleness. Buckingham makes a start in lines 70–9, in which he contrasts Richard with Edward.

a As one person speaks Buckingham's lines slowly, the second person echoes each example of Edward's wantonness, and the third person echoes each example of Richard's piety.

b Prepare two tableaux of Richard – the first showing how Buckingham is presenting him, and the second showing his true personality.

Write about it

Catesby's role (by yourself)

What is the dramatic significance of Catesby acting as a mediator between Richard and Buckingham during this 'performance'?

- In role as Buckingham, write a paragraph explaining why you wanted Catesby to be involved and what you hoped to achieve.

intend some fear pretend to be afraid

mighty suit strenuous pleading

descant variety of musical variations on a theme

Play the maid's part pretend to be shy and timid like a girl

still always

issue conclusion

leads flat roof covered in lead

dance attendance wait obsequiously

spoke withal spoken with

Divinely bent devoutly inclined

holy exercise worship

deep designs important matters

No less importing concerning nothing less

lulling lolling

brace pair

deep divines learned clergymen

engross fatten

watchful unsleeping

sovereignty kingship

BUCKINGHAM   The Mayor is here at hand; intend some fear.
      Be not you spoke with but by mighty suit.   45
      And look you get a prayer book in your hand
      And stand between two churchmen, good my lord,
      For on that ground I'll make a holy descant.
      And be not easily won to our requests;
      Play the maid's part: still answer nay and take it. 50
RICHARD I go; and if you plead as well for them
      As I can say nay to thee for myself,
      No doubt we bring it to a happy issue.
BUCKINGHAM   Go, go, up to the leads. The Lord Mayor knocks.

                 Exit [*Richard*]

      Enter the MAYOR *and Citizens*

      Welcome, my lord. I dance attendance here.   55
      I think the duke will not be spoke withal.

         Enter CATESBY

BUCKINGHAM   Now, Catesby, what says your lord to my request?
CATESBY He doth entreat your grace, my noble lord,
      To visit him tomorrow or next day.
      He is within, with two right reverend fathers, 60
      Divinely bent to meditation,
      And in no worldly suits would he be moved
      To draw him from his holy exercise.
BUCKINGHAM   Return, good Catesby, to the gracious duke.
      Tell him myself, the Mayor, and aldermen 65
      In deep designs, in matter of great moment,
      No less importing than our general good,
      Are come to have some conference with his grace.
CATESBY I'll signify so much unto him straight.   *Exit*
BUCKINGHAM   Ah ha, my lord, this prince is not an Edward. 70
      He is not lulling on a lewd love-bed
      But on his knees at meditation,
      Not dallying with a brace of courtesans
      But meditating with two deep divines,
      Not sleeping to engross his idle body   75
      But praying to enrich his watchful soul.
      Happy were England, would this virtuous prince
      Take on his grace the sovereignty thereof,
      But sure I fear we shall not win him to it.

1 Richard and the bishops

Richard's appearance with the two bishops has been played on stage in all kinds of ways. The bishops have been portrayed as medieval monks in cowls and robes, as modern clergymen, as bishops wearing mitres and copes (elaborate gowns), and as 'holy fools' (almost naked religious prophets).

- How would you choose to present them? Why? What effect might be gained by your particular presentation of the bishops? Write down your thoughts in your Director's Journal.

▼ Richard appearing between two bishops. Compare this picture with the picture on page x. How are they similar? In what ways are they different?

Marry by Our Lady (a mild oath)

at their beads saying their rosary, praying

much to draw them thence difficult to attract their attention

stay stop

know recognise

right true, genuine

Deferred the visitation put off visiting

ungoverned without a proper ruler

disgracious displeasing, unacceptable

MAYOR   Marry, God defend his grace should say us nay.   80

BUCKINGHAM I fear he will. Here Catesby comes again.

Enter CATESBY

Now, Catesby, what says his grace?

CATESBY   He wonders to what end you have assembled

Such troops of citizens to come to him,

His grace not being warned thereof before.   85

He fears, my lord, you mean no good to him.

BUCKINGHAM Sorry I am my noble cousin should

Suspect me that I mean no good to him.

By heaven, we come to him in perfect love,

And so once more return and tell his grace.   90

Exit [*Catesby*]

When holy and devout religious men

Are at their beads, 'tis much to draw them thence,

So sweet is zealous contemplation.

Enter RICHARD *aloft, between two Bishops*

MAYOR   See where his grace stands, 'tween two clergymen.

BUCKINGHAM Two props of virtue for a Christian prince,   95

To stay him from the fall of vanity.

And see, a book of prayer in his hand,

True ornaments to know a holy man –

Famous Plantagenet, most gracious prince,

Lend favourable ear to our requests,   100

And pardon us the interruption

Of thy devotion and right Christian zeal.

RICHARD   My lord, there needs no such apology.

I do beseech your grace to pardon me,

Who, earnest in the service of my God,   105

Deferred the visitation of my friends.

But leaving this, what is your grace's pleasure?

BUCKINGHAM Even that, I hope, which pleaseth God above

And all good men of this ungoverned isle.

RICHARD   I do suspect I have done some offence   110

That seems disgracious in the city's eye,

And that you come to reprehend my ignorance.

BUCKINGHAM You have, my lord. Would it might please your grace

On our entreaties to amend your fault.

Buckingham puts forward several reasons to persuade Richard to become King. He claims it is the citizens' wish. Richard debates whether he should reply or remain silent.

1 Buckingham's rhetoric (in pairs)

The plot to fool the Lord Mayor and citizens into accepting Richard as King continues with a brilliant display of rhetoric:

- **Lines 116–21** Buckingham tells Richard that he is wrong to give up his right to the crown in favour of corrupt members of his family.
- **Lines 122–8** He urges Richard to take action because England is sick and its royal family at the point of death.
- **Lines 129–35** The people beg Richard to cure England by becoming not the agent of another, but the true King in his own right.
- **Lines 136–9** All this is the wish of the citizens; he speaks for them.

Take turns to speak Buckingham's lines 116–39, experimenting with a range of tone, volume, pitch and pace to be as persuasive as you can.

2 Mock-modest Richard (I) (in pairs)

In lines 140–72 – in which Richard responds to Buckingham's offer of the crown – his formal language masks his ambition. The first twelve lines are like an internal debate in which he attempts to balance two opposing arguments: speak or be silent.

a Write out in your own words what Richard means by this response to Buckingham's offer of the crown. Which of his two arguments do you think will carry the most weight with the Mayor and the citizens?

b Provide two (or more) asides that show what Richard is really thinking as he describes his dilemma between speaking out or remaining silent.

Write about it

A citizen's perspective (by yourself)

Consider these events from the perspective of one of the citizens of London who was present at both Buckingham's addresses.

- Write a diary entry giving an account of the events described in this scene and your understanding of what is really happening. How do you feel about Richard becoming King and about Buckingham's persuasive performance? Why do you remain silent at the beginning of the scene (see lines 1–42)? What is your response when Richard speaks for himself?

sceptered office position as King
your state of fortune position you deserve by fortune
lineal glory inherited
blemished stock impure family

proper limbs own true parts

graft with united to, joined with
ignoble plants illegitimate offspring
shouldered pushed into
recure cure

factor agent
successively by inheritance
empery dominion, empire
consorted associated

vehement instigation strong
move persuade

degree status

fondly foolishly
suit request
seasoned made agreeable
checked rebuked

| RICHARD | Else wherefore breathe I in a Christian land? | 115 |
| BUCKINGHAM | Know, then, it is your fault that you resign | |

The supreme seat, the throne majestical,
The sceptered office of your ancestors,
Your state of fortune and your due of birth,
The lineal glory of your royal house, 120
To the corruption of a blemished stock;
While in the mildness of your sleepy thoughts,
Which here we waken to our country's good,
The noble isle doth want her proper limbs;
Her face defaced with scars of infamy, 125
Her royal stock graft with ignoble plants,
And almost shouldered in the swallowing gulf
Of dark forgetfulness and deep oblivion.
Which to recure, we heartily solicit
Your gracious self to take on you the charge 130
And kingly government of this your land,
Not as protector, steward, substitute,
Or lowly factor for another's gain,
But as successively from blood to blood,
Your right of birth, your empery, your own. 135
For this, consorted with the citizens,
Your very worshipful and loving friends,
And by their vehement instigation,
In this just cause come I to move your grace.

RICHARD I cannot tell if to depart in silence 140
Or bitterly to speak in your reproof
Best fitteth my degree or your condition.
If not to answer, you might haply think
Tongue-tied ambition, not replying, yielded
To bear the golden yoke of sovereignty, 145
Which fondly you would here impose on me.
If to reprove you for this suit of yours,
So seasoned with your faithful love to me,
Then on the other side I checked my friends.
Therefore, to speak, and to avoid the first, 150
And then, in speaking, not to incur the last,
Definitively thus I answer you:

Richard argues that he is unworthy to be King and that young Edward will in time become a successful monarch. Buckingham reminds Richard of the Prince of Wales's suspect family history.

1 Mock-modest Richard (II)

- In lines 155–65, Richard argues he is unfit for such a high position. He compares himself to a ship ('bark') unfit to endure a great ocean ('brook no mighty sea'), claiming that he would rather avoid kingship ('greatness') than desire it ('covet to be hid') and would be overwhelmed by such an awesome responsibility.

- In lines 166–72, he asserts that the Prince of Wales is the rightful heir who will mature ('mellowed by the stealing hours of time') into a distinguished monarch. But Richard's 'no doubt' is a sting in the tail of his praise of Edward.

a Make notes on the main points of Richard's speech, using the information above and on page 138. Use your notes to help you deliver Richard's lines 140–72. Try to bring out his hypocrisy.

b How would you advise the actor playing Richard at this point in the play? Write notes in your Director's Journal.

Characters

Sneering at Queen Elizabeth

Buckingham repeats the accusations of Prince Edward's illegitimacy and King Edward's breaking of two marriage contracts. In highly insulting language, he turns his attention to Elizabeth Grey.

a List the words and phrases Buckingham uses to describe the Queen. Then write out his description of her in modern English. What picture is he painting of her and her son?

b Write a defence of the Queen in the form of an opinion article submitted to the national newspaper. What other perspectives can you put forward to save the Queen's reputation and that of her family?

desert / Unmeritable unworthy merit

shuns rejects

even smooth

As the ripe ... birth as what is rightly mine

need (line 165) lack

defend forbid

a poor petitioner a person of low status

beauty-waning fading beauty

the afternoon of her best days her middle age

Made prize ... wanton eye seduced Edward

pitch importance, high rank

base declension ignoble decline

bigamy (Buckingham argues that Edward's contracts to other women caused him to commit bigamy when he married Elizabeth)

our manners courtesy

Your love deserves my thanks, but my desert
Unmeritable shuns your high request.
First, if all obstacles were cut away, 155
And that my path were even to the crown
As the ripe revenue and due of birth,
Yet so much is my poverty of spirit,
So mighty and so many my defects,
That I would rather hide me from my greatness, 160
Being a bark to brook no mighty sea,
Than in my greatness covet to be hid
And in the vapour of my glory smothered.
But, God be thanked, there is no need of me,
And much I need to help you, were there need. 165
The royal tree hath left us royal fruit,
Which, mellowed by the stealing hours of time,
Will well become the seat of majesty
And make (no doubt) us happy by his reign.
On him I lay that you would lay on me, 170
The right and fortune of his happy stars,
Which God defend that I should wring from him.

BUCKINGHAM   My lord, this argues conscience in your grace,
But the respects thereof are nice and trivial,
All circumstances well considerèd. 175
You say that Edward is your brother's son.
So say we too, but not by Edward's wife,
For first was he contràct to Lady Lucy,
Your mother lives a witness to his vow,
And afterward by substitute betrothed 180
To Bona, sister to the King of France.
These both put off, a poor petitioner,
A care-crazed mother to a many sons,
A beauty-waning and distressèd widow,
Even in the afternoon of her best days, 185
Made prize and purchase of his wanton eye,
Seduced the pitch and height of his degree
To base declension and loathed bigamy.
By her, in his unlawful bed, he got
This Edward, whom our manners call the prince. 190

Buckingham says he will refrain from further criticism. He begs Richard to accept the crown, echoed by the Lord Mayor on behalf of the people. Richard refuses. Buckingham threatens to enthrone another. Catesby adds his pleas.

1 Richard the unwilling King? (in large groups)

The unsettling macabre humour and dramatic irony continue to the end of the scene, as Richard and his co-conspirators act out their charade for the Lord Mayor and citizens.

a Decide whether they really are deceived by Richard. Take parts as the Lord Mayor and citizens, Richard, Buckingham and Catesby. Work out a performance of lines 191–245 to bring out the humour and hypocrisy in the episode. Use the following to help you:

- Read through lines 191–9 to work out how Buckingham might speak as much to the Lord Mayor and citizens as he does to Richard.
- The Lord Mayor's plea at line 200 is (probably) sincere. Buckingham's and Catesby's lines 201–2 are deeply insincere. Use tones and gestures to bring out what is really in each man's mind.
- How can Richard speak or act in lines 203–4 to reveal his hypocrisy?
- How does Richard react to Buckingham's description of him in lines 209–10?

b Write notes in your Director's Journal about how you want the script opposite to be staged. Remember to include your thoughts about what the crowd is doing and thinking during this 'performance'.

Themes

Acting the part (in pairs)

Both Buckingham and Richard give convincing performances, and they work well together, with each man offering the other the opportunity to develop his part.

- In role as Richard and Buckingham, write asides at suitable points in the script opposite to allow them to comment on their own and each other's performance.
- Take turns to perform your asides to the rest of the class, while three others read out the scripted lines from the page opposite, pausing for you to give your character's comments.

---

expostulate argue

give … my tongue refuse to speak further of King Edward's scandalous past

proffered benefit of dignity (the crown)

draw forth rescue

amiss wrongly

zeal enthusiasm

gentle refined

effeminate remorse tender, nurturing pity

kindred family

all estates people of all ranks

whe'er whether

	More bitterly could I expostulate,	
	Save that for reverence to some alive,	
	I give a sparing limit to my tongue.	
	Then, good my lord, take to your royal self	
	This proffered benefit of dignity,	195
	If not to bless us and the land withal,	
	Yet to draw forth your noble ancestry	
	From the corruption of abusing times	
	Unto a lineal true-derivèd course.	
MAYOR	Do, good my lord, your citizens entreat you.	200
BUCKINGHAM	Refuse not, mighty lord, this proffered love.	
CATESBY	Oh, make them joyful. Grant their lawful suit.	
RICHARD	Alas, why would you heap this care on me?	
	I am unfit for state and majesty.	
	I do beseech you, take it not amiss;	205
	I cannot nor I will not yield to you.	
BUCKINGHAM	If you refuse it, as in love and zeal	
	Loath to depose the child, your brother's son,	
	As well we know your tenderness of heart	
	And gentle, kind, effeminate remorse,	210
	Which we have noted in you to your kindred	
	And equally indeed to all estates,	
	Yet know, whe'er you accept our suit or no,	
	Your brother's son shall never reign our king,	
	But we will plant some other in the throne	215
	To the disgrace and downfall of your house.	
	And in this resolution here we leave you.	
	Come, citizens. We will entreat no more.	

Exeunt

CATESBY	Call him again, sweet prince; accept their suit.	
	If you deny them, all the land will rue it.	220

Richard orders Catesby to recall everyone. He grudgingly accepts the burden of kingship, but says that if discord follows, he is free of blame. He is proclaimed King, with the coronation to take place the following day.

1 'Call them again' (in small groups)

The stage direction *Exeunt* at line 218 implies that only Richard, the bishops and Catesby remain on stage. In some productions, following a long pause after line 221, Richard is genuinely afraid that the citizens will not come back.

- Use that interpretation to suggest how Richard speaks his words 'Call them again' to get a laugh from the audience.

Language in the play
Denying responsibility

Richard's lines 225–34 reveal more of his cunning. He says he must patiently accept the burden of kingship that they are fastening like armour on his back. As this role has been imposed upon him, so those who forced him to become King must acquit him of any future blame.

- Experiment with ways of performing these lines. Are they spoken grudgingly, sorrowfully, gravely or threateningly? In your delivery, show how Richard's language shifts responsibility away from himself and reinforces his appearance of grudgingly accepting the crown (for example, in his use of 'you' and 'your' and 'I', and in the words that mean burden and faults).

Stagecraft
Long live King Richard (in small groups)

Many stage productions place the interval at this point, closing with a striking image, as a triumphant Richard achieves his aim and is proclaimed King. In one stage production, Richard threw away his prayer book and the bishops revealed themselves as armed soldiers. In Laurence Olivier's movie of the play, Richard's final action was to force Buckingham to kneel and kiss his hand in an act of submission.

- Work out a final, effective dramatic image of your own to close the scene.

penetrable open
Albeit although you forced me

sage wise
buckle armour

Attend the sequel appear as a result
Your mere enforcement the mere fact
acquittance acquit
impure blots slanders

cousins (Richard includes the citizens in this term of intimacy)

RICHARD   Will you enforce me to a world of cares?
Call them again. I am not made of stones,
But penetrable to your kind entreaties,
Albeit against my conscience and my soul.

Enter BUCKINGHAM *and the rest*

Cousin of Buckingham, and sage, grave men,   225
Since you will buckle fortune on my back,
To bear her burden, whe'er I will or no,
I must have patience to endure the load.
But if black scandal or foul-faced reproach
Attend the sequel of your imposition,   230
Your mere enforcement shall acquittance me
From all the impure blots and stains thereof;
For God doth know, and you may partly see,
How far I am from the desire of this.

MAYOR   God bless your grace; we see it and will say it.   235

RICHARD   In saying so, you shall but say the truth.

BUCKINGHAM   Then I salute you with this royal title:
Long live King Richard, England's worthy king.

ALL   Amen.

BUCKINGHAM   Tomorrow may it please you to be crowned?   240

RICHARD   Even when you please, for you will have it so.

BUCKINGHAM   Tomorrow, then, we will attend your grace,
And so most joyfully we take our leave.

RICHARD   [*To the Bishops*] Come, let us to our holy work again. –
Farewell, my cousins, farewell, gentle friends.   245

Exeunt

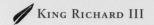

Looking back at Act 3
Activities for groups or individuals

1 Richard plays many parts

Richard takes a malicious delight in acting out a variety of parts as he plots and kills his way to the throne. Act 3 contains many examples of Richard's duplicity, from his ironic warning to Prince Edward to beware 'false friends' (Scene 1) to the full-scale production put on for the benefit of the Lord Mayor and citizens (Scene 7).

a Trace all Richard's 'performances' in the act and discuss how they compare with other examples from Acts 1 and 2 of Richard's techniques for dissembling and cynically using others.

b Analyse each performance and give a score out of ten for his acting abilities. Then write a report on his acting skills and his ability to influence the people around him.

2 The rat, the cat, the dog

Sir Richard Ratcliffe's power and influence has steadily increased through his unquestioning loyalty to Richard since his first appearance (Act 2 Scene 1). His two friends, Catesby and Lovell, have similarly flourished under Richard's patronage as they carry out his sinister commands. Catesby is entrusted to test Hastings's loyalty, and Lovell brings in Hastings's severed head. The three men featured in a contemporary verse:

> The Cat, the Rat and Lovell the dog
> Do rule all England under the Hog.

• Look back through the play and write down what other services the three have performed for Richard so far. Suggest how a director might emphasise their new-found status. As you read on, look out for what else they do.

3 Buckingham the spin-doctor

Buckingham uses a variety of methods to ensure that Richard gains the crown. The techniques he employs are similar to those used by present-day political spin-doctors, who manipulate unpleasant facts to make them appear attractive to the voting public (see the picture on p. 158).

• Look back at Buckingham's words and actions in Scenes 1, 4, 5 and 7, then step into role as Buckingham and write yourself a memo setting out your intention to make Richard King and the methods you will use to achieve this aim.

4 Depicting the two princes

The plight of the two young princes, sent off to the Tower by their scheming and murderous uncle, has been depicted in moving detail by artists since Shakespeare's play was first performed.

a Look at the representation of the princes in the Tower opposite. Is this how you imagine them to look?

b How else might the princes be represented? You might like to refer back to Act 3 Scene 1 and at the image on page 102.

c Describe in your own words the significance of the princes in developing the character of Richard III.

Queen Elizabeth, the Duchess of York, Dorset and Anne meet outside the Tower, where they have come to visit the princes. Brakenbury, on Richard's orders, refuses them entry.

1 Family tree: a reminder (whole class)

At the opening of Act 4, the three main female characters emphasise their close family ties, united in opposition to Richard.

- To remind yourself of their relationship to each other and to Richard, three volunteers take parts as the Duchess, Anne and Elizabeth and speak lines 1–11. Project the Plantagenet family tree (see p. 266) onto a whiteboard or screen. Everyone points to the appropriate name on the family tree as any words showing relationships are spoken.

Themes

The role of women (in fours)

Women start to play an increasingly significant role in the play. In depicting the main female characters as a group, united in adversity, Shakespeare was probably drawing on early Renaissance Resurrection plays. These popular dramas enacted stories from the Christian Bible, particularly focusing on the crucifixion and resurrection of Jesus. Here, Anne, Elizabeth and the Duchess of York take on a similar role to the three Biblical Marys (Mary Magdalene, Mary Salome and Mary, the mother of James). They shift attention away from the figure of Richard and focus instead on the victims of his crimes.

a The stage direction at the start suggests that Clarence's young daughter accompanies the delegation, but she is sometimes omitted in productions. What difference do you think this would make to the scene?

b Take parts as Brakenbury, Elizabeth, the Duchess and Anne, then read lines 12–28. How do you think the women react to Brakenbury's refusal to allow them to see the princes in the Tower? For example, do you think they are pleading and desperate, assertive and accustomed to giving orders, fearful, angry and dismissive, or something else?

c Is it important that all the women react in the same way, or do you think they can each behave differently? Make a decision and then explain your reasons. Write your thoughts in your Director's Journal.

niece granddaughter
kind family or kind-hearted
for my life I stake my life on it

sister sister-in-law
Whither away? where are you going?
devotion duty
gratulate greet

in good time with good timing

suffer permit

bounds barriers

thy office your responsibility
on my peril with danger to myself
leave it so let it be so

Act 4 Scene 1
Outside the Tower of London

Enter QUEEN ELIZABETH, *the* DUCHESS OF YORK, *and*
MARQUESS DORSET, *meeting* ANNE DUCHESS OF GLOUCESTER
and Clarence's daughter

DUCHESS   Who meets us here? My niece Plantagenet
Led in the hand of her kind aunt of Gloucester?
Now, for my life, she's wand'ring to the Tower,
On pure heart's love to greet the tender prince.
Daughter, well met.

ANNE   God give your graces both   5
A happy and a joyful time of day.

ELIZABETH   As much to you, good sister. Whither away?

ANNE   No farther than the Tower, and, as I guess,
Upon the like devotion as yourselves,
To gratulate the gentle princes there.   10

ELIZABETH   Kind sister, thanks. We'll enter all together.

Enter the Lieutenant [BRAKENBURY]

And in good time, here the Lieutenant comes.
Master Lieutenant, pray you, by your leave,
How doth the prince and my young son of York?

BRAKENBURY   Right well, dear madam. By your patience,   15
I may not suffer you to visit them.
The king hath strictly charged the contrary.

ELIZABETH   The king? Who's that?

BRAKENBURY   I mean the Lord Protector.

ELIZABETH   The Lord protect him from that kingly title.   20
Hath he set bounds between their love and me?
I am their mother. Who shall bar me from them?

DUCHESS   I am their father's mother. I will see them.

ANNE   Their aunt I am in law, in love their mother.
Then bring me to their sights; I'll bear thy blame   25
And take thy office from thee, on my peril.

BRAKENBURY   No, madam, no; I may not leave it so.
I am bound by oath, and therefore pardon me.

Exit Lieutenant

Stanley's news of Richard's intended coronation dismays the women. Elizabeth tells Dorset to flee to join Richmond. Stanley's son will help him. Anne says she would prefer to die than to be Queen.

1 Events gather pace (in small groups)

The speed with which Richard's coronation takes place surprises all the characters. Realising that her son Dorset is in danger, Elizabeth shows political astuteness in urging him to leave the country and join Richmond in France.

a Read the script opposite and write down all the words and phrases that help create the impression of speed and urgency.

b Take parts and read lines 29–63 in a way that emphasises this sense of urgency. Consider tone and pace when speaking, then experiment with appropriate movements.

2 Remembering Margaret's curse (in pairs)

In lines 46–7, Elizabeth recalls Margaret's curse.

- Turn back to Act 1 Scene 3, line 207, and compare Margaret's curse with Elizabeth's words here.

Language in the play

Images of outrage (in small groups)

Elizabeth, the Duchess and Anne express their emotions through a number of powerful images, including those linked with hell, death and monstrous animals.

a Choose three images from the script opposite that you find particularly striking and construct a series of tableaux. Show your tableaux to other groups and ask them to guess which images you are representing. If you have access to a digital camera, take some photographs of each of the tableaux and create a classroom display. Add to this as you progress through the rest of this act, collecting the most graphic images used to describe Richard.

b Discuss the effectiveness of this vivid language in the play. How does it affect an audience's view of Richard and of the three women?

---

reverend respectful
Westminster Westminster Abbey (where coronations are held)
lace cord used to lace up a tight bodice or corset
pent imprisoned
scope room
Despiteful cruel

outstrip outrun

thrall slave
counted acknowledged

ta'en tardy slowed, captured later

cockatrice basilisk (serpent whose look could kill)

inclusive verge encircling rim

deadly venom poison from a snake

feed my humour cheer my unhappy mood

Enter STANLEY [EARL OF DERBY]

STANLEY   Let me but meet you ladies one hour hence,
            And I'll salute your grace of York as mother   30
            And reverend looker-on of two fair queens.
            [*To Anne*] Come, madam, you must straight to Westminster,
            There to be crownèd Richard's royal queen.

ELIZABETH   Ah, cut my lace asunder,
            That my pent heart may have some scope to beat,   35
            Or else I swoon with this dead-killing news.

ANNE   Despiteful tidings. Oh, unpleasing news.

DORSET   Be of good cheer, mother; how fares your grace?

ELIZABETH   O Dorset, speak not to me; get thee gone.
            Death and destruction dogs thee at thy heels.   40
            Thy mother's name is ominous to children.
            If thou wilt outstrip death, go, cross the seas
            And live with Richmond, from the reach of hell.
            Go hie thee, hie thee from this slaughterhouse,
            Lest thou increase the number of the dead   45
            And make me die the thrall of Margaret's curse,
            Nor mother, wife, nor England's counted queen.

STANLEY   Full of wise care is this your counsel, madam –
            [*To Dorset*] Take all the swift advantage of the hours.
            You shall have letters from me to my son   50
            In your behalf, to meet you on the way.
            Be not ta'en tardy by unwise delay.

DUCHESS   O ill-dispersing wind of misery.
            O my accursèd womb, the bed of death.
            A cockatrice hast thou hatched to the world,   55
            Whose unavoided eye is murderous.

STANLEY   Come, madam, come. I in all haste was sent.

ANNE   And I with all unwillingness will go.
            Oh, would to God that the inclusive verge
            Of golden metal that must round my brow   60
            Were red-hot steel, to sear me to the brains.
            Anointed let me be with deadly venom
            And die ere men can say 'God save the queen.'

ELIZABETH   Go, go, poor soul, I envy not thy glory.
            To feed my humour, wish thyself no harm.   65

1 Bad dreams

Line 85 suggests that Richard has nightmares that keep Anne awake. Shakespeare appears to have been fascinated by dreams and the way a guilty conscience could play on a person's subconscious mind.

- Imagine you are making a movie version of *King Richard III*. You have decided to create a scene in which Richard's nightmares are briefly visualised for the audience. Make a list of Richard's past crimes, then choose one or two that you think would work well in the shape of a nightmarish vision, and storyboard the scene. How will you highlight the disorienting effect that nightmares often have? Add notes to suggest suitable lighting, sound effects and music.

2 Taking leave (in fours)

Elizabeth, Anne, Dorset and the Duchess of York bid each other farewell in lines 88–94.

a As you read through the script aloud, identify which lines are addressed to which character. What actions might they use?

b Anne voices her fear that Richard will want to get rid of her, now that he has gained the throne (line 87). This is the last time that Anne will see Elizabeth and the Duchess. What advice would you give to the actor playing Anne so that the sombre finality of this farewell is communicated to the audience?

Stagecraft

Set the scene

Elizabeth's plea for the Tower to show pity towards the two princes contrasts the impersonal, menacing prison ('Rough cradle') with the vulnerable, innocent boys ('those tender babes'). She addresses the Tower as if it is alive: it is the only 'nurse' her children now have.

- How might a stage designer present a strong visual image of the Tower's menace to contrast with Elizabeth's pleas? Think about set design and lighting. Compile some notes and sketches in your Director's Journal.

accursed cursed

wed'st get married

ere before

Grossly stupidly
honey sweet-sounding
hitherto until now

still awaked always kept awake

adieu farewell
complaining reasons to complain
glory position of Queen

teen grief
Stay wait

immured imprisoned

Rude rough

ANNE	No? Why? When he that is my husband now
	Came to me as I followed Henry's corpse,
	When scarce the blood was well washed from his hands
	Which issued from my other angel husband
	And that dear saint which then I weeping followed,
	Oh, when, I say, I looked on Richard's face,
	This was my wish: 'Be thou', quoth I, 'accursed
	For making me, so young, so old a widow.
	And when thou wed'st, let sorrow haunt thy bed;
	And be thy wife, if any be so mad,
	More miserable by the life of thee
	Than thou hast made me by my dear lord's death.'
	Lo, ere I can repeat this curse again,
	Within so small a time, my woman's heart
	Grossly grew captive to his honey words
	And proved the subject of mine own soul's curse,
	Which hitherto hath held mine eyes from rest.
	For never yet one hour in his bed
	Did I enjoy the golden dew of sleep,
	But with his timorous dreams was still awaked.
	Besides, he hates me for my father Warwick,
	And will, no doubt, shortly be rid of me.
ELIZABETH	Poor heart, adieu; I pity thy complaining.
ANNE	No more than with my soul I mourn for yours.
DORSET	Farewell, thou woeful welcomer of glory.
ANNE	Adieu, poor soul, that tak'st thy leave of it.
DUCHESS	Go thou to Richmond, and good fortune guide thee –
	Go thou to Richard, and good angels tend thee –
	Go thou to sanctuary, and good thoughts possess thee;
	I to my grave, where peace and rest lie with me.
	Eighty-odd years of sorrow have I seen,
	And each hour's joy wracked with a week of teen.
ELIZABETH	Stay, yet look back with me unto the Tower.
	Pity, you ancient stones, those tender babes
	Whom envy hath immured within your walls,
	Rough cradle for such little pretty ones.
	Rude, ragged nurse, old sullen playfellow
	For tender princes, use my babies well.
	So foolish sorrows bids your stones farewell.

70

75

80

85

90

95

100

Exeunt

The newly crowned Richard sits on the throne. He implies that Buckingham should kill the princes. At first, Buckingham pretends not to understand, then he asks for time to think. Richard shows his anger.

Characters

Richard the King (in groups of six or more)

a Richard, now the crowned King, makes a stately entrance and then seats himself on the throne. Stage these two moments, showing each as a tableau:

- Enter King Richard. Where and how is Richard standing? How might you suggest his state of anticipation? How are his courtiers positioned around him? Think carefully about body language and facial expressions. Who looks at whom?
- What is the manner of Richard's taking the throne? Is he triumphant? Gracious? Cynical and sneering? Or does he feel insecure? How will you show Buckingham's closeness to Richard?

b Share your tableaux with the rest of the class. Can they identify the participants? Be prepared to bring your character to life if asked to do so, to express his innermost thoughts at this moment.

Write about it

Buckingham's doubts

Buckingham is reluctant to carry out Richard's orders to murder the young princes, and does not give the answer that the new King is hoping for. Imagine Buckingham's political diaries have just been published. Write the entry for this day. Consider the following questions as you write:

- What has the day of coronation been like?
- What does it feel like to have succeeded in finally getting Richard crowned? Has it all been worthwhile?
- What is your immediate reaction when you learn that Richard wants to have the princes killed?

fanfare a ceremonial trumpet blast
in pomp in stately splendour

apart aside

Sound another fanfare

Still ever
touch touchstone (used to test the genuineness of gold)
current genuine

thrice-renownèd
three times famous

consequence reply

thou wast not … dull
you used not to be so stupid

suddenly swiftly

may do your pleasure
can do whatever you wish

herein in this matter
presently at once

Act 4 Scene 2
London: the throne-room of the palace

A fanfare sounds. RICHARD, *newly crowned as king enters in pomp with* BUCKINGHAM, CATESBY, RATCLIFFE, LOVELL, *a* PAGE, *and others*

RICHARD	Stand all apart. Cousin of Buckingham.
BUCKINGHAM	My gracious sovereign.
RICHARD	Give me thy hand.

Sound

	Thus high, by thy advice and thy assistance,	
	Is King Richard seated.	5
	But shall we wear these glories for a day?	
	Or shall they last, and we rejoice in them?	
BUCKINGHAM	Still live they, and forever let them last.	
RICHARD	Ah, Buckingham, now do I play the touch	
	To try if thou be current gold indeed.	10
	Young Edward lives; think now what I would speak.	
BUCKINGHAM	Say on, my loving lord.	
RICHARD	Why, Buckingham, I say I would be king.	
BUCKINGHAM	Why, so you are, my thrice-renownèd lord.	
RICHARD	Ha, am I king? 'Tis so. But Edward lives.	15
BUCKINGHAM	True, noble prince.	
RICHARD	O bitter consequence,	
	That Edward still should live, true noble prince.	
	Cousin, thou wast not wont to be so dull.	
	Shall I be plain? I wish the bastards dead,	
	And I would have it suddenly performed.	20
	What say'st thou now? Speak suddenly, be brief.	
BUCKINGHAM	Your grace may do your pleasure.	
RICHARD	Tut, tut, thou art all ice; thy kindness freezes.	
	Say, have I thy consent that they shall die?	
BUCKINGHAM	Give me some little breath, some pause, dear lord,	25
	Before I positively speak in this.	
	I will resolve you herein presently. *Exit Buckingham*	
CATESBY	The king is angry; see, he gnaws his lip.	

Richard orders Tyrrel to be brought to him. He will no longer confide in Buckingham. Stanley brings news of Dorset's escape. Richard plots against Anne and Clarence's daughter and resolves to marry Princess Elizabeth.

1 Where is Anne?

The stage direction at the start of Scene 2 leaves Anne out of the coronation. However, some directors choose to include her in this scene. In one production, Richard callously talks about her illness and imminent death right in front of her (see lines 51–8).

- If you were staging this scene, would you include Anne or not? Give reasons for your choice.
- If you would include her, what advice would you give to the actor playing Anne? Remember, she has no lines in this scene.

▼ What does this image suggest about Richard and his relationship with Anne?

2 Richard and Buckingham (in pairs)

At the beginning of this scene, Richard takes Buckingham's hand as he seats himself on the throne. Within the space of twenty lines, Richard is gnawing his lip with anger (according to Catesby) when Buckingham hesitates to carry out an order.

- **a** Read lines 43–6, in which Richard reflects upon Buckingham. He ends with the ambiguous line 'Well, be it so'. How does Richard say this? Experiment with a number of different interpretations – for example, lightly dismissive, ominously, obviously intending to harm Buckingham, resigned or with a sigh. What gesture might accompany the words?

- **b** Is anyone else on stage at this point in the play? What difference (if any) might that make?

iron-witted dull
unrespective unfeeling
considerate thoughtful

close exploit secret deed

partly slightly

deep-revolving thoughtful
witty clever

Rumour it abroad
spread rumours widely

take order give orders
keeping close confinement
mean of low social status
boy Clarence's son
give out announce

it stands me much upon
it is to my advantage

Uncertain way of gain
risky business
pluck on encourage

RICHARD   I will converse with iron-witted fools
And unrespective boys. None are for me   30
That look into me with considerate eyes.
High-reaching Buckingham grows circumspect. –
Boy!

PAGE   My lord.

RICHARD   Know'st thou not any whom corrupting gold   35
Will tempt unto a close exploit of death?

PAGE   I know a discontented gentleman
Whose humble means match not his haughty spirit.
Gold were as good as twenty orators
And will, no doubt, tempt him to anything.   40

RICHARD   What is his name?

PAGE   His name, my lord, is Tyrrel.

RICHARD   I partly know the man. Go call him hither, boy.

Exit [*Page*]

The deep-revolving, witty Buckingham
No more shall be the neighbour to my counsels.
Hath he so long held out with me, untired,   45
And stops he now for breath? Well, be it so.

Enter STANLEY [EARL OF DERBY]

How now, Lord Stanley, what's the news?

STANLEY   Know, my loving lord, the Marquess Dorset,
As I hear, is fled to Richmond
In the parts where he abides.   50

RICHARD   Come hither, Catesby. Rumour it abroad
That Anne my wife is very grievous sick.
I will take order for her keeping close.
Inquire me out some mean poor gentleman,
Whom I will marry straight to Clarence' daughter.   55
The boy is foolish, and I fear not him.
Look how thou dream'st! I say again, give out
That Anne my queen is sick and like to die.
About it, for it stands me much upon
To stop all hopes whose growth may damage me.   60
I must be married to my brother's daughter,
Or else my kingdom stands on brittle glass.
Murder her brothers, and then marry her:
Uncertain way of gain. But I am in
So far in blood that sin will pluck on sin.   65
Tear-falling pity dwells not in this eye.

Richard orders Tyrrel to kill the princes and warns Stanley not to support Richmond. Richard ignores Buckingham's request for the promised earldom of Hereford and recalls Henry VI's prophecy that Richmond will become King.

Characters

Tyrrel: cast the part

What kind of man is Tyrrel and how should he be played?

a Re-read lines 35–40, which describe the kind of man Richard is looking for, and the Page's reply. Then summarise the characteristics that Tyrrel displays.

b Read the dialogue between Richard and Tyrrel in lines 67–83. How does Tyrrel react to Richard's proposal? Does he hesitate at all?

c If you were casting a new production of the play, who would you choose to play the part of Tyrrel? Consider television and film actors you are familiar with, then go online and download a couple of photos of actors you would recommend. Give reasons for your choices.

d Write some notes to the actor playing Tyrrel.

▼ The once-influential Buckingham is now ignored by Richard. How would you show his desperation on stage?

Prove test

Please you if it pleases you

deal upon act against

open means an easy way

Go by gain access with

prefer advance, reward
dispatch it straight do it immediately

late last
sound me in ask me about

pawned pledged

look to keep watch on
you shall answer it you'll suffer the consequences

peevish silly

vein mood

158

Enter TYRREL

	Is thy name Tyrrel?	
TYRREL	James Tyrrel, and your most obedient subject.	
RICHARD	Art thou indeed?	
TYRREL	Prove me, my gracious lord.	
RICHARD	Dar'st thou resolve to kill a friend of mine?	70
TYRREL	Please you.	
	But I had rather kill two enemies.	
RICHARD	Why then thou hast it: two deep enemies,	
	Foes to my rest and my sweet sleep's disturbers	
	Are they that I would have thee deal upon.	75
	Tyrrel, I mean those bastards in the Tower.	
TYRREL	Let me have open means to come to them,	
	And soon I'll rid you from the fear of them.	
RICHARD	Thou sing'st sweet music. Hark, come hither, Tyrrel.	
	Go by this token. Rise, and lend thine ear. *Whispers*	80
	There is no more but so; say it is done,	
	And I will love thee and prefer thee for it.	
TYRREL	I will dispatch it straight. *Exit*	

Enter BUCKINGHAM

BUCKINGHAM	My lord, I have considered in my mind	
	The late request that you did sound me in.	85
RICHARD	Well, let that rest. Dorset is fled to Richmond.	
BUCKINGHAM	I hear the news, my lord.	
RICHARD	Stanley, he is your wife's son. Well, look unto it.	
BUCKINGHAM	My lord, I claim the gift, my due by promise,	
	For which your honour and your faith is pawned:	90
	Th'earldom of Hereford and the movables	
	Which you have promisèd I shall possess.	
RICHARD	Stanley, look to your wife. If she convey	
	Letters to Richmond, you shall answer it.	
BUCKINGHAM	What says your highness to my just request?	95
RICHARD	I do remember me, Henry the Sixth	
	Did prophesy that Richmond should be king,	
	When Richmond was a little peevish boy.	
	A king, perhaps.	
BUCKINGHAM	May it please you to resolve me in my suit?	100
RICHARD	Thou troublest me; I am not in the vein. *Exit*	

Buckingham resolves to flee to safety in Wales. Tyrrel describes the remorse of the murderers who smothered the princes.

1 The death of the princes (in fours)

The murder of the princes in the Tower is a famous piece of English history, although historians do not know for sure whether Richard III was responsible for their deaths. Over the centuries, many artists and writers have recreated this event, but Shakespeare chooses not to show the boys' murder on stage.

- Read Tyrrel's description of the princes' murder (lines 1–22) and then mime the scene, making your actions and emotions clear through body language, facial expressions and gesture. You might like to look at the picture on this page and the one on page 147, which show how two different artists have interpreted the scene. How do they differ? What emotional impact is each artist striving for?
- Perform your mime for the rest of the class as someone reads the script aloud. What differences in interpretation emerge in the different mimes?

▼ The murder of the princes in the Tower.

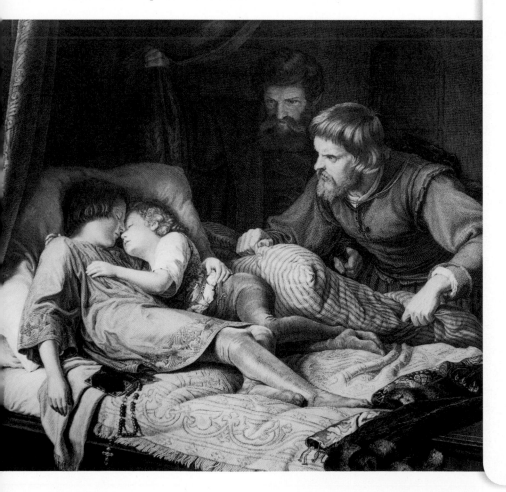

Brecknock (Buckingham's estate in Wales)

most arch highest

suborn procure, bribe
ruthful pitiful
Albeit although
fleshed hardened
in their deaths' sad story in telling how they died
girdling embracing
alabaster marble, tomb-like

replenishèd perfect
prime creation world's beginning
she (i.e. nature)

160

BUCKINGHAM And is it thus? Repays he my deep service
With such contempt? Made I him king for this?
Oh, let me think on Hastings and be gone
To Brecknock, while my fearful head is on.   105

Exeunt

Act 4 Scene 3
London: a room in King Richard's palace

Enter TYRREL

TYRREL The tyrannous and bloody act is done,
The most arch deed of piteous massacre
That ever yet this land was guilty of.
Dighton and Forrest, who I did suborn
To do this piece of ruthful butchery,   5
Albeit they were fleshed villains, bloody dogs,
Melted with tenderness and mild compassion,
Wept like to children in their deaths' sad story.
'Oh, thus', quoth Dighton, 'lay the gentle babes.'
'Thus, thus', quoth Forrest, 'girdling one another   10
Within their alabaster innocent arms.
Their lips were four red roses on a stalk,
And in their summer beauty kissed each other.
A book of prayers on their pillow lay,
Which once', quoth Forrest, 'almost changed my mind.   15
But oh, the devil', there the villain stopped.
When Dighton thus told on: 'we smotherèd
The most replenishèd sweet work of nature
That from the prime creation e'er she framed'.
Hence both are gone; with conscience and remorse   20
They could not speak, and so I left them both
To bear this tidings to the bloody king.

Enter RICHARD

And here he comes. All health, my sovereign lord.

Tyrrel assures Richard that the princes are dead. Richard plans marriage to Elizabeth. Ratcliffe's news is that Ely has joined Richmond and Buckingham has raised an army in Wales. Richard resolves to fight.

1 Does Tyrrel show his feelings? (in pairs)

Tyrrel's soliloquy in lines 1–22 reveals his real feelings about the murder, but his words to Richard mask his emotion.

a Talk about how Tyrrel might react to Richard's entrance and decide if he would hint at his real feelings in the way he speaks the lines or in his body language. Then take parts as Richard and Tyrrel and act out lines 24–35.

b Look back at the 'Characters' box on page 158. What additional notes would you make about Tyrrel's character now? Extend your initial advice for the actor playing Tyrrel to encompass his lines in Scene 3.

2 Richard's achievements

Richard lists the successes he has rapidly achieved (lines 36–43). Remind yourself of the plans Richard made straight after his coronation (Scene 2, lines 51–63) and then copy and complete the table below, using quotations from Richard's two speeches where possible.

Richard's plan (Scene 2)	Lines	Outcome (Scene 3)
'Rumour it abroad … Anne my queen is sick and like to die'	51–8	
	63	'The sons of Edward sleep in Abraham's bosom'

Characters

Richard: from 'woo-er' to soldier (in pairs)

Richard is about to play the role of 'jolly thriving wooer' (line 43), intending to claim the hand of Elizabeth's daughter and thus strengthen his power-base. However, within the space of fourteen lines he has abandoned that plan in reaction to Ratcliffe's news, and is taking up arms against his enemies.

• Choose two or three words or phrases that demonstrate the change in Richard's attitude and tone at this point in the play.

Kind like-minded
gave in charge ordered

process story

be inheritor of thy desire your wish will come true

meanly to a low-ranking husband
sleep … bosom are dead

Breton (Richmond had taken refuge in Brittany, France)
by that knot by means of that marriage

Morton the Bishop of Ely
Is in the field has begun military operations
power army
rash-levied strength hastily recruited army
fearful commenting nervous talk
leaden servitor slow servant
leads precedes
beggary ruin
fiery expedition speedy action
Jove's Mercury messenger of the gods
My counsel is my shield I have no time to talk
brave the field confront upon the battlefield

RICHARD	Kind Tyrrel, am I happy in thy news?	
TYRREL	If to have done the thing you gave in charge	25
	Beget your happiness, be happy then,	
	For it is done.	
RICHARD	But did'st thou see them dead?	
TYRREL	I did, my lord.	
RICHARD	And buried, gentle Tyrrel?	
TYRREL	The chaplain of the Tower hath buried them,	
	But where, to say the truth, I do not know.	30
RICHARD	Come to me, Tyrrel, soon and after supper,	
	When thou shalt tell the process of their death.	
	Meantime, but think how I may do thee good,	
	And be inheritor of thy desire.	
	Farewell till then.	
TYRREL	I humbly take my leave. *[Exit]*	35
RICHARD	The son of Clarence have I pent up close,	
	His daughter meanly have I matched in marriage,	
	The sons of Edward sleep in Abraham's bosom,	
	And Anne my wife hath bid this world good night.	
	Now, for I know the Breton Richmond aims	40
	At young Elizabeth, my brother's daughter,	
	And by that knot looks proudly on the crown,	
	To her go I, a jolly thriving wooer.	

Enter RATCLIFFE

RATCLIFFE	My lord.	
RICHARD	Good or bad news, that thou com'st in so bluntly?	45
RATCLIFFE	Bad news, my lord. Morton is fled to Richmond,	
	And Buckingham, backed with the hardy Welshmen,	
	Is in the field, and still his power increaseth.	
RICHARD	Ely with Richmond troubles me more near	
	Than Buckingham and his rash-levied strength.	50
	Come. I have learned that fearful commenting	
	Is leaden servitor to dull delay.	
	Delay leads impotent and snail-paced beggary.	
	Then fiery expedition be my wing,	
	Jove's Mercury, and herald for a king!	55
	Go muster men. My counsel is my shield.	
	We must be brief when traitors brave the field.	

Exeunt

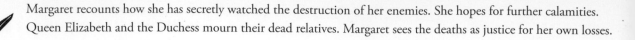

Margaret recounts how she has secretly watched the destruction of her enemies. She hopes for further calamities. Queen Elizabeth and the Duchess mourn their dead relatives. Margaret sees the deaths as justice for her own losses.

1 United in grief (in threes)

a Lines 1–135 involve only Queen Margaret, the Duchess and Elizabeth. To gain a first impression of the whole episode, take parts and read it through without pausing. The following may help you.

- **Queen Margaret** Hiding within the walls of the court ('confines'), Margaret has watched the loss of power ('the waning') of the Yorkists and Woodvilles. Margaret's asides show how she views each death as justice or repayment for her own losses ('right for right', 'doth quit', 'pays a dying debt').

- **Elizabeth** Grieving for her two sons murdered in the Tower, Elizabeth speaks of them as flowers in bud ('unblowed', 'new-appearing') and hopes they have escaped limbo ('doom perpetual') to become angels.

- **The Duchess of York** She mourns for her son, King Edward. She feels she has lived long enough.

b Talk together how the tone changes between this and the last scene. How does Shakespeare create this change of tone?

c Look carefully at the language used by the women. Pick out any images referring to nature or infancy and motherhood. What do these images contribute to the scene? How do they convey the mood?

2 Oxymorons

The Duchess of York describes herself as 'Dead life', 'blind sight' and a 'poor mortal living ghost' (lines 26–8). Opposite ideas linked together in this way are called **oxymorons**.

a Choose one of the three oxymorons listed above and create a human statue that you feel illustrates the image suggested by the Duchess's words. Show your statue to the rest of the class and see if they can guess which oxymoron you are portraying.

b Write a paragraph explaining the significance of these oxymorons.

prosperity success
mellow ripen
confines boundaries (of England)

induction prologue, beginning
will will go
consequence sequel, future
withdraw thee step aside

unblowed still in bud
sweets sweet-scented flowers
doom perpetual limbo

lamentation grief
right for right justice for justice
your infant morn the bright hope of children
agèd night death
crazed cracked

gentle lambs (the dead princes)
entrails belly

holy Harry (Henry VI)
mortal living living dead
grave's due by life usurped
I should be in the grave, but I am still alive
abstract précis, summary
Rest cease

Act 4 Scene 4
London: outside King Richard's palace

Enter old QUEEN MARGARET

MARGARET	So now prosperity begins to mellow
	And drop into the rotten mouth of death.
	Here in these confines slyly have I lurked
	To watch the waning of mine enemies.
	A dire induction am I witness to,
	And will to France, hoping the consequence
	Will prove as bitter, black, and tragical.
	Withdraw thee, wretched Margaret. Who comes here?

Enter DUCHESS [OF YORK] *and* QUEEN [ELIZABETH]

ELIZABETH	Ah, my poor princes! Ah, my tender babes!
	My unblowed flowers, new-appearing sweets!
	If yet your gentle souls fly in the air
	And be not fixed in doom perpetual,
	Hover about me with your airy wings
	And hear your mother's lamentation.
MARGARET	[*Aside*] Hover about her; say that right for right
	Hath dimmed your infant morn to agèd night.
DUCHESS	So many miseries have crazed my voice
	That my woe-wearied tongue is still and mute.
	Edward Plantagenet, why art thou dead?
MARGARET	[*Aside*] Plantagenet doth quit Plantagenet;
	Edward for Edward pays a dying debt.
ELIZABETH	Wilt thou, O God, fly from such gentle lambs
	And throw them in the entrails of the wolf?
	When didst thou sleep when such a deed was done?
MARGARET	[*Aside*] When holy Harry died, and my sweet son.
DUCHESS	Dead life, blind sight, poor mortal living ghost;
	Woe's scene, world's shame, grave's due by life usurped;
	Brief abstract and recòrd of tedious days,
	Rest thy unrest on England's lawful earth,
	Unlawfully made drunk with innocent blood.

Line numbers: 5, 10, 15, 20, 25, 30

Margaret asks to join the women in grieving. She and the Duchess list the deaths. Margaret blames the Duchess for giving birth to Richard. The Duchess asks for sympathy from Margaret, who expresses satisfaction in gaining revenge.

1 Listing the victims

Margaret and the Duchess of York list the dead (lines 35–70). To help you sort out who is who, copy and complete the following table. The family tree on page 266 may also help you. Colour code the killers and victims according to whether they are the house of York or the house of Lancaster.

Line	Victim	Killed by	Other Information?
39	Margaret's son, Prince Edward	Edward IV, Richard and Clarence	Killed after the Battle of Tewkesbury
40	Margaret's husband, Henry VI		Murdered in the Tower
41		Dighton and Forrest (ordered by Richard)	
42		Dighton and Forrest	
43			
44			
45			
63			
64			
65			
69	Hastings, Rivers, Vaughan and Grey	Ratcliffe and Lovell	Executed on Richard's orders

Language in the play
A disturbing image

Margaret accuses the Duchess of York of giving birth to a dog-like creature (Richard).

- Look at exactly what she says (lines 47–58) and consider the various animal-related metaphors she uses to convey a deeply disturbing image of Richard. Create a collage of words and pictures that you think captures the image that Margaret draws in words.

thou (line 31) England's earth

reverend worthy of deference
benefit of seniory advantage of age
let my griefs ... hand let my sorrows take precedence
society friendship, unity

holp'st helped

worry bite the throat (like a wolf or hunting dog)
God's handiwork human beings
gallèd sore

carnal cur murderous dog
issue children
pew-fellow fellow church-goer

cloy me gorge myself

quit revenge
boot lightweight
both they (i.e. both Edwards)

beholders of this frantic play spectators of this mad drama
Th'adulterate the adulterous

ELIZABETH	Ah, that thou wouldst as soon afford a grave
	As thou canst yield a melancholy seat.
	Then would I hide my bones, not rest them here.
	Ah, who hath any cause to mourn but we?
MARGARET	If ancient sorrow be most reverend,
	Give mine the benefit of seniory,
	And let my griefs frown on the upper hand,
	If sorrow can admit society.
	I had an Edward, till a Richard killed him;
	I had a husband, till a Richard killed him.
	Thou hadst an Edward, till a Richard killed him;
	Thou hadst a Richard, till a Richard killed him.
DUCHESS	I had a Richard too, and thou didst kill him;
	I had a Rutland too, thou holp'st to kill him.
MARGARET	Thou hadst a Clarence, too,
	And Richard killed him.
	From forth the kennel of thy womb hath crept
	A hell-hound that doth hunt us all to death:
	That dog, that had his teeth before his eyes
	To worry lambs and lap their gentle blood,
	That foul defacer of God's handiwork
	That reigns in gallèd eyes of weeping souls,
	That excellent grand tyrant of the earth
	Thy womb let loose to chase us to our graves.
	O upright, just, and true-disposing God,
	How do I thank thee, that this carnal cur
	Preys on the issue of his mother's body
	And makes her pew-fellow with others' moan.
DUCHESS	O Harry's wife, triumph not in my woes.
	God witness with me, I have wept for thine.
MARGARET	Bear with me. I am hungry for revenge,
	And now I cloy me with beholding it.
	Thy Edward he is dead that killed my Edward;
	The other Edward dead to quit my Edward;
	Young York he is but boot, because both they
	Matched not the high perfection of my loss.
	Thy Clarence he is dead that stabbed my Edward,
	And the beholders of this frantic play,
	Th'adulterate Hastings, Rivers, Vaughan, Grey,
	Untimely smothered in their dusky graves.

Line numbers: 35, 40, 45, 50, 55, 60, 65, 70

Margaret calls Richard an agent of hell. Elizabeth remembers Margaret's prophecy that she would ask her help to curse Richard. Margaret recalls her descriptions of Elizabeth and contrasts Elizabeth's past situation with her present situation.

Write about it

Hell's agent

Margaret says that Richard is a spy operating on behalf of the Devil. Write a modern-day story of about 500 words involving a spy from hell. When planning your story, consider the following:

- What is their mission?
- What do they do and with what consequences?
- How is it resolved?

Decide whether you are going to write it from the perspective of the evil agent or that of another character. Use some characteristics of Richard in your own spy.

Language in the play

'Bottled spider', 'bunch-backed toad' (in pairs)

In Act 1 Scene 3, Margaret called Richard a 'bottled spider' and a 'bunch-backed toad' (lines 242 and 246). Now Elizabeth repeats the insults.

a Discuss what properties of spiders and toads are appropriate when describing Richard.

b Sketch some ideas to show ways in which spiders and/or toads might be used as a central visual motif in stage design or costumes. (For example, if you look at the picture of Richard on p. 255, you will see that he has the appearance of a spider in the way he is dressed and positioned.)

1 Where are they now? (in small groups)

In lines 92–6, Margaret asks a series of rhetorical questions designed to emphasise the extent of Elizabeth's personal losses. This is a poetic convention from classical and medieval poetry known as *ubi sunt* (Latin for 'where are they?'). Margaret then proceeds to answer her own questions, listing in order all the miseries that Elizabeth has endured (lines 97–110).

a Take it in turn to read each of Margaret's questions, then match each question with an answer.

b Divide the questions and answers between you, then devise a dramatic presentation of these lines. Use movement and your voices to emphasise the tone of grief and sense of loss contained in the words.

intelligencer spy
reserved kept alive
factor agent
at hand soon
piteous dreadful

bond lease

vain flourish empty show
painted queen picture of a queen
presentation copy, reproduction
pageant play

sign image
fill the scene play a small part

sues asks for favours
bending bowing

Decline recite in order

caitiff wretch

one (line 103) Richard

whirled about wheeled around
Having … wast having only the memory of what you were

Richard yet lives, hell's black intelligencer,
Only reserved their factor to buy souls
And send them thither. But at hand, at hand
Ensues his piteous and unpitied end.
Earth gapes, hell burns, fiends roar, saints pray,   75
To have him suddenly conveyed from hence.
Cancel his bond of life, dear God, I pray,
That I may live and say the dog is dead.

ELIZABETH   Oh, thou didst prophesy the time would come
That I should wish for thee to help me curse   80
That bottled spider, that foul bunch-backed toad.

MARGARET   I called thee then vain flourish of my fortune;
I called thee then poor shadow, painted queen,
The presentation of but what I was,
The flattering index of a direful pageant,   85
One heaved a-high to be hurled down below,
A mother only mocked with two fair babes,
A dream of what thou wast, a garish flag
To be the aim of every dangerous shot,
A sign of dignity, a breath, a bubble,   90
A queen in jest, only to fill the scene.
Where is thy husband now? Where be thy brothers?
Where be thy two sons? Wherein dost thou joy?
Who sues and kneels and says 'God save the queen'?
Where be the bending peers that flattered thee?   95
Where be the thronging troops that followed thee?
Decline all this, and see what now thou art:
For happy wife, a most distressèd widow;
For joyful mother, one that wails the name;
For one being sued to, one that humbly sues;   100
For queen, a very caitiff crowned with care;
For she that scorned at me, now scorned of me;
For she being feared of all, now fearing one;
For she commanding all, obeyed of none.
Thus hath the course of justice whirled about   105
And left thee but a very prey to time,
Having no more but thought of what thou wast
To torture thee the more, being what thou art.
Thou didst usurp my place, and dost thou not
Usurp the just proportion of my sorrow?   110

Elizabeth asks Margaret to teach her how to curse. Margaret offers harsh advice. The Duchess tells Elizabeth to complain bitterly and often to Richard. Richard enters and the women verbally attack him.

Write about it

How to curse successfully

a In Margaret's final appearance in the play, she gives Elizabeth a lesson in how to curse someone successfully (lines 118–25). Read Margaret's advice. List each item of advice in modern English.

b Imagine you are an 'agony aunt' working for a teenage magazine. You receive the following letter:

> *Dear Marge,*
> *About six months ago, I fell out badly with my best friend*
> *and she is now being really nasty to me. I am in danger of*
> *dropping out of school if things carry on. She is evil; I think she*
> *might be an agent from hell (no, really!). I want to put a curse*
> *on her that will get her out of my life for ever. Can you help?*
> *Liz*

- Write Marge's reply.

Themes

Words as weapons (in threes)

Elizabeth and the Duchess of York realise, like Margaret, that words are the only weapons they have against Richard (lines 126–35).

a Read lines 136–146 and pick out all the insults (e.g. 'wretch') and accusations (e.g. 'all the slaughters … thou hast done').

b Two of you hurl insults and accusations, one at a time, at the third person, who repeats the words as if in shocked disbelief, contemptuous anger or in any other style you feel is appropriate. Experiment with pace and tone.

Stagecraft

Marching to battle

The stage direction at line 135 tells us that Richard enters with his 'train' (accompanied by soldiers, drummers, flag bearers and so on) marching to war ('expedition', line 136).

- Make notes suggesting how you might stage this entrance, firstly for a film version of the play and then for a stage production. How do your two versions differ? Why do you think this is?

Forbear refuse

Bett'ring exaggerating
causer perpetrator
Revolving thinking about, brooding on
quicken sharpen

Windy attorneys long-winded lawyers
Airy … joys too much talk that follows profound happiness
scope room, space

Be copious in exclaims use many bitter words
train retinue, followers
intercepts stops
expedition military campaign

owed owned

Ned (diminutive of Edward)

	Now thy proud neck bears half my burdened yoke,	
	From which even here I slip my wearied head	
	And leave the burden of it all on thee.	
	Farewell, York's wife, and queen of sad mischance.	
	These English woes shall make me smile in France.	115
ELIZABETH	O thou well skilled in curses, stay awhile,	
	And teach me how to curse mine enemies.	
MARGARET	Forbear to sleep the night, and fast the day;	
	Compare dead happiness with living woe;	
	Think that thy babes were sweeter than they were	120
	And he that slew them fouler than he is.	
	Bett'ring thy loss makes the bad causer worse;	
	Revolving this will teach thee how to curse.	
ELIZABETH	My words are dull. Oh, quicken them with thine.	
MARGARET	Thy woes will make them sharp, and pierce like mine.	125

Exit Margaret

DUCHESS	Why should calamity be full of words?	
ELIZABETH	Windy attorneys to their clients' woes,	
	Airy succeeders of intestine joys,	
	Poor breathing orators of miseries,	
	Let them have scope. Though what they will impart	130
	Help nothing else, yet do they ease the heart.	
DUCHESS	If so, then be not tongue-tied. Go with me,	
	And in the breath of bitter words let's smother	
	My damnèd son that thy two sweet sons smothered.	
	The trumpet sounds. Be copious in exclaims.	135

Enter RICHARD *and his train*

RICHARD	Who intercepts me in my expedition?	
DUCHESS	Oh, she that might have intercepted thee,	
	By strangling thee in her accursèd womb,	
	From all the slaughters, wretch, that thou hast done.	
ELIZABETH	Hid'st thou that forehead with a golden crown	140
	Where should be branded, if that right were right,	
	The slaughter of the prince that owed that crown	
	And the dire death of my poor sons and brothers?	
	Tell me, thou villain slave, where are my children?	
DUCHESS	Thou toad, thou toad, where is thy brother Clarence,	145
	And little Ned Plantagenet, his son?	
ELIZABETH	Where is the gentle Rivers, Vaughan, Grey?	

Richard tries to drown out the women's words with drums and trumpets. His mother catalogues all his faults from birth onwards. She demands a final hearing, and vows never to speak to him afterwards.

1 A mother's view (in small groups)

In lines 168–73, the Duchess of York's view of her son, Richard, is a chilling one. She lists his characteristics from birth to the present, piling up the adjectives that made 'the earth my hell'. She divides his life into four periods:

1 'infancy' – bad-tempered and disobedient

2 'schooldays' – rebellious

3 'prime of manhood' – always taking risks

4 'age confirmed' (maturity) – cunning and untrustworthy.

On television in the UK there used to be a programme called *This Is Your Life*, where famous people's lives were celebrated by friends, family and other celebrities. Each person recounted an incident from the celebrity's life, or introduced a short piece of film. A studio presenter hosted the show.

- In your groups, put together a *Richard III: This Is Your Life* programme, from the perspective of his mother. One person should be the presenter, one Richard's mother and the rest of the group act out four brief scenes from Richard's life. Share your finished programme with the rest of the class.

Rail on criticise
Lord's anointed King
Flourish trumpet fanfare
Alarum the call to arms (drum roll)
entreat me fair treat me politely
report noises, cannon fire

condition personality
brook the accent of reproof bear being criticised

stayed waited

the holy rood Christ's cross

Tetchy irritable

age confirmed full maturity
kind in hatred naturally hating; hating with a smile
comfortable comforting
Humphrey Hower (Elizabethans used the phrase 'dining with Duke Humphrey' to mean to go without a meal, so this might be a joke)
forth of away from
disgracious ungracious

DUCHESS	Where is kind Hastings?	
RICHARD	A flourish, trumpets! Strike alarum, drums!	
	Let not the heavens hear these telltale women	150
	Rail on the Lord's anointed. Strike, I say!	

Flourish. Alarums

	Either be patient and entreat me fair,	
	Or with the clamorous report of war	
	Thus will I drown your exclamations.	
DUCHESS	Art thou my son?	155
RICHARD	Ay, I thank God, my father, and yourself.	
DUCHESS	Then patiently hear my impatience.	
RICHARD	Madam, I have a touch of your condition,	
	That cannot brook the accent of reproof.	
DUCHESS	Oh, let me speak.	
RICHARD	Do then, but I'll not hear.	160
DUCHESS	I will be mild and gentle in my words.	
RICHARD	And brief, good mother, for I am in haste.	
DUCHESS	Art thou so hasty? I have stayed for thee,	
	God knows, in torment and in agony.	
RICHARD	And came I not at last to comfort you?	165
DUCHESS	No, by the holy rood, thou know'st it well,	
	Thou cam'st on earth to make the earth my hell.	
	A grievous burden was thy birth to me.	
	Tetchy and wayward was thy infancy;	
	Thy schooldays frightful, desperate, wild, and furious;	170
	Thy prime of manhood, daring, bold, and venturous;	
	Thy age confirmed, proud, subtle, sly, and bloody:	
	More mild, but yet more harmful, kind in hatred.	
	What comfortable hour canst thou name	
	That ever graced me with thy company?	175
RICHARD	Faith, none but Humphrey Hower, that called your grace	
	To breakfast once, forth of my company.	
	If I be so disgracious in your eye,	
	Let me march on and not offend you, madam.	
	Strike up the drum!	
DUCHESS	I prithee, hear me speak.	180
RICHARD	You speak too bitterly.	
DUCHESS	Hear me a word,	
	For I shall never speak to thee again.	
RICHARD	So.	

The Duchess prophesies she will never see Richard again. She lays a curse to ensure his defeat. Elizabeth echoes the curse. She says she will do anything to save her daughter's life, and blames Richard for her son's death.

1 A mother's last words to her son (in fours)

- The Duchess of York's farewell to her son is in the form of a curse (lines 184–96). Read her speech through at least twice, handing over to the next person at each full stop. Discuss what each section of the curse means, then memorise your lines.
- Explore ways of performing the speech together, using movement, choral speech and gestures. Can you find a piece of music to accompany your performance? What overall tone are you hoping to achieve? Share your performances, and discuss how you think Richard might react to each.

2 Richard versus Elizabeth (in pairs)

To gain a first impression of this long exchange between Richard and Elizabeth, take parts and read it straight through. Then work on one or more of the following activities.

a Talk together about whether you think Elizabeth has any suspicion of Richard's marriage intentions towards her daughter in the script opposite.

b Richard and Elizabeth's verbal battle in lines 212–22 recalls the rapidly alternating lines (known as stichomythia) between Richard and Anne in the 'wooing scene' (Act 1 Scene 2). Speak the lines in turn to bring out their speed and balance.

c Watch two different filmed productions of this scene. Write at least three paragraphs comparing how the directors set the scene and present the character of Elizabeth. Try to include quotations from the original script to illustrate how the director has made changes.

3 Mock innocence? (in pairs)

Elizabeth refers to her sons' death (lines 219–21), to which Richard replies, 'You speak as if that I had slain my cousins' (line 222). How does he say this line? In pairs try it in various ways:

- with mock innocence
- with knowing menace (as if daring Elizabeth to accuse him to his face)
- flatly and inscrutably
- casual and uncaring.

Decide which delivery you like best. Discuss what this line says about Richard and the way you would want to present him on stage.

---

turn return

tire thee (i.e. I hope will tire you)
còmplete head to toe
adverse party the opposite side

Whisper whisper to

attend wait upon

For my as for my

level not don't aim

veil of infamy protection of a bad reputation
So provided that

in her birth in her high position

good stars were opposite their star signs were unfavourable
ill friends bad persons
unavoided unavoidable
avoided grace rejection of God

DUCHESS	Either thou wilt die by God's just ordinance	
	Ere from this war thou turn a conqueror,	185
	Or I with grief and extreme age shall perish	
	And nevermore behold thy face again.	
	Therefore take with thee my most grievous curse,	
	Which in the day of battle tire thee more	
	Than all the còmplete armour that thou wear'st.	190
	My prayers on the adverse party fight,	
	And there the little souls of Edward's children	
	Whisper the spirits of thine enemies	
	And promise them success and victory.	
	Bloody thou art, bloody will be thy end;	195
	Shame serves thy life and doth thy death attend.	*Exit*
ELIZABETH	Though far more cause, yet much less spirit to curse	
	Abides in me. I say amen to her.	
RICHARD	Stay, madam. I must talk a word with you.	
ELIZABETH	I have no more sons of the royal blood	200
	For thee to slaughter. For my daughters, Richard,	
	They shall be praying nuns, not weeping queens,	
	And therefore level not to hit their lives.	
RICHARD	You have a daughter called Elizabeth,	
	Virtuous and fair, royal and gracious.	205
ELIZABETH	And must she die for this? Oh, let her live,	
	And I'll corrupt her manners, stain her beauty,	
	Slander myself as false to Edward's bed,	
	Throw over her the veil of infamy.	
	So she may live unscarred of bleeding slaughter,	210
	I will confess she was not Edward's daughter.	
RICHARD	Wrong not her birth; she is a royal princess.	
ELIZABETH	To save her life, I'll say she is not so.	
RICHARD	Her life is safest only in her birth.	
ELIZABETH	And only in that safety died her brothers.	215
RICHARD	Lo, at their birth good stars were opposite.	
ELIZABETH	No, to their lives ill friends were contrary.	
RICHARD	All unavoided is the doom of destiny.	
ELIZABETH	True, when avoided grace makes destiny.	
	My babes were destined to a fairer death,	220
	If grace had blest thee with a fairer life.	
RICHARD	You speak as if that I had slain my cousins.	

Elizabeth continues to accuse Richard of the murder of the princes and wishes she could die assaulting him. Richard declares that he will banish her grief by giving all honour and dignity to her daughter, Elizabeth.

Characters

Interpreting Elizabeth (in pairs)

a Read through the script opposite and discuss what impressions you gain of Elizabeth at this point in the play. Do you see her as:

- a strong, principled woman, not afraid to stand up to Richard
- nervous and fearful, pleading with Richard at times to spare her daughter
- scheming just as much as Richard, thinking that she might win some advantage by marrying her daughter to him
- behaving in another way?

b Find examples from the text to support your interpretation and note them down. Prepare a short presentation to deliver to the class. When everyone has given their presentations, discuss any differences in interpretation. Why is it possible to read the script in a number of different ways?

Richard argues that he should marry Elizabeth's daughter to consolidate his position as King. Choose a line to make an effective caption for the picture.

cozened cheated

kindred family

Whose hand soever whoever's hand it was

lanch'd lanced, pierced

direction command

whetted sharpened

But that only because

still use of grief repeated expression of grief

in such a desperate bay desperately at bay (as an animal hunted by hounds)

bark boat

reft bereft

so thrive I may I only thrive

As only as far as

discovered uncovered

high imperial type the crown

demise assign, grant

So provided that

Lethe (in classical mythology, the river of forgetfulness)

thy kindness' date the duration of your kindness

from apart from

ELIZABETH	Cousins indeed, and by their uncle cozened	
	Of comfort, kingdom, kindred, freedom, life.	
	Whose hand soever lanch'd their tender hearts,	225
	Thy head all indirectly gave direction.	
	No doubt the murderous knife was dull and blunt	
	Till it was whetted on thy stone-hard heart	
	To revel in the entrails of my lambs.	
	But that still use of grief makes wild grief tame,	230
	My tongue should to thy ears not name my boys	
	Till that my nails were anchored in thine eyes,	
	And I in such a desperate bay of death,	
	Like a poor bark of sails and tackling reft,	
	Rush all to pieces on thy rocky bosom.	235
RICHARD	Madam, so thrive I in my enterprise	
	And dangerous success of bloody wars	
	As I intend more good to you and yours	
	Than ever you and yours by me were harmed.	
ELIZABETH	What good is covered with the face of heaven	240
	To be discovered, that can do me good?	
RICHARD	Th'advancement of your children, gentle lady.	
ELIZABETH	Up to some scaffold, there to lose their heads.	
RICHARD	Unto the dignity and height of fortune,	
	The high imperial type of this earth's glory.	245
ELIZABETH	Flatter my sorrow with report of it.	
	Tell me what state, what dignity, what honour,	
	Canst thou demise to any child of mine?	
RICHARD	Even all I have, ay, and myself and all,	
	Will I withal endow a child of thine,	250
	So in the Lethe of thy angry soul	
	Thou drown the sad remembrance of those wrongs	
	Which thou supposest I have done to thee.	
ELIZABETH	Be brief, lest that the process of thy kindness	
	Last longer telling than thy kindness' date.	255
RICHARD	Then know that from my soul I love thy daughter.	
ELIZABETH	My daughter's mother thinks it with her soul.	
RICHARD	What do you think?	
ELIZABETH	That thou dost love my daughter from thy soul.	
	So from thy soul's love didst thou love her brothers,	260
	And from my heart's love I do thank thee for it.	

Richard states his intention to marry Elizabeth's daughter and make her Queen. Elizabeth mockingly suggests ways in which he should woo her daughter. Richard promises to make amends through the marriage.

Write about it

A grisly love letter

Richard now reveals that he wants to marry Elizabeth's daughter and make her Queen of England. On the grounds that a mother best knows how to win her daughter's heart, Richard asks for help in proposing marriage. Elizabeth's reply is probably not quite what he had in mind …

- Sketch and label Elizabeth's suggested gifts as outlined in lines 274–86). Then write the accompanying letter from Richard to the young Elizabeth.

1 Play it for laughs? (in pairs)

Faced with Elizabeth's elaborate challenge to his proposals, Richard's response in lines 287–8 could be delivered in a 'deadpan' tone to cause amusement. In the following lines, Richard goes on to defend himself. Such bloody acts have been committed because of his love for Elizabeth's daughter (line 292). When Elizabeth rejects this excuse, he suggests that sometimes men can act thoughtlessly ('Men shall deal unadvisedly sometimes'). This line usually gains a laugh in the theatre because 'deal unadvisedly' is totally out of proportion to the enormity of his crimes.

a Take parts and play around with this section of script (lines 270–99), trying to emphasise the preposterous nature of Richard's proposal and the possible humour in this part of the scene.

b Talk together about the advantages and disadvantages of highlighting the humour here.

Stagecraft

Direct the army

Richard entered at line 135 with his followers ('*train*'), which presumably included armed soldiers and military drummers, but there has been no stage direction to indicate what the army is doing all this time.

- Step into role as director and decide on some possible solutions. Make notes in your Director's Journal.

confound confuse

humour moods, temperament

by on behalf of

purple sap blood
sweet brother (Prince Edward)

mad'st away murdered, did away with

mad'st quick conveyance with quickly disposed of

spoil destruction
Look what whatever
deal unadvisedly act thoughtlessly

RICHARD	Be not so hasty to confound my meaning.	
	I mean that with my soul I love thy daughter	
	And do intend to make her Queen of England.	
ELIZABETH	Well then, who dost thou mean shall be her king?	265
RICHARD	Even he that makes her queen. Who else should be?	
ELIZABETH	What, thou?	
RICHARD	Even so. How think you of it?	
ELIZABETH	How canst thou woo her?	
RICHARD	That I would learn of you,	270
	As one being best acquainted with her humour.	
ELIZABETH	And wilt thou learn of me?	
RICHARD	Madam, with all my heart.	
ELIZABETH	Send to her by the man that slew her brothers	
	A pair of bleeding hearts; thereon engrave	275
	Edward and York; then haply will she weep.	
	Therefore present to her, as sometime Margaret	
	Did to thy father, steeped in Rutland's blood,	
	A handkerchief, which, say to her, did drain	
	The purple sap from her sweet brother's body,	280
	And bid her wipe her weeping eyes withal.	
	If this inducement move her not to love,	
	Send her a letter of thy noble deeds.	
	Tell her thou mad'st away her uncle Clarence,	
	Her uncle Rivers, ay, and for her sake	285
	Mad'st quick conveyance with her good aunt Anne.	
RICHARD	You mock me, madam, this is not the way	
	To win your daughter.	
ELIZABETH	There is no other way,	
	Unless thou couldst put on some other shape	290
	And not be Richard that hath done all this.	
RICHARD	Say that I did all this for love of her.	
ELIZABETH	Nay, then indeed she cannot choose but hate thee,	
	Having bought love with such a bloody spoil.	
RICHARD	Look what is done, cannot be now amended.	295
	Men shall deal unadvisedly sometimes,	
	Which after-hours gives leisure to repent.	
	If I did take the kingdom from your sons,	
	To make amends I'll give it to your daughter.	

Richard lists all the gains Queen Elizabeth will enjoy if her daughter becomes his wife. Her son, Dorset, will also benefit. He asks her to prepare Elizabeth for his wooing while he defeats Buckingham.

1 Intercut Richard's argument (in pairs)

Read lines 300–40, in which Richard lays out his argument as to why Elizabeth should accept his offer. He speaks without interruption, but what might Elizabeth be thinking all this time?

a Divide Richard's speech into sections and work out what Elizabeth's unspoken response might be. Use the following summary to help you understand Richard's lines:

- **Lines 298–9** If I took the kingdom from your sons, I'll make your daughter Queen.

- **Lines 300–2** If I killed your children, I will now give life to heirs through your daughter.

- **Lines 303–8** A grandmother is loved only a little less than a child's mother, but the grandmother does not have to suffer the pain of labour to produce a grandchild.

- **Lines 309–10** Your children were an annoyance when you were young. Grandchildren will comfort you in age.

- **Lines 311–12** Your loss is not having a son as King, but that has resulted in your daughter becoming Queen.

- **Lines 313–14** I can't offer you what I'd really like, but please accept what I'm able to offer.

- **Lines 315–20** Your son, Dorset, can return home to a position of power, as brother-in-law to the King.

- **Lines 321–3** You will be the mother-in-law to the King and the troubles of the past will be resolved.

- **Lines 324–8** The future will be far, far better and happier than the past.

- **Lines 329–34** Go to your daughter and use your maturity to prepare her to be wooed. Make her ambitious to be Queen and tell her of the joys of marriage.

- **Lines 335–40** When I've defeated Buckingham, I'll marry your daughter and she will be my commander.

Look back at Elizabeth's responses to Richard so far in this scene. How has she addressed Richard up to now? What is her manner and what kind of language does she use? Perform Richard's speech, pausing at the end of each section to allow Elizabeth to voice her innermost thoughts.

b Turn the page to find out how Elizabeth actually responds. As a class, discuss any major differences between the script and your prediction.

quicken your increase put new life in your family

doting title fond name

They (i.e. grandchildren)

metal substance, body, being

Of all one pain children and grandchildren cause the same amount of pain

bid like sorrow endured similar pain

discontented steps rebellious followers

Familiarly in the manner of a family

orient bright, valuable

Advantaging adding value to

my mother (Elizabeth would become his mother-in-law)

aspiring flame fire of ambition

triumphant garlands wreaths that Roman military heroes wore

retail retell

If I have killed the issue of your womb,   300
To quicken your increase I will beget
Mine issue of your blood upon your daughter.
A grandam's name is little less in love
Than is the doting title of a mother;
They are as children but one step below,   305
Even of your metal, of your very blood,
Of all one pain, save for a night of groans
Endured of her for whom you bid like sorrow.
Your children were vexation to your youth,
But mine shall be a comfort to your age.   310
The loss you have is but a son being king,
And by that loss your daughter is made queen.
I cannot make you what amends I would;
Therefore accept such kindness as I can.
Dorset, your son, that with a fearful soul   315
Leads discontented steps in foreign soil,
This fair alliance quickly shall call home
To high promotions and great dignity.
The king that calls your beauteous daughter wife
Familiarly shall call thy Dorset brother.   320
Again shall you be mother to a king,
And all the ruins of distressful times
Repaired with double riches of content.
What? We have many goodly days to see.
The liquid drops of tears that you have shed   325
Shall come again, transformed to orient pearl,
Advantaging their love with interest
Of ten times double gain of happiness.
Go then, my mother, to thy daughter go.
Make bold her bashful years with your experience;   330
Prepare her ears to hear a wooer's tale;
Put in her tender heart th'aspiring flame
Of golden sovereignty; acquaint the princess
With the sweet silent hours of marriage joys.
And when this arm of mine hath chastisèd   335
The petty rebel, dull-brained Buckingham,
Bound with triumphant garlands will I come
And lead thy daughter to a conqueror's bed;
To whom I will retail my conquest won,
And she shall be sole victoress, Caesar's Caesar.   340

Elizabeth again mocks Richard's proposal to woo Princess Elizabeth. She challenges every one of his arguments and statements, and dismisses his attempt to swear on the symbols of kingship.

Language in the play

Claims and counter-claims (whole class, then in pairs)

Elizabeth's list of questions (lines 341–6) is a response to Richard's long speech ending in the proposal that he should marry young Elizabeth. What follows returns to the quick-fire exchanges, often using balanced, antithetical pairing of sentences. This rapid exchange ends on a set of split lines (378–81).

a Divide the class into two and stand on different sides of the classroom in two long opposing lines:

- One line reads Richard's words, the other line reads Elizabeth's (lines 347–71). Start off quite slowly to get used to the words, but as you become more confident, start to experiment with pace, volume and tone, and how each side answers the other.

- Can you add gestures to the words? Remember, everyone on your side of the room needs to do the same. Make sure there is no gap between one side speaking and the other taking over. Aim for a slight overlap so that the rapid exchange is maintained.

b Divide into pairs and look again at each two-line claim and counter-claim separately.

- Talk together about the way one line leads to the next (that is, how one character picks up a word or phrase spoken by the other and returns it in a different form).

- Dramatically, what is the effect of this style of writing? What does it convey to an audience about Elizabeth and Richard? Make notes in your Director's Journal.

Infer imply
Still-lasting everlasting
entreats begs

vail yield, lose

speeds best succeeds best

quick hastily invented

Harp not on that string don't keep repeating that, change the subject
George St George (patron saint of England)
Garter badge signifying membership of the Order of the Garter, the highest order of knighthood
profaned treated irreverently and contemptuously
his its

ELIZABETH	What were I best to say? Her father's brother	
	Would be her lord? Or shall I say her uncle?	
	Or he that slew her brothers and her uncles?	
	Under what title shall I woo for thee	
	That God, the law, my honour, and her love	345
	Can make seem pleasing to her tender years?	
RICHARD	Infer fair England's peace by this alliance.	
ELIZABETH	Which she shall purchase with still-lasting war.	
RICHARD	Tell her the king, that may command, entreats.	
ELIZABETH	That at her hands which the king's King forbids.	350
RICHARD	Say she shall be a high and mighty queen.	
ELIZABETH	To vail the title, as her mother doth.	
RICHARD	Say I will love her everlastingly.	
ELIZABETH	But how long shall that title ever last?	
RICHARD	Sweetly in force unto her fair life's end.	355
ELIZABETH	But how long fairly shall her sweet life last?	
RICHARD	As long as heaven and nature lengthens it.	
ELIZABETH	As long as hell and Richard likes of it.	
RICHARD	Say I, her sovereign, am her subject low.	
ELIZABETH	But she, your subject, loathes such sovereignty,	360
RICHARD	Be eloquent in my behalf to her.	
ELIZABETH	An honest tale speeds best being plainly told.	
RICHARD	Then plainly to her tell my loving tale.	
ELIZABETH	Plain and not honest is too harsh a style.	
RICHARD	Your reasons are too shallow and too quick.	365
ELIZABETH	Oh, no, my reasons are too deep and dead,	
	Too deep and dead, poor infants, in their graves.	
RICHARD	Harp not on that string, madam. That is past.	
ELIZABETH	Harp on it still shall I till heartstrings break.	
RICHARD	Now, by my George, my Garter, and my crown –	370
ELIZABETH	Profaned, dishonoured, and the third usurped.	
RICHARD	I swear –	
ELIZABETH	By nothing, for this is no oath.	
	Thy George, profaned, hath lost his lordly honour;	
	Thy Garter, blemished, pawned his knightly virtue;	
	Thy crown, usurped, disgraced his kingly glory:	375
	If something thou wouldst swear to be believed,	
	Swear then by something that thou hast not wronged.	

Elizabeth will not accept any oath sworn by Richard based on himself, the world, his father's death, on God or the future. Richard claims that he intends to reform if he is successful in battle.

1 God, honour and the state

In line 345, Elizabeth accused Richard of disregarding three basic principles that govern a stable society ('God', 'law', 'honour'). Later, in line 370, Richard swears by Saint George (Church), his Garter (honour) and his crown (law and kingship). By swearing on these symbols of his kingship, Richard is not only invoking the Church, chivalry and honour, but also the divinity connected with kingship.

a Carry out an internet search to find out more about St George and what he stands for as the patron saint of England. Do the same for the Order of the Garter.

b Identify the three reasons Elizabeth gives in lines 373–5 that show Richard's oath is worthless.

c Using the symbolism of St George, the Garter and the crown, design a graphic representation (a drawing or a collage) of Richard's crown, religion and knightly honour all profaned and tarnished.

2 Richard's oath (in pairs)

Richard continues to search for an oath that is acceptable to Elizabeth. Today an oath is mainly sworn in a formal situation, such as when swearing in a jury or making marriage vows. The swearers pledge their word by using something they venerate as a symbol, perhaps a holy book or the safety of those they love.

Elizabeth says that Richard cannot swear an oath, as through his actions he has devalued all he might swear by. He has destroyed the value of himself, his kingdom and the honour of his dead father (lines 378–80). Richard does not answer Elizabeth's charges, but tries another oath based on the future. She dismisses this with contempt, because the future will be filled with the children and parents grieving for their loved ones whom Richard has killed.

- Take parts as Richard and Elizabeth, and speak the whole 'oath' episode (lines 370–401). Emphasise Richard's increasing desperation and Elizabeth's determined rejection of each attempt.

- As you rehearse this episode, experiment with positioning – for example, with the two characters standing very close to each other, then gradually further apart. Also, try making them move onto different levels. Who might gain the highest position by the end of this exchange?

Thyself is self-misused you have devalued yourself

Him God

Th'imperial metal the crown

bedfellows for dust both in their graves

time o'erpast past

Hereafter time the time to come, the future

Ungoverned unguided, fatherless

by times ill-used repassed times badly used in the past

confound destroy

bar me stop my

opposite hostile

proceeding success

Immaculate devotion pure prayer

tender not don't win

RICHARD	Then by myself.
ELIZABETH	Thyself is self-misused.
RICHARD	Now, by the world –
ELIZABETH	'Tis full of thy foul wrongs.
RICHARD	My father's death.
ELIZABETH	Thy life hath it dishonoured.

380

RICHARD	Why then, by heaven.
ELIZABETH	Heaven's wrong is most of all.

If thou didst fear to break an oath with Him,
The unity the king my husband made
Thou hadst not broken, nor my brothers died.
If thou hadst feared to break an oath by Him,   385
Th'imperial metal circling now thy head
Had graced the tender temples of my child,
And both the princes had been breathing here,
Which now, two tender bedfellows for dust,
Thy broken faith hath made the prey for worms.   390
What canst thou swear by now?

RICHARD   The time to come.

ELIZABETH   That thou hast wrongèd in the time o'erpast,
For I myself have many tears to wash
Hereafter time, for time past wronged by thee.   395
The children live whose fathers thou hast slaughtered,
Ungoverned youth, to wail it with their age;
The parents live whose children thou hast butchered,
Old barren plants, to wail it with their age.
Swear not by time to come, for that thou hast   400
Misused ere used, by times ill-used repassed.

RICHARD   As I intend to prosper and repent,
So thrive I in my dangerous affairs
Of hostile arms. Myself myself confound!
Heaven and fortune bar me happy hours!   405
Day, yield me not thy light, nor night, thy rest!
Be opposite, all planets of good luck
To my proceeding if, with dear heart's love,
Immaculate devotion, holy thoughts,
I tender not thy beauteous, princely daughter!   410
In her consists my happiness and thine.

Richard says that total destruction will result if he does not marry young Elizabeth. Her mother says she will let Richard know later. Ratcliffe brings news of a threatened invasion and unreliable allies.

Stagecraft

Is Elizabeth persuaded? (in pairs)

For the Plantagenets, marriages of political expediency were commonplace and morally acceptable. Therefore, Richard's final argument to Elizabeth is the strongest – without this alliance the state will collapse. Richard paints a picture of the country ruined if Princess Elizabeth will not marry him.

In the end, does Richard feel he has been successful? His comment about Elizabeth at line 436 ('Relenting fool and shallow, changing woman') suggests that he thinks he has won her over.

- With a partner, take parts and read through the script from line 423 to Elizabeth's exit. Rehearse a version that suggests Elizabeth has been persuaded by Richard and will allow him to marry her daughter.
- Then rehearse a second version, in which it is clear that Elizabeth has rejected the idea. Think carefully about how Elizabeth speaks her lines and about the way she exits in each version.

Characters

'Rounding out' Elizabeth

Many commentators claim that until Act 4 Scene 4, the female roles are rather 'flat' and formulaic, fulfilling a specific thematic function. Here, however, the actor playing Elizabeth is given space to develop the character dramatically.

Write approximately four paragraphs outlining how you think the role of Elizabeth should be played. Focus your attention on Act 4 and provide evidence from the script to support your view of her. You might find it helpful to look at the following episodes:

- **Act 4 Scene 1** The three women meet outside the Tower, where Elizabeth's sons are imprisoned.
- **Act 4 Scene 4** Elizabeth and the Duchess meet Margaret. Note particularly the points where Elizabeth mourns her sons; where she takes cursing lessons, and how she immediately responds to Richard's entrance; and where she sustains a verbal fencing match with Richard.

mother mother-in-law
attorney pleader, match-maker

necessity and state of times urgent political situation
be not ... designs do not be discovered fretfully complaining when great deeds are planned

in that nest ... they will breed in that phoenix's nest they will be reborn
recomforture renewed happiness

Relenting forgiving

puissant powerful
shores beaches
hollow-hearted cowardly

hull ride at anchor
expecting but only waiting for
light-foot swift
post ride speedily

	Without her follows to myself and thee,	
	Herself, the land, and many a Christian soul,	
	Death, desolation, ruin, and decay.	
	It cannot be avoided but by this.	415
	It will not be avoided but by this.	
	Therefore, dear mother, I must call you so,	
	Be the attorney of my love to her.	
	Plead what I will be, not what I have been,	
	Not my deserts, but what I will deserve.	420
	Urge the necessity and state of times,	
	And be not peevish found in great designs.	
ELIZABETH	Shall I be tempted of the devil thus?	
RICHARD	Ay, if the devil tempt you to do good.	
ELIZABETH	Shall I forget myself to be myself?	425
RICHARD	Ay, if your self's remembrance wrong yourself.	
ELIZABETH	Yet thou didst kill my children.	
RICHARD	But in your daughter's womb I bury them,	
	Where in that nest of spicery they will breed	
	Selves of themselves, to your recomforture.	430
ELIZABETH	Shall I go win my daughter to thy will?	
RICHARD	And be a happy mother by the deed.	
ELIZABETH	I go. Write to me very shortly,	
	And you shall understand from me her mind.	
RICHARD	Bear her my true love's kiss, and so farewell.	435

Exit Q[ueen Elizabeth]

	Relenting fool and shallow, changing woman.	
	How now, what news?	

Enter RATCLIFFE [*and* CATESBY]

RATCLIFFE	Most mighty sovereign, on the western coast	
	Rideth a puissant navy. To our shores	
	Throng many doubtful, hollow-hearted friends,	440
	Unarmed and unresolved to beat them back.	
	'Tis thought that Richmond is their admiral;	
	And there they hull, expecting but the aid	
	Of Buckingham to welcome them ashore.	
RICHARD	Some light-foot friend post to the Duke of Norfolk:	445
	Ratcliffe, thyself, or Catesby; where is he?	
CATESBY	Here, my good lord.	

Richard's orders to Catesby and Ratcliffe cause them some puzzlement. Stanley confirms that Richmond is leading a force by sea to seize the crown. Richard suspects Stanley's loyalty.

Characters

Is Richard an effective general? (in threes)

a Catesby and Ratcliffe have problems with Richard's orders. Take parts and read lines 437–62 aloud. Think about:

- the clarity of Richard's commands
- possible reasons for Richard's forgetfulness
- how Catesby and Ratcliffe react to each other and to Richard
- how effective you think Richard is as a military commander.

b Write two paragraphs about the way Richard appears to be developing at this point in the play. Try to include quotations to support your comments.

liege lord
deliver to tell
levy straight recruit immediately
make assemble
suddenly at once

1 Is Stanley loyal? (in fours)

In Act 3, Stanley urged Hastings to flee to the north to escape Richard's vindictiveness (Act 3 Scene 2, lines 17–18), yet here he appears to still be working for Richard and passing on valuable information.

a Two group members take on the roles of Richard and Stanley. Read the script through, pausing at the end of each character's lines. In the pause, the other two group members voice the inner thoughts of the character. How far does what they say match what they really mean? How does this contribute to the theme of appearance and reality as the play moves towards its conclusion?

b Do you think Stanley is loyal to Richard? How much does Richard suspect him?

Hoyday what's this

nearest simplest

White-livered runagate cowardly fugitive

Stagecraft

'Is the chair empty?'

Line 476 can be a great moment on stage, and every actor playing Richard tries to create a striking dramatic effect with the words 'Is the chair empty?'

- What would you do to make this a thrilling dramatic moment? What stage sets or delivery might give meaning to Richard's line? Write some notes in your Director's Journal.

chair throne
sword ceremonial sword of office
unswayed not wielded
The empire unpossessed the country unruled
York the house of York
makes he is he doing
Welshman Richmond (grandson of Owen Tudor)

RICHARD	Catesby, fly to the duke.
CATESBY	I will, my lord, with all convenient haste.
RICHARD	Ratcliffe, come hither. Post to Salisbury.
	When thou com'st thither – Dull, unmindful villain,
	Why stay'st thou here, and go'st not to the duke?
CATESBY	First, mighty liege, tell me your highness' pleasure,
	What from your grace I shall deliver to him.
RICHARD	Oh, true, good Catesby. Bid him levy straight
	The greatest strength and power that he can make
	And meet me suddenly at Salisbury.
CATESBY	I go. *Exit*
RATCLIFFE	What, may it please you, shall I do at Salisbury?
RICHARD	Why, what wouldst thou do there before I go?
RATCLIFFE	Your highness told me I should post before.
RICHARD	My mind is changed.

Enter LORD STANLEY [EARL OF DERBY]

	Stanley, what news with you?
STANLEY	None good, my liege, to please you with the hearing,
	Nor none so bad but well may be reported.
RICHARD	Hoyday, a riddle! Neither good nor bad.
	What need'st thou run so many miles about,
	When thou mayst tell thy tale the nearest way?
	Once more, what news?
STANLEY	Richmond is on the seas.
RICHARD	There let him sink, and be the seas on him!
	White-livered runagate, what doth he there?
STANLEY	I know not, mighty sovereign, but by guess.
RICHARD	Well, as you guess.
STANLEY	Stirred up by Dorset, Buckingham, and Morton,
	He makes for England, here to claim the crown.
RICHARD	Is the chair empty? Is the sword unswayed?
	Is the king dead? The empire unpossessed?
	What heir of York is there alive but we?
	And who is England's king but great York's heir?
	Then tell me, what makes he upon the seas?
STANLEY	Unless for that, my liege, I cannot guess.
RICHARD	Unless for that he comes to be your liege,
	You cannot guess wherefore the Welshman comes.
	Thou wilt revolt and fly to him, I fear.

Line numbers: 450, 455, 460, 465, 470, 475, 480

Stagecraft

Growing distrust? (in pairs)

Richard accuses Stanley of sending his army to help Richmond's troops disembark safely in Wales. Stanley claims to be loyal and says he will raise an army to fight against Richmond. Still distrusting Stanley, Richard insists that his son, George, be left as a hostage to be killed if Stanley is disloyal.

- Take parts as Stanley and Richard and speak lines 463–505, emphasising Richard's distrust and Stanley's evasive replies. What stage business could you include to show that Richard means his threat? How might Stanley react?

1 Mapping the action (in pairs)

- Create a large-scale map based on the one on pages 2–3. Locate all the places mentioned in the script and where the separate forces ranged against Richard are active. (Richard is in London.)
- Use the Internet to find production photographs of different characters from the play. Print them out and attach them to the map in such a way that they can be moved around. Consider ways of colour-coding those loyal to Richard and those fighting with Richmond.
- Put the clearest versions up on the wall and add/move/remove characters as the next act unfolds.

2 Don't shoot the messenger (in sixes)

Two messengers tell of increasing support for Richmond 'in Devonshire' and 'In Kent'. The Third Messenger brings news of Buckingham, but Richard strikes him, fearing more bad news.

- Freeze the moment when Richard strikes the Third Messenger. Work out who else is on stage at this moment. How exactly does Richard strike him and does the messenger stay on his feet or fall over? Show the expressions of those nearby as they see Richard strike the messenger.
- Bring some characters in the tableau to life and explain what they are thinking at this moment.
- What does this action contribute to an audience's impression of Richard?

---

power military force

Cold unfriendly

Pleaseth if it pleases

false disloyal
muster men recruit an army

assurance security

advertisèd informed
haughty prelate proud Bishop

confederates … in arms armed men in league together

competitors associates, collaborators

owls (an owl's cries were thought to predict death)

STANLEY	No, my good lord; therefore mistrust me not.	485
RICHARD	Where is thy power then, to beat him back?	
	Where be thy tenants and thy followers?	
	Are they not now upon the western shore,	
	Safe-cònducting the rebels from their ships?	
STANLEY	No, my good lord, my friends are in the north.	490
RICHARD	Cold friends to me. What do they in the north	
	When they should serve their sovereign in the west?	
STANLEY	They have not been commanded, mighty king.	
	Pleaseth your majesty to give me leave,	
	I'll muster up my friends and meet your grace	495
	Where and what time your majesty shall please.	
RICHARD	Ay, thou wouldst be gone, to join with Richmond.	
	But I'll not trust thee.	
STANLEY	Most mighty sovereign,	
	You have no cause to hold my friendship doubtful.	500
	I never was nor never will be false.	
RICHARD	Go then and muster men, but leave behind	
	Your son George Stanley. Look your heart be firm,	
	Or else his head's assurance is but frail.	
STANLEY	So deal with him as I prove true to you. _Exit Stanley_	505

Enter a MESSENGER

MESSENGER	My gracious sovereign, now in Devonshire,	
	As I by friends am well advertisèd,	
	Sir Edward Courtney and the haughty prelate,	
	Bishop of Exeter, his elder brother,	
	With many more confederates, are in arms.	510

Enter another MESSENGER

SECOND MESSENGER	In Kent, my liege, the Guilfords are in arms,	
	And every hour more competitors	
	Flock to the rebels, and their power grows strong.	

Enter another MESSENGER

| THIRD MESSENGER | My lord, the army of great Buckingham – | |
| RICHARD | Out on ye, owls, nothing but songs of death! | 515 |

He striketh him

There, take thou that, till thou bring better news.

The messengers report that Buckingham's army is scattered, Buckingham declared a traitor, Yorkshire in rebellion, and Richmond's navy dispersed. Catesby's news is of Buckingham's capture and Richmond's landing at Milford Haven.

Stagecraft
Unwelcome news (in small groups)

In lines 506–43, four messengers and Catesby report growing unrest and tell of Richmond's invasion. Richard's reactions to the unwelcome news show that he feels under increasing pressure. He gives confused orders and changes his mind. He strikes a messenger. He makes hasty decisions without seeking counsel.

• Take parts as Richard, Catesby and the messengers, then speak lines 506–47. Work out how to stage the sequence to bring out the increasing pace of events, their effect on Richard, and whether he retains any of his grotesque sense of humour.

Write about it
Wanted!

Richard proclaims that Buckingham is a traitor with a price on his head (lines 523–5).

a Write the proclamation (a brief statement that was 'proclaimed' or shouted out publicly).

b Design a 'Wanted' poster for Buckingham. Include: a picture; a list of his alleged crimes; the price on his head; and where to bring him if caught.

Characters
Richard in Scene 4: a reminder

Scene 4 is a very long scene in which a great deal happens. Richard's fortunes change dramatically. Glance back over the whole scene to remind yourself of its major episodes:

• **Lines 1–135** Margaret, Elizabeth and the Duchess's grieving (and cursing of Richard).
• **Lines 136–96** Richard's relationship with his mother.
• **Lines 197–436** Richard's proposal of marriage
• **Lines 437–547** Richard dealing with military matters.

Write four paragraphs, briefly describing each sequence and explaining what each reveals about Richard. Include evidence from the script to support your ideas.

---

fall of waters storms

I cry thee mercy I ask forgiveness

well-advisèd prudent, sensible

Breton navy ships from Brittany
dispersed scattered
banks edges of the land
assistants allies
Upon his party to join his forces
Hoised hoisted
Bretagne Brittany

reason debate
royal battle battle in which the throne is in dispute

THIRD MESSENGER   The news I have to tell your majesty
     Is that by sudden floods and fall of waters
     Buckingham's army is dispersed and scattered,
     And he himself wandered away alone,   520
     No man knows whither.
RICHARD   I cry thee mercy.
     There is my purse to cure that blow of thine.
     Hath any well-advisèd friend proclaimed
     Reward to him that brings the traitor in?   525
THIRD MESSENGER   Such proclamation hath been made, my lord.

Enter another MESSENGER

FOURTH MESSENGER   Sir Thomas Lovell and Lord Marquess Dorset,
     'Tis said, my liege, in Yorkshire are in arms.
     But this good comfort bring I to your highness:
     The Breton navy is dispersed by tempest.   530
     Richmond, in Dorsetshire, sent out a boat
     Unto the shore, to ask those on the banks
     If they were his assistants, yea or no,
     Who answered him they came from Buckingham
     Upon his party. He, mistrusting them,   535
     Hoised sail and made his course again for Bretagne.
RICHARD   March on, march on, since we are up in arms,
     If not to fight with foreign enemies,
     Yet to beat down these rebels here at home.

Enter CATESBY

CATESBY   My liege, the Duke of Buckingham is taken. 540
     That is the best news. That the Earl of Richmond
     Is with a mighty power landed at Milford
     Is colder news, but yet they must be told.
RICHARD   Away towards Salisbury! While we reason here
     A royal battle might be won and lost.   545
     Someone take order Buckingham be brought
     To Salisbury. The rest march on with me.

Flourish. Exeunt

Stanley discloses that his son is Richard's hostage, so he cannot openly support Richmond, and that Queen Elizabeth has agreed to Richmond marrying her daughter. Urswick reports that Richmond's army is marching to London.

Stagecraft
Scene change

A very swift change of scene is suggested here, where Stanley feels safe enough to confess his disloyalty to Richard. This change of location is easy to effect in a film, but how might a director manage it on stage without holding up the action? Consider some of the following suggestions and make some notes in your Director's Journal:

- Use a change of lighting (for example, dim the lights to suggest an indoor scene).
- Bring on two or three pieces of furniture to suggest a domestic interior.
- Simply have Stanley return once Richard and his followers have left.

Write about it
Stanley's letter

In the previous scene, Stanley declared his loyalty to Richard. Now he shows that he is really loyal to Richmond, but cannot openly support his stepson because Richard has taken his son, George, hostage and threatens to execute him if Stanley is disloyal.

- Imagine that Stanley sends a letter to Richmond to explain his predicament. Write the letter. Refer to the growing number of nobles who are turning against Richard in order to bolster Richmond's confidence in attacking Richard's army. What frame of mind do you believe Richard to be in? Why do you think this?

1 Growing opposition

Sir Christopher Urswick reports that more noblemen are joining Richmond. (Urswick is the Stanley family priest, used as a messenger.)

- Create a chart (or add to the map you began on p. 190), in which you collect the growing list of Richard's enemies. Use the list of characters on pages 4–5 to help you identify who's who.

franked up in hold shut up in a prison

present aid immediate help

espouse marry

Pembroke (a town in Wales)

Ha'rfordwest Haverford west, west Wales

men of name powerful, high-status people

redoubted brave

bend their power march their army

by the way along the way

hie thee to thy lord go to Richmond

resolve tell

Act 4 Scene 5
The house of Stanley, Earl of Derby

Enter STANLEY EARL OF DERBY, *and* SIR CHRISTOPHER
URSWICK, *a priest*

STANLEY   Sir Christopher, tell Richmond this from me,
That in the sty of the most deadly boar
My son George Stanley is franked up in hold.
If I revolt, off goes young George's head;
The fear of that holds off my present aid.   5
So get thee gone; commend me to thy lord.
Withal say that the queen hath heartily consented
He should espouse Elizabeth her daughter.
But tell me, where is princely Richmond now?

CHRISTOPHER   At Pembroke, or at Ha'rfordwest, in Wales.   10

STANLEY   What men of name resort to him?

CHRISTOPHER   Sir Walter Herbert, a renownèd soldier,
Sir Gilbert Talbot, Sir William Stanley,
Oxford, redoubted Pembroke, Sir James Blunt,
And Rice ap Thomas, with a valiant crew,   15
And many other of great name and worth;
And towards London do they bend their power,
If by the way they be not fought withal.

STANLEY   Well, hie thee to thy lord; I kiss his hand.
My letter will resolve him of my mind.   20
Farewell.

Exeunt

Looking back at Act 4
Activities for groups or individuals

1 Grieving women

Anne, the Duchess of York, Elizabeth and Margaret do
not appear again after this act (although Anne returns
as a ghost in Act 5). This activity is designed to help you
consider the four women characters and what dramatic
tension they add to the play in Act 4.

a Make a list or draw a diagram for each of the women
to illustrate what each says she has suffered or is
about to suffer. The following table may help you
locate relevant information in the script.

	Scene 1	Scene 4
Anne	Lines 66–87	
Elizabeth	Lines 98–104	Lines 9–14; 206–11
Duchess		Lines 44–5; lines 166–75
Margaret		see her asides on page 165; lines 35–70

b In groups of four, select a key line or phrase for each
woman that you agree best sums up the nature of
her grief. Create a tableau entitled 'Grief', making sure
all four group members are included. Once you are
happy with the look of the tableau (think about shapes,
posture, facial expressions), you can add the words
you selected from the script and begin to move and
speak. Compare your performance with other groups'.
Which one seems to convey most effectively the
overwhelming emotion of the four female characters?

2 Richard as King

Imagine you are a spy in Richard's camp, secretly working
for Richmond. You see everything, from Richard's
entrance in Scene 3 to the end of the act. Write a report
explaining Richard's military and political situation and
describing his mental state. You might like to include:

- how Richard greets the news of the princes' deaths
- the various pieces of bad news Richard receives and
how he reacts to them.

- Richard's public encounter with his mother
- any other gossip you have picked up (e.g. about
Lord Stanley)
- what conclusions you come to: should Richmond
feel confident about victory?

3 Richard as lover

In Act 1, Richard's brazen wooing results in Anne
succumbing to his menacing charm and agreeing to
marry him. In Act 4 Scene 3, he is confidently making
plans to go wooing again. But in Scene 4, he appears to
be less successful in his manoeuvres when he attempts
to court the young Elizabeth through her mother. Has he
lost his touch or do you think that Elizabeth is, in the end,
persuaded of the benefits of allowing Richard to marry
her daughter?

Imagine you are directing the play. You are
considering three possible interpretations of the
scene between Richard and Elizabeth:

- Elizabeth pretends to agree to Richard's proposal in
order to stall for time, knowing that Richmond's army
is on its way.
- Elizabeth eventually gives in and genuinely agrees to
the marriage.
- Richard's power and confidence are visibly weaker in
this 'wooing scene', and Elizabeth senses this.

In groups of three, one person takes the role of director,
while the other two take the parts of Richard and
Elizabeth. Read through lines 197–435 in Scene 4, then
choose one of the interpretations listed above. Work out
a way of enacting the script so that this interpretation
is clearly conveyed to an audience. Get together with
another group that has chosen a different interpretation
and compare a short section of your performances.
In what ways do they differ?

197

Buckingham, escorted to execution, begs all Richard's dead victims to mock him. He remembers he wished God to punish him when he was proved a traitor, and recalls Margaret's prophecy that Richard would betray him.

Stagecraft

Set the scene (in pairs)

The setting for Act 5 Scene 1 in this edition of the play is 'Salisbury: a place of execution', and from Buckingham's words we know he is about to be beheaded ('the block of shame', line 28). In a film version of the play, it would be easy to show this change of scene from Stanley's house in Act 4 Scene 5, but on stage this is more complicated.

* Take on the roles of director and set designer. Talk about your ideas for this scene change on stage, bearing in mind that it needs to be swift. How might you use lighting, sound, props and/or set change in a way that effectively, but efficiently, conveys meaning?

1 How does Buckingham leave?

The tone of this short scene is important. It helps to establish whether or not the director wants the audience to sympathise with the figure of Buckingham.

* Talk about how you could portray Buckingham (for example, how the guards deal with him, how he moves and speaks, what lighting and sounds could highlight the desperateness of his situation). In Buckingham's final line, does he say that he gets what he deserves? How would you stage his departure for execution?

2 All Souls' Day (in pairs)

Buckingham reveals that he is about to be executed on the Christian festival of All Souls' Day (line 12).

* Use the Internet to conduct some research into All Souls' Day. Suggest why this might be an appropriate day for Buckingham's death.

Themes

Curses

Buckingham remembers Margaret's earlier curse as he walks to his execution (line 25).

* Turn back to Act 1 Scene 3, lines 299–301 to check how accurately he remembers her words. As you read on through Act 5, keep a record of all the curses that come true.

thy (line 4) King Henry's
miscarrièd been killed

moody angry

doomsday day of death

fall on me condemn me to die

determined ... my wrongs
end of reprieve from
my punishment
All-Seer God
dallied pretended
in earnest in reality

Act 5 Scene 1
Salisbury: a place of execution

Enter SHERIFF *and officers lead* BUCKINGHAM *to execution*

BUCKINGHAM   Will not King Richard let me speak with him?

SHERIFF   No, my good lord. Therefore be patient.

BUCKINGHAM   Hastings and Edward's children, Grey and Rivers,
Holy King Henry, and thy fair son Edward,
Vaughan, and all that have miscarrièd   5
By underhand corrupted foul injustice,
If that your moody, discontented souls
Do through the clouds behold this present hour,
Even for revenge mock my destruction.
This is All Souls' Day, fellow, is it not?   10

SHERIFF   It is.

BUCKINGHAM   Why, then, All Souls' Day is my body's doomsday.
This is the day which, in King Edward's time,
I wished might fall on me when I was found
False to his children and his wife's allies.   15
This is the day wherein I wished to fall
By the false faith of him whom most I trusted.
This, this All Souls' Day to my fearful soul
Is the determined respite of my wrongs.
That high All-Seer which I dallied with   20
Hath turned my feignèd prayer on my head
And given in earnest what I begged in jest.
Thus doth he force the swords of wicked men
To turn their own points in their masters' bosoms.
Thus Margaret's curse falls heavy on my neck: 25
'When he', quoth she, 'shall split thy heart with sorrow,
Remember Margaret was a prophetess.'
Come, lead me, officers, to the block of shame;
Wrong hath but wrong, and blames the due of blame.

Exeunt Buckingham with officers

Richmond has received a letter of support from Stanley. He vows to defeat Richard's troops and bring peace. Doubts are voiced about the loyalty of Richard's followers.

Characters

Richmond rallies his troops (in groups of four or five)

a Read through Richmond's speech in lines 1–16. Identify each of the following features of his speech:

- the way he refers to Richard
- how he talks about peace
- what he says about trust and hope
- how he mentions God and faith.

b Read the speech aloud in your group, with one person in role as Richmond. The rest of the group (as soldiers) should cheer at any references to God, peace, trust, faith/hope and Richard.

c At the end of the speech, the person reading Richmond should add the final three lines on the page (lines 22–4). How does his 'soldier audience' react? Discuss Richmond's choice of words – how good is he at motivating his men?

Language in the play

Richard as rampaging boar (in threes)

Richmond employs a particularly vivid extended metaphor to describe Richard's rule over England (lines 7–12).

a Use pictures from magazines or the Internet to create a large collage that captures all the different aspects of the metaphor. Underneath your collage, add a few lines of writing explaining the effect your group was hoping to achieve with your collage.

b Consider how effective Richmond's words are in creating a particular view of Richard. Write a paragraph either for display or as notes in your Director's Journal.

Stagecraft

Richmond's 'colours'

The stage direction in this edition directs Richmond and his followers to enter with drums and banners.

- Suggest an appropriate colour for Richmond (different from Richard's white rose) and an appropriate image. What qualities do you want to suggest?

bowels interior

Lines of fair comfort a letter of support

spoiled plundered

Swills swallows greedily

wash scraps given to pigs, hogwash

embowelled bosoms disembowelled bodies

cheerly cheerfully

homicide murderer

dearest greatest

Act 5 Scene 2
Tamworth: the camp of Richmond

Enter RICHMOND, OXFORD, BLUNT, HERBERT, *and others,*
with drum and colours

RICHMOND	Fellows in arms, and my most loving friends,	
	Bruised underneath the yoke of tyranny,	
	Thus far into the bowels of the land	
	Have we marched on without impediment;	
	And here receive we from our father Stanley	5
	Lines of fair comfort and encouragement.	
	The wretched, bloody, and usurping boar,	
	That spoiled your summer fields and fruitful vines,	
	Swills your warm blood like wash, and makes his trough	
	In your embowelled bosoms, this foul swine	10
	Is now even in the centre of this isle,	
	Near to the town of Leicester, as we learn.	
	From Tamworth thither is but one day's march.	
	In God's name, cheerly on, courageous friends,	
	To reap the harvest of perpetual peace	15
	By this one bloody trial of sharp war.	
OXFORD	Every man's conscience is a thousand men	
	To fight against this guilty homicide.	
HERBERT	I doubt not but his friends will turn to us.	
BLUNT	He hath no friends but what are friends for fear,	20
	Which in his dearest need will fly from him.	
RICHMOND	All for our vantage. Then in God's name march!	
	True hope is swift and flies with swallow's wings;	
	Kings it makes gods, and meaner creatures kings.	

Exeunt

Richard orders his tent to be pitched and declares his army to be three times larger than Richmond's. He begins his battle plans. Richmond also begins to prepare for the coming battle.

1 Rival camps, sunset to sunrise

Scene 3 portrays events from sunset to early morning. The action alternates between the rival camps of Richard and Richmond, as the two leaders reflect upon their personal situations and prepare for the coming battle.

a **Time passing** As you read the whole scene, look out for ways in which Shakespeare's language indicates the passage of time (sunset, 9 o'clock at night, midnight, 4 o'clock in the morning, dawn). Make a note of how this is indicated in the words and stage directions.

b **Staging** Many modern productions have two tents erected on either side of the stage. Whether inside or outside their tents, Richard and Richmond are in full view of the audience, but do not acknowledge each other's presence. Design the insignia on the two tents to denote Richard and Richmond. Think about appropriate symbols, colours, coats of arms and mottos.

2 Similarities and differences

The alternating episodes in the scene, between Richard and Richmond and their troops, enable the audience to make direct comparisons and contrasts between the rival camps.

*   Copy the table below and make notes on the differences and similarities between the two leaders and their followers as you read through the scene. Begin with Richard and Richmond's initial comments in the script opposite.

Richmond as leader	Richard as leader
	Dismisses number of traitors as unimportant; boasts that his status as King more than makes up for it (11–13).
Discusses battle strategy with trusted nobles (22–34).	Talks battle tactics with trusted nobles (14–18).
Regards the beautiful sunset as a good omen (19–21).	

have knocks suffer blows

all's one for that never mind that
descried counted

battalia large army
account number

vantage best strategic position
men of sound direction good leaders

tract track
car cart, chariot
standard flag, banner

form and model organisation and tactics

Limit assign

several charge separate position, duty

part in ... power proportionately divide our small army

Act 5 Scene 3
Bosworth Field

Enter RICHARD *in arms, with* NORFOLK, RATCLIFFE,
the EARL OF SURREY *and others*

RICHARD	Here pitch our tent, even here in Bosworth field.
	My lord of Surrey, why look you so sad?
SURREY	My heart is ten times lighter than my looks.
RICHARD	My lord of Norfolk.
NORFOLK	Here, most gracious liege.
RICHARD	Norfolk, we must have knocks, ha, must we not?

RICHARD   Here pitch our tent, even here in Bosworth field.
           My lord of Surrey, why look you so sad?
SURREY   My heart is ten times lighter than my looks.
RICHARD   My lord of Norfolk.
NORFOLK   Here, most gracious liege.
RICHARD   Norfolk, we must have knocks, ha, must we not?   5
NORFOLK   We must both give and take, my loving lord.
RICHARD   Up with my tent. Here will I lie tonight,
           But where tomorrow? Well, all's one for that.
           Who hath descried the number of the traitors?
NORFOLK   Six or seven thousand is their utmost power.   10
RICHARD   Why, our battalia trebles that account.
           Besides, the king's name is a tower of strength,
           Which they upon the adverse faction want.
           Up with the tent. Come, noble gentlemen,
           Let us survey the vantage of the ground.   15
           Call for some men of sound direction.
           Let's lack no discipline, make no delay,
           For lords, tomorrow is a busy day.

                                                    Exeunt

Enter RICHMOND, SIR WILLIAM BRANDON, OXFORD,
and DORSET, [HERBERT, BLUNT, *and others*]

RICHMOND   The weary sun hath made a golden set,
           And by the bright tract of his fiery car,   20
           Gives token of a goodly day tomorrow.
           Sir William Brandon, you shall bear my standard.
           Give me some ink and paper in my tent.
           I'll draw the form and model of our battle,
           Limit each leader to his several charge,   25
           And part in just proportion our small power.
           My lord of Oxford, you, Sir William Brandon,
           And you, Sir Walter Herbert, stay with me.

Richmond asks Blunt to attempt to take an important message to Stanley. He proposes a battle-plan meeting. Richard checks his armour is ready and orders trustworthy guards to be placed on watch.

keeps remains with

quartered camped (Stanley cannot openly support Richmond because his son is being held hostage by Richard)
colours flags

make some good means try your best
needful important

▲ Richard (top left) and Richmond (top right) encourage their supporters to fight. How would you design the set for this scene to show the difference between rival camps?

beaver face guard of helmet, visor
easier working more smoothly

hie thee to thy charge hasten to your duty
sentinels guards

warrant guarantee

1 Meanwhile, back at Richard's camp … (in pairs)

In sharp contrast to Richmond, all is not well with Richard.

a Many productions show Richard's camp with a boar symbol. Discuss why this is appropriate for Richard. In particular, consider the animal imagery that has been used earlier in the play.

b Suggest what Richard's manner of speaking and general behaviour should be like at this point in the play. Make some notes in your Director's Journal, using what you have learned about Richard as the play has progressed.

	The Earl of Pembroke keeps his regiment.	
	Good Captain Blunt, bear my goodnight to him	30
	And by the second hour in the morning	
	Desire the earl to see me in my tent.	
	Yet one thing more, good captain, do for me:	
	Where is Lord Stanley quartered, do you know?	
BLUNT	Unless I have mista'en his colours much,	35
	Which well I am assured I have not done,	
	His regiment lies half a mile at least	
	South from the mighty power of the king.	
RICHMOND	If without peril it be possible,	
	Sweet Blunt, make some good means to speak with him	40
	And give him from me this most needful note.	
BLUNT	Upon my life, my lord, I'll undertake it.	
	And so, God give you quiet rest tonight.	
RICHMOND	Good night, good Captain Blunt.	
	Come, gentlemen,	45
	Let us consult upon tomorrow's business.	
	Into my tent; the dew is raw and cold.	

They withdraw into the tent

Enter RICHARD, RATCLIFFE, NORFOLK, *and* CATESBY

RICHARD	What is't o'clock?	
CATESBY	It's supper time, my lord; it's nine o'clock.	
RICHARD	I will not sup tonight.	50
	Give me some ink and paper.	
	What, is my beaver easier than it was,	
	And all my armour laid into my tent?	
CATESBY	It is, my liege, and all things are in readiness.	
RICHARD	Good Norfolk, hie thee to thy charge.	55
	Use careful watch; choose trusty sentinels.	
NORFOLK	I go, my lord.	
RICHARD	Stir with the lark tomorrow, gentle Norfolk.	
NORFOLK	I warrant you, my lord.	

Exit

RICHARD	Ratcliffe.	60
RATCLIFFE	My lord.	

Richard sends a message that Stanley's son will be killed if Stanley does not bring troops to him. He reflects on the loss of his previously high spirits. Stanley pledges, if possible, to aid Richmond in the battle.

Characters

Richard: a changed man? (in pairs)

Richard observes that he has lost his normal cheerfulness of mind ('alacrity of spirit').

a Take parts and read aloud lines 62–81. Make a list of key words or phrases from the script that convey Richard's mood at this point in the play.

b What advice would you give to the actor playing Richard here? How should he act and speak during this scene? Write notes for the actor, emphasising the importance of certain lines, words or phrases.

1 Stanley: the balance of power? (in threes)

Stanley acts as a catalyst to reveal the differences between Richard and Richmond. Both commanders need his support, but they try to win this support in very different ways. Stanley's relationship with Richmond (lines 82–105) provides a sharp contrast to the way he relates to Richard.

a Each person takes the role of Richmond, Richard or Stanley. Create two tableaux: one of Stanley and Richard together, the other depicting an 'eve-of-war' photograph showing Stanley with Richmond. Think about the way they stand (or perhaps one is seated?), the distance between the two men, their facial expressions and the direction of their gaze. When you present your tableaux, it should be obvious to other groups who each character is. If you have a camera, take a photograph of each pairing.

b Produce a slow-motion transition sequence between the first tableau (Stanley and Richard) and the second (Stanley with Richmond). As Stanley moves, what might Richard and Richmond do?

c Talk together about the relationship between the three men at this point in the play. How does it contribute to the dramatic tension?

d Continue adding to your notes on the similarities and differences between Richard and Richmond (see p. 202).

pursuivant at arms junior officer

watch watch-light (a candle marked into sections to measure time)
white Surrey (a particular horse)
staves lances
Saw'st have you seen

cockshut twilight

alacrity lightness

Fortune ... sit on thy helm may you be lucky and victorious

by attorney by proxy

flaky darkness streaks of light

Prepare thy battle draw up your army
arbitrement test
mortal-staring fatally glaring
With best advantage at the best opportunity

RICHARD	Send out a pursuivant at arms
	To Stanley's regiment. Bid him bring his power
	Before sunrising, lest his son George fall
	Into the blind cave of eternal night. 65
	Fill me a bowl of wine. Give me a watch.
	Saddle white Surrey for the field tomorrow.
	Look that my staves be sound and not too heavy. Ratcliffe!
RATCLIFFE	My lord.
RICHARD	Saw'st the melancholy Lord Northumberland? 70
RATCLIFFE	Thomas the Earl of Surrey and himself,
	Much about cockshut time, from troop to troop
	Went through the army, cheering up the soldiers.
RICHARD	So, I am satisfied. Give me a bowl of wine.
	I have not that alacrity of spirit 75
	Nor cheer of mind that I was wont to have.
	Set it down. Is ink and paper ready?
RATCLIFFE	It is, my lord.
RICHARD	Bid my guard watch. Leave me.
	Ratcliffe, about the mid of night come to my tent 80
	And help to arm me. Leave me, I say.

Exeunt Ratcliffe [and Catesby]

Enter [STANLEY EARL OF] DERBY *to* RICHMOND *in his tent*

STANLEY	Fortune and victory sit on thy helm.
RICHMOND	All comfort that the dark night can afford
	Be to thy person, noble father-in-law.
	Tell me, how fares our noble mother? 85
STANLEY	I by attorney bless thee from thy mother,
	Who prays continually for Richmond's good.
	So much for that. The silent hours steal on,
	And flaky darkness breaks within the east.
	In brief, for so the season bids us be, 90
	Prepare thy battle early in the morning,
	And put thy fortune to th'arbitrement
	Of bloody strokes and mortal-staring war.
	I, as I may (that which I would I cannot),
	With best advantage will deceive the time 95
	And aid thee in this doubtful shock of arms.

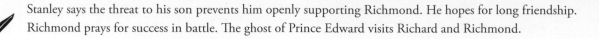
Themes

Sin and salvation: Richmond's prayer (in pairs)

In lines 111–20, Richmond prays to God, asking him to bless his army ('Look on my forces with a gracious eye') and support them as they fight against Richard. The army will then be agents of God ('ministers of chastisement') and it will be God's victory that is celebrated.

- Discuss possible reasons why Shakespeare gave Richmond a prayer here, but not Richard.

1 Ghostly visitors (in large groups)

In lines 121–79, the action continues to alternate between the rival camps as no fewer than eleven ghosts of Richard's victims visit the two sleeping leaders, condemning Richard and supporting Richmond.

- Divide the parts up between your group members and read lines 121–79.
- Split into pairs. Share out the different ghosts between you and, for each one, pick out a key phrase or line that he or she says to the sleeping Richard or Richmond.
- Each pair then presents to the larger group a brief scene in which the ghosts chant their phrase repeatedly. Compare each pair's chosen words and decide which you think is truly key to that particular ghost.
- Draw a table similar to the one below on a large sheet of paper. The whole group should now contribute to completing it.

Lines	Ghost	What does s/he say to Richard?	What does s/he say to Richmond?
121–6	Prince Edward	'thou stab'st me in my prime of youth … Despair … and die'	'King Henry's issue … comforts thee'
127–33	Henry VI		
	Clarence		

forward obvious

brother (George Stanley, Richmond's stepbrother)

tender young

leisure (line 100) available time

ample … sweet discourse long and pleasant conversation

sundered parted

speed prosper

strive contend

peise weigh

thou (line 111) God

captain subordinate officer

irons weapons

chastisement punishment

windows eyelids

still always

issue child

208

But on thy side I may not be too forward,
Lest being seen, thy brother, tender George,
Be executed in his father's sight.
Farewell. The leisure and the fearful time   100
Cuts off the ceremonious vows of love
And ample interchange of sweet discourse
Which so long sundered friends should dwell upon.
God give us leisure for these rites of love.
Once more adieu. Be valiant, and speed well.   105

RICHMOND Good lords, conduct him to his regiment.
I'll strive with troubled noise to take a nap,
Lest leaden slumber peise me down tomorrow,
When I should mount with wings of victory.
Once more, good night, kind lords and gentlemen.   110

Exeunt [all but Richmond]

O thou whose captain I account myself,
Look on my forces with a gracious eye.
Put in their hands thy bruising irons of wrath,
That they may crush down with a heavy fall
Th'usurping helmets of our adversaries.   115
Make us thy ministers of chastisement,
That we may praise thee in thy victory.
To thee I do commend my watchful soul
Ere I let fall the windows of mine eyes.
Sleeping, and waking, oh, defend me still. *Sleeps*   120

Enter the GHOST OF PRINCE EDWARD, *son to Henry the Sixth*

GHOST [OF PRINCE EDWARD] (*To Richard*) Let me sit heavy on thy
    soul tomorrow.
Think how thou stab'st me in my prime of youth
At Tewkesbury. Despair therefore, and die.
(*To Richmond*) Be cheerful, Richmond, for the wrongèd souls
Of butchered princes fight in thy behalf.   125
King Henry's issue, Richmond, comforts thee.

Stagecraft

The ghosts (in pairs)

The ghost sequence offers any director an exciting opportunity to think creatively. On stage, the ghosts have been presented in many different ways. In one production, they did not appear to the dreaming commanders in their tents, but took part in the Battle of Bosworth (which happens in Scenes 4 and 5). They wounded Richard in the fighting, emphasising that although Richmond physically killed Richard in a real sword fight, Richard had already been defeated psychologically. How would you present the ghosts?

- What do they look like? Would you use real actors or not? Alternatives might be puppets or film projected onto a large screen.
- How do they dress? Are the ghosts all very similar or different to each other?
- How do they move? What gestures do they use?
- How do they speak? Do they talk individually or in chorus? Do they speak in different tones when wishing good luck to Richmond or repeatedly cursing Richard?
- Do they simply walk on stage and stand near the sleeping Richard or Richmond? Or do they appear on a balcony, or emerge through the audience? Are they all on stage together?

mortal alive

punched pierced

Tower Tower of London (where Richard murdered Henry VI)

washed drowned

fulsome too much

guile deceit

fall thy edgeless sword drop your useless weapon

battle army

bosom conscience

Enter the GHOST OF HENRY THE SIXTH

GHOST [OF HENRY] [*To Richard*] When I was mortal, my anointed body
　　　　　By thee was punchèd full of holes.
　　　　　Think on the Tower and me. Despair, and die.
　　　　　Harry the Sixth bids thee despair and die.　　　　　130
　　　　　(*To Richmond*) Virtuous and holy, be thou conqueror.
　　　　　Harry, that prophesied thou shouldst be king,
　　　　　Doth comfort thee in sleep. Live and flourish.

Enter the GHOST OF CLARENCE

GHOST [OF CLARENCE] [*To Richard*] Let me sit heavy in thy soul tomorrow,
　　　　　I, that was washed to death with fulsome wine,　　　　135
　　　　　Poor Clarence, by thy guile betrayed to death.
　　　　　Tomorrow in the battle think on me,
　　　　　And fall thy edgeless sword, despair, and die.
　　　　　(*To Richmond*) Thou offspring of the house of Lancaster,
　　　　　The wrongèd heirs of York do pray for thee.　　　　　140
　　　　　Good angels guard thy battle. Live and flourish.

Enter the GHOSTS OF RIVERS, GREY, *and* VAUGHAN

[GHOST OF] RIV[ERS] [*To Richard*] Let me sit heavy in thy soul tomorrow.
　　　　　Rivers that died at Pomfret. Despair, and die.
[GHOST OF] GREY　Think upon Grey, and let thy soul despair.
[GHOST OF] VAUGHAN　Think upon Vaughan, and with guilty fear　145
　　　　　Let fall thy lance. Despair, and die.
ALL [THREE GHOSTS] (*To Richmond*) Awake, and think our wrongs in
　　　　　　　Richard's bosom
　　　　　Will conquer him. Awake, and win the day.

Enter the GHOST OF LORD HASTINGS

GHOST [OF HASTINGS] [*To Richard*] Bloody and guilty, guiltily awake
　　　　　And in a bloody battle end thy days.　　　　　150
　　　　　Think on Lord Hastings. Despair, and die.
　　　　　(*Hast*[*ings*] *to Richmond*) Quiet untroubled soul, awake, awake.
　　　　　Arm, fight, and conquer, for fair England's sake.

The ghosts of the princes in the Tower, Anne and Buckingham bring messages of death and despair to Richard and success to Richmond.

Language in the play
The ghosts' messages

The ghosts' messages to the sleeping commanders are delivered in formal, highly patterned language.

a Re-read the ghosts' speeches and find an example of each of the following linguistic devices:

- repetition
- balance and contrast.

b Write two paragraphs describing the ghosts' language, suggesting why the ghosts speak in this way. Share what you have written with two or three other students.

1 More ghosts

The picture below shows a stylised, formal presentation of the ghost scene, where all the ghosts gather on stage together to accuse Richard (seated, wearing crown).

- Compare this picture with the ghosts shown in the image on page xii (left) in the photo gallery and that of the ghost on page 210. How do these images compare with your own ideas for staging and representing the ghosts?

the boar's annoy injury from Richard

beget father

race of kings royal dynasty

perturbations disturbances, anxieties

adversary's enemy's

Fainting growing faint of heart, losing confidence

yield give up

I died for hope … aid I died before I could support you

Richard fall Richard may fall

Enter the GHOSTS OF THE TWO YOUNG PRINCES

GHOSTS [OF PRINCES] [*To Richard*] Dream on thy cousins smothered in
      the Tower.
    Let us be laid within thy bosom, Richard,   155
    And weigh thee down to ruin, shame, and death.
    Thy nephews' soul bids thee despair and die.
    (*To Richmond*) Sleep, Richmond, sleep in peace, and wake in joy.
    Good angels guard thee from the boar's annoy.
    Live, and beget a happy race of kings.   160
    Edward's unhappy sons do bid thee flourish.

Enter the GHOST OF ANNE, *his wife*

GHOST [OF ANNE] (*To Richard*) Richard, thy wife, that wretched Anne, thy wife,
    That never slept a quiet hour with thee,
    Now fills thy sleep with perturbations.
    Tomorrow in the battle think on me,   165
    And fall thy edgeless sword. Despair, and die.
    (*To Richmond*) Thou quiet soul, sleep thou a quiet sleep.
    Dream of success and happy victory.
    Thy adversary's wife doth pray for thee.

Enter the GHOST OF BUCKINGHAM

GHOST [OF BUCKINGHAM] (*To Richard*) The first was I that helped thee to
      the crown.   170
    The last was I that felt thy tyranny.
    Oh, in the battle think on Buckingham,
    And die in terror of thy guiltiness.
    Dream on, dream on, of bloody deeds and death.
    Fainting, despair; despairing, yield thy breath.   175
    (*To Richmond*) I died for hope ere I could lend thee aid.
    But cheer thy heart and be thou not dismayed.
    God and good angels fight on Richmond's side,
    And Richard fall in height of all his pride.

Richard starts from sleep and questions the reasons for his fear. He wrestles with his troubled conscience, which reminds him of the ghosts' accusations of murder and threats of vengeance.

Language in the play
Dramatic punctuation (whole class)

You will need a large space for this activity, such as a hall, drama studio, or cleared classroom. All class members should hold a copy of Richard's soliloquy in lines 180–209.

a Everyone walks around the room while reading the first few lines of the script in unison. At every punctuation mark, change direction (don't change direction at speech marks or apostrophes).

b Now, try the whole speech – but this time it's a race to see who can perform the speech fastest, making sure everyone continues to turn at each punctuation mark. As you finish, freeze and wait for everyone else to reach the end.

c Discuss the way this speech is punctuated, including sentence length and structure, use of questions and exclamations. How does the punctuation (and repeated use of first person pronoun) help guide an actor playing the part of Richard?

d On your own, write two paragraphs analysing the way this speech is written and what it suggests about Richard's state of mind at this point in the play.

Themes
'Shadows', dreams and sleep (in pairs)

Earlier in this scene, the ghost of Anne takes delight in disturbing Richard's sleep, while wishing dreams of success for Richmond (lines 163–8). Earlier in the play (Act 1 Scene 4), Clarence wakes from a hellish dream and realises he should repent his sins. Here, Richard also wakes from a terrible dream.

a Read from line 180 to line 220 and consider how Richard reacts to his nightmares, firstly during his soliloquy (up to line 209) and secondly in dialogue with Ratcliffe (210–20).

b Read lines 224–34 and summarise how Richmond reacts to his dreams.

c Devise a short presentation for the rest of the class, in which you talk about Richard's dream and the significance of dreams in the play as a whole. Include two or three short quotations from both Richard's and Richmond's speeches.

Soft but wait

The lights burn blue (believed to be the sign of a ghost)
not dead midnight not exactly midnight
none else by no one else here

Wherefore? why?

Perjury lying under oath

several separate
all used in each degree committed often at every level
bar place in a courtroom where the prisoner hears the sentence

done salutation greeted

Richard starts out of his dream

RICHARD   Give me another horse! Bind up my wounds!   180
Have mercy, Jesu! Soft, I did but dream.
O coward conscience, how dost thou afflict me?
The lights burn blue. It is not dead midnight.
Cold, fearful drops stand on my trembling flesh.
What? Do I fear myself? There's none else by.   185
Richard loves Richard, that is, I am I.
Is there a murderer here? No. Yes, I am.
Then fly. What, from myself? Great reason why:
Lest I revenge. What, myself upon myself?
Alack, I love myself. Wherefore? For any good   190
That I myself have done unto myself?
Oh, no. Alas, I rather hate myself
For hateful deeds committed by myself.
I am a villain. Yet I lie, I am not.
Fool, of thyself speak well. Fool, do not flatter.   195
My conscience hath a thousand several tongues,
And every tongue brings in a several tale,
And every tale condemns me for a villain.
Perjury in the highest degree,
Murder, stern murder, in the direst degree,   200
All several sins, all used in each degree,
Throng all to th'bar, crying all 'Guilty, guilty!'
I shall despair. There is no creature loves me,
And if I die no soul shall pity me.
Nay, wherefore should they, since that I myself   205
Find in myself no pity to myself?
Methought the souls of all that I had murdered
Came to my tent, and every one did threat
Tomorrow's vengeance on the head of Richard.

Enter RATCLIFFE

RATCLIFFE   My lord.   210
RICHARD   Who's there?
RATCLIFFE   Ratcliffe, my lord, 'tis I. The early village cock
Hath twice done salutation to the morn.
Your friends are up and buckle on their armour.
RICHARD   O Ratcliffe, I fear, I fear.   215

Richard plans to eavesdrop on his troops to discover deserters. Richmond tells of his happiness about his dream and its message of victory. He tells his army that God and right are on their side.

1 Motivating the troops (in pairs)

Richmond motivates his soldiers through a formal address ('oration') before the battle (Richard also speaks an oration to his troops later). In pairs, practise reading the speech in lines 238–71 in a manner that will instil confidence in those who hear it. Use the following outline of the speech to help you decide what tone and manner to use for each section:

- **Lines 238–40** He regrets he has little time for his speech.
- **Lines 240–3** He assures the soldiers that God is on their side and that they fight for a just cause.
- **Lines 244–53** He claims that all Richard's followers want Richmond to win because they know Richard is a usurper and not the true King.
- **Lines 254–63** He again reminds his soldiers that God is on their side, and he lists the advantages for the future that will be gained by fighting now.
- **Lines 264–71** If he succeeds, the soldiers will all share his victory; they should go cheerfully into battle for the sake of God, their country, Richmond and victory.

Write about it

A soldier's letter home

It is customary for soldiers to write letters to their loved ones on the eve of battle, in case they never return. Imagine you are a soldier in Richmond's army. You have just listened to his speech and now have just enough time to write your letter home. You might like to use the following prompts to help you shape your letter, but feel free to develop ideas of your own:

- What is your impression of Richmond as a leader – do you feel confident with him in charge?
- Were you impressed by his speech to the troops? What kind of things did he say?
- What is the mood of the troops around you?
- Why did you join up to fight against the King? Do you still believe it was the right thing to do?
- End by sending loving messages to your family.

shadows ghosts, premonitions

Armèd in proof in strongest armour

shallow insignificant

shrink from desert

Cry mercy I beg your pardon

ta'en a tardy sluggard caught a slow late-riser

fairest-boding happiness-promising

cried on called out

jocund happy

leisure and enforcement available time and constraint

high-reared bulwarks high battlements

except apart

raised in blood promoted by means of bloodshed

made means contrived, plotted

RATCLIFFE	Nay, good my lord, be not afraid of shadows.
RICHARD	By the apostle Paul, shadows tonight
	Have struck more terror to the soul of Richard
	Than can the substance of ten thousand soldiers
	Armèd in proof and led by shallow Richmond. 220
	'Tis not yet near day. Come, go with me.
	Under our tents I'll play the eavesdropper,
	To hear if any mean to shrink from me.

Exeunt Richard and Ratcliffe

Enter the LORDS *to Richmond sitting in his tent*

LORDS	Good morrow, Richmond.
RICHMOND	Cry mercy, lords and watchful gentlemen, 225
	That you have ta'en a tardy sluggard here.
LORD	How have you slept, my lord?
RICHMOND	The sweetest sleep and fairest-boding dreams
	That ever entered in a drowsy head
	Have I since your departure had, my lords. 230
	Methought their souls whose bodies Richard murdered
	Came to my tent and cried on victory.
	I promise you, my heart is very jocund
	In the remembrance of so fair a dream.
	How far into the morning is it, lords? 235
LORD	Upon the stroke of four.
RICHMOND	Why, then 'tis time to arm and give direction.

His oration to his soldiers

More than I have said, loving countrymen,
The leisure and enforcement of the time
Forbids to dwell upon. Yet remember this: 240
God and our good cause fight upon our side.
The prayers of holy saints and wrongèd souls,
Like high-reared bulwarks, stand before our faces.
Richard except, those whom we fight against
Had rather have us win than him they follow. 245
For what is he they follow? Truly, gentlemen,
A bloody tyrant, and a homicide;
One raised in blood, and one in blood established;
One that made means to come by what he hath,
And slaughtered those that were the means to help him; 250

Write about it

Motivational speech

Imagine you manage a sports team, or you have organised a big charity event. You need to make a key motivational speech before the event opens or the match begins. You want to make people feel confident, believe that the event is important and that it will be a great success – and to assure them that the hard work will be worthwhile.

- Write the speech (it should last no more than two minutes when read aloud). Make it as inspirational as possible.
- Summarise the speech on cards, and practise performing it so that you are confident enough to make eye contact with your audience as you speak.
- Listen to each other's speeches, then discuss what features help to make a motivational speech really effective. Relate your conclusions to Richmond's speech in the play. What specific persuasive and motivational elements can you find in his speech?

▼ Richmond is often portrayed as the bright young hero saving England from Richard's dark oppression. Discuss the way Richmond is presented in this production photograph. How would you describe him in this picture? Could there be another way of presenting Richmond? How do you imagine him? Find the lines in the script that have shaped your views.

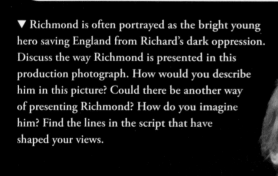

stone gem
foil … chair setting of the throne

ward guard, reward

Your country's fat England's riches
hire compensation

quits makes up for, rewards
age old age
standards flags
ransom penalty for failure

Tell the clock count the chimes

calendar almanac

by the book according to the calendar

braved made bright, risen in

A base, foul stone made precious by the foil
Of England's chair, where he is falsely set;
One that hath ever been God's enemy.
Then if you fight against God's enemy,
God will in justice ward you as his soldiers;   255
If you do swear to put a tyrant down,
You sleep in peace, the tyrant being slain;
If you do fight against your country's foes,
Your country's fat shall pay your pains the hire;
If you do fight in safeguard of your wives,   260
Your wives shall welcome home the conquerors;
If you do free your children from the sword,
Your children's children quits it in your age.
Then in the name of God and all these rights,
Advance your standards, draw your willing swords.   265
For me, the ransom of my bold attempt
Shall be this cold corpse on the earth's cold face.
But if I thrive, the gain of my attempt
The least of you shall share his part thereof.
Sound drums and trumpets boldly and cheerfully.   270
God and Saint George, Richmond and victory!

Enter RICHARD, RATCLIFFE, *and* CATESBY

RICHARD	What said Northumberland as touching Richmond?
RATCLIFFE	That he was never trainèd up in arms.
RICHARD	He said the truth. And what said Surrey then?
RATCLIFFE	He smiled and said 'The better for our purpose'. 275
RICHARD	He was in the right, and so indeed it is.
	Tell the clock there.

Clock strikes

Give me a calendar. Who saw the sun today?

RATCLIFFE	Not I, my lord.
RICHARD	Then he disdains to shine, for by the book 280
	He should have braved the east an hour ago.
	A black day will it be to somebody. Ratcliffe!
RATCLIFFE	My lord.

Richard tries to calm his misgivings about the lack of sun. He sets out his battle plan and dismisses a mocking verse. His address to his troops begins by insulting Richmond's followers.

Characters

Richard's changing mood (in pairs)

Read the script from line 272 to line 343. This activity will help you analyse Richard's changing mood.

a Find lines in the script that suggest the following:
  - Richard is concerned about traitors and deserters.
  - Richard takes notice of good or bad omens.
  - Richard is an experienced general and is happiest when he is busy issuing commands.
  - Richard is a confident tactician.
  - Richard is back to his old swaggering self.
  - Richard cynically claims that only cowards have a conscience.
  - Richard believes that his troops are better fighters than Richmond's.

b For each statement above, write a sentence explaining whether you think this is a fair comment about Richard. Provide a short quotation from the script as evidence to support each of your points.

c Sum up what you think about Richard's state of mind at this point in the play. Has he completely recovered from his nightmares or not?

Write about it

Richard's diary

Write Richard's diary entry for the day of the battle, just before the fighting starts. What are his hopes and fears? You might like to mention:

- his dreams and how he feels about them
- his concern about disloyalty in his ranks
- his superstitious belief in omens (for example, the lack of sun, his consultation of a calendar)
- what he thinks about Richmond as a military man
- what he thinks about Richmond's troops (see Richard's speech in lines 316–39).

lour look angrily
from gone from

vaunts swaggers
bustle hurry, get busy
Caparison equip for battle

foreward vanguard
drawn extended
horse and foot cavalry (mounted soldiers) and foot soldiers

main battle main division of soldiers
puissance force
wingèd with flanked by
chiefest horse best cavalry
This, and … to boot! not only a great plan, but helped by St George as well!
direction battle plan
Jockey (a familiar form of John)
Dickon (disrespectful form of the name Richard)
bought and sold finished

Join engage in battle
pell mell hand-to-hand fighting, furiously
inferred stated
cope withal fight against
A sort of assorted
lackey servile

RICHARD   The sun will not be seen today;
           The sky doth frown and lour upon our army.   285
           I would these dewy tears were from the ground.
           Not shine today? Why, what is that to me
           More than to Richmond? For the self-same heaven
           That frowns on me looks sadly upon him.

Enter NORFOLK

NORFOLK   Arm, arm, my lord! The foe vaunts in the field!   290
RICHARD   Come, bustle, bustle. Caparison my horse.
           Call up Lord Stanley; bid him bring his power.
           I will lead forth my soldiers to the plain,
           And thus my battle shall be orderèd:
           My foreward shall be drawn in length,   295
           Consisting equally of horse and foot;
           Our archers shall be placèd in the midst.
           John Duke of Norfolk, Thomas Earl of Surrey,
           Shall have the leading of the foot and horse.
           They thus directed, we will follow   300
           In the main battle, whose puissance on either side
           Shall be well-wingèd with our chiefest horse.
           This, and Saint George to boot! What think'st thou, Norfolk?
NORFOLK   A good direction, warlike sovereign.
           This found I on my tent this morning: 305
           'Jockey of Norfolk, be not so bold,
           For Dickon thy master is bought and sold.'
RICHARD   A thing devisèd by the enemy.
           Go, gentlemen, every man to his charge.
           Let not our babbling dreams affright our souls,   310
           For conscience is a word that cowards use,
           Devised at first to keep the strong in awe.
           Our strong arms be our conscience, swords our law!
           March on! Join bravely! Let us to't pell mell,
           If not to heaven, then hand in hand to hell.   315
                     [*His oration to his army*]
           What shall I say more than I have inferred?
           Remember whom you are to cope withal:
           A sort of vagabonds, rascals, and runaways,
           A scum of Bretons and base lackey peasants,

Richard calls Richmond's followers beggars and rapists. He mocks Richmond as a spoilt weakling and reminds his soldiers of past victories over the French. Hearing of Stanley's refusal to join him, Richard orders Stanley's son's death.

1 Richard spurs on his troops (in threes)

In a stirring oration (lines 316–43), Richard attempts to galvanise his troops into action.

a Read Richard's speech, then pick out all the words or phrases he uses to describe Richmond's army. Discuss what he is trying to suggest by these descriptions. You might find it helpful to copy out and complete the table below.

Lines	Richard's description of the enemy	What he means
318 331	Vagabonds, rascals and runaways; famished beggars	They are all beggars and thieves
319	Scum, lackey peasants	The lowest of the low
319	Bretons	They are not even English
	their o'ercloy'd country vomits forth	
	led by a 'milksop'	
	rats	

b Create a tableau that represents Richard's view of Richmond's army. Remember, a tableau does not have to be realistic – it should be suggestive of some of the images Richard uses. Make sure everyone in your group is involved.

c Share your tableau with others in the class and talk about how successful Richard is in making the enemy seem less of a threat.

d Re-read Richmond's oration and compare it with Richard's. Add some more information to your table, charting the differences between the two men (see p. 202).

o'ercloyèd sickeningly overfull

restrain seize
distain rape
paltry insignificant
Bretagne Brittany
our mother's England's
milksop weakling
overweening presumptuous, boastful
fond exploit foolish invasion
means riches, income

bobbed buffeted
on recòrd as is written

yeomen landowners (lower status than 'gentlemen')

welkin sky

spleen anger

Whom their o'ercloyèd country vomits forth 320
To desperate adventures and assured destruction.
You sleeping safe, they bring you to unrest;
You having lands, and blest with beauteous wives,
They would restrain the one, distain the other.
And who doth lead them but a paltry fellow, 325
Long kept in Bretagne at our mother's cost?
A milksop, one that never in his life
Felt so much cold as over shoes in snow.
Let's whip these stragglers o'er the seas again;
Lash hence these overweening rags of France, 330
These famished beggars, weary of their lives,
Who, but for dreaming on this fond exploit,
For want of means, poor rats, had hanged themselves.
If we be conquered, let men conquer us,
And not these bastard Bretons, whom our fathers 335
Have in their own land beaten, bobbed, and thumped,
And on recòrd left them the heirs of shame.
Shall these enjoy our lands, lie with our wives?
Ravish our daughters?
                    (*Drum afar off*)
Hark, I hear their drum!
Fight, gentlemen of England! Fight boldly, yeomen! 340
Draw, archers, draw your arrows to the head!
Spur your proud horses hard and ride in blood;
Amaze the welkin with your broken staves!

                    Enter a MESSENGER

What says Lord Stanley? Will he bring his power?
MESSENGER My lord, he doth deny to come. 345
RICHARD Off with his son George's head!
NORFOLK My lord, the enemy is past the marsh;
After the battle let George Stanley die.
RICHARD A thousand hearts are great within my bosom.
Advance our standards! Set upon our foes! 350
Our ancient word of courage, fair Saint George,
Inspire us with the spleen of fiery dragons!
Upon them! Victory sits on our helms!
                                        [*Exeunt*]

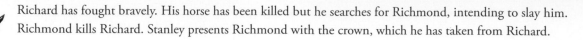

Richard has fought bravely. His horse has been killed but he searches for Richmond, intending to slay him. Richmond kills Richard. Stanley presents Richmond with the crown, which he has taken from Richard.

1 'my kingdom for a horse!' (in pairs)

The actor Anthony Sher, who played Richard III, once remarked that 'A horse, a horse, my kingdom for a horse!' is one of the most famous of all Shakespeare's lines. How can an actor make it sound fresh and new? Take parts as Richard and Catesby and read Scene 4. Explore ways of speaking Richard's lines to find the most dramatically effective delivery. For example, is Richard:

- bullish, overly confident and deluding himself
- terrified and panicking
- full of despair
- resigned to his fate
- noble, dignified?

Excursions battles

Daring an opposite
challenging an opponent

Slave wretch
cast throw of a die (plural: dice)
stand the hazard of the die
accept the outcome of the dice

Stagecraft

Richard's death (in small groups)

In some stage productions, Richard and Richmond perform a choreographed fight in heavy medieval armour. In the 1997 film version, Ian McKellen plays Richard in a jeep like a World War II general. Eventually, he greets death with a sardonic smile. Al Pacino (*Looking for Richard*, 1996) portrays him in medieval costume with arrows in his chest and back, killed by Richmond's longsword.

a The stage direction calls for '*Excursions*', or battles. Would you have some fighting on stage, or simply use sound effects to suggest the battle is happening off stage? Why?

b Work out how you would stage Richard's death. Turn back to the picture on page xii (right) in the photo gallery, showing how one stage production portrayed Richard's death. Then work out your own imaginative staging of that moment.

c Create a series of three tableaux capturing the moment of Richard's death. As a class, select one group's tableau and ask them to extend the final frame. One person in the role of Stanley mimes removing the crown from dead Richard's head and ceremonially presents it to Richmond. Read Stanley's lines 3–7. As a class, discuss the dramatic effect you would want to achieve here.

acquit thee acquitted yourself
usurpèd royalties (the crown)
wrongfully seized symbol of kingship

Act 5 Scene 4
Bosworth: the battlefield

Alarum. Excursions. Enter CATESBY

CATESBY	Rescue, my lord of Norfolk, rescue, rescue!
	The king enacts more wonders than a man,
	Daring an opposite to every danger.
	His horse is slain, and all on foot he fights,
	Seeking for Richmond in the throat of death.
	Rescue, fair lord, or else the day is lost.

5

Alarums. Enter RICHARD

RICHARD	A horse, a horse, my kingdom for a horse!
CATESBY	Withdraw, my lord; I'll help you to a horse.
RICHARD	Slave, I have set my life upon a cast,
	And I will stand the hazard of the die.
	I think there be six Richmonds in the field;
	Five have I slain today instead of him.
	A horse, a horse, my kingdom for a horse!

10

[*Exeunt*]

Act 5 Scene 5
Bosworth: the battlefield

Alarum. Enter RICHARD *and* RICHMOND. *They fight.*
Richard is slain. A trumpet sounds retreat. Enter STANLEY EARL
OF DERBY *bearing the crown, with several other lords*

RICHMOND	God and your arms be praised, victorious friends!
	The day is ours; the bloody dog is dead.
STANLEY	Courageous Richmond, well hast thou acquit thee.
	Lo, here these long usurpèd royalties
	From the dead temples of this bloody wretch
	Have I plucked off to grace thy brows withal.
	Wear it and make much of it.

5

Richmond learns that George Stanley is safe but that four noblemen have died. He declares the civil war at an end, and that his marriage to Elizabeth will unite the houses of York and Lancaster.

1 A new beginning

Richmond's crowning is highly significant historically, as it marks the end of the Wars of the Roses and the beginning of Tudor rule. His actions and language are intended to bring peace after bloody civil war.

a By marrying Elizabeth, Richmond will unite the houses of York and Lancaster. Use the family tree on page 266 to discover just how the 'white rose and the red' are now united. Design a new emblem that could be used to mark the unification of the white and red rose.

b One commentator suggests that Richmond's closing speech refers to 'all things an Elizabethan cared about', in that it upholds the 'Tudor myth' (see pp. 236–7). Pick out three aspects of Richmond's speech that you think support this view.

Stagecraft

The final image (in small groups)

The final 'stage picture' can underline the director's overall approach and interpretation of the main themes. For example, a director might want to end the play on an optimistic note, suggesting that England's troubles are now over and a good King is in place. Or a director might want to raise doubts about the ambitious Richmond, emphasising the fact that he, too, has gained the throne by use of bloody force.

a What final image would the audience see at the end of your production of *King Richard III*? Firstly, create a freeze-frame of Richmond's final words, 'God say amen'. Consider who is on stage and where they are standing. Think about body language and facial expressions.

b What do you plan to do with the dead Richard? Is his corpse on stage right to the end? If so, where and why? For example, does he have prominence in the scene or is he already an irrelevance?

c Consider what lighting and sound or music you might use as Richmond finishes his speech. What tone or mood do you want to create – and why? How do characters leave the stage?

d Show your freeze-frames to the rest of the class and explain your ideas, trying to relate them to your overall understanding of the play.

men of name men of high rank

Inter bury

in submission in defeat
ta'en the sacrament previously sworn, taken a holy vow
Smile heaven may heaven smile
conjunction union
enmity hatred

sire father

fair ordinance pleasing command
conjoin together marry
smooth-faced carefree

Abate the edge blunt the swords
reduce return to

increase bountiful harvest

civil wounds wounds caused by civil war
are stopped have stopped bleeding

RICHMOND	Great God of heaven, say amen to all.	
	But tell me, is young George Stanley living?	
STANLEY	He is, my lord, and safe in Leicester town,	10
	Whither, if you please, we may withdraw us.	
RICHMOND	What men of name are slain on either side?	
STANLEY	John Duke of Norfolk, Walter Lord Ferris,	
	Sir Robert Brakenbury, and Sir William Brandon.	
RICHMOND	Inter their bodies as become their births.	15
	Proclaim a pardon to the soldiers fled	
	That in submission will return to us,	
	And then, as we have ta'en the sacrament,	
	We will unite the white rose and the red.	
	Smile heaven upon this fair conjunction,	20
	That long have frowned upon their enmity.	
	What traitor hears me and says not amen?	
	England hath long been mad, and scarred herself;	
	The brother blindly shed the brother's blood;	
	The father rashly slaughtered his own son;	25
	The son, compelled, been butcher to the sire;	
	All this divided York and Lancaster,	
	Divided in their dire division.	
	Oh, now let Richmond and Elizabeth,	
	The true succeeders of each royal house,	30
	By God's fair ordinance conjoin together.	
	And let thy heirs, God, if thy will be so,	
	Enrich the time to come with smooth-faced peace,	
	With smiling plenty and fair prosperous days.	
	Abate the edge of traitors, gracious Lord,	35
	That would reduce these bloody days again	
	And make poor England weep in streams of blood.	
	Let them not live to taste this land's increase	
	That would with treason wound this fair land's peace.	
	Now civil wounds are stopped; peace lives again.	40
	That she may long live here, God say amen.	

Exeunt

FINIS.

Looking back at the play
Activities for groups or individuals

1 Headlines

Split into five groups. Each group is assigned a different act. Your challenge is to tell the story of each act in four or five headlines that could be used on the main evening television news. For example, the group assigned Act 1 might begin with the following two headlines:

> 'The Royal Family is in turmoil today as the Duke of Clarence is arrested on the grounds of possible treason.'

> 'And today's long-term weather forecast is for glorious summer…'

Present your headlines in the style of your favourite newsreader. Share the headlines in the order of the five acts. After each presentation, other groups could suggest a 'missing' headline – what they would have included if they had been working on your act.

2 The case against Hastings and Buckingham

Imagine that Hastings and Buckingham are brought to public trial, accused of treason against Richard. The King would not appear in court in person to give evidence, but he might submit a written statement in which he gives details of the men's crimes. Write Richard's two statements. Consider how he might describe certain events in such a way as to hide his own complicity in some of their crimes.

3 Changing fortunes

a Characters' fortunes (status, happiness and so on) rise and fall frequently in the play. Chart the fluctuating fortunes of Hastings, Buckingham and Anne in graph form, accompanied by quotations to illustrate their changing circumstances.

b Do you see Richard as a tragic hero figure (as suggested by the picture opposite, for example)? Or more as a comic rogue (as suggested in the picture on p. 197)?

4 Tragedy, history or comedy?

The title of the play is sometimes printed as *The Tragedy of Richard III*. Some critics view this play as a tragedy, others as a history play – some even see it as a comedy.

a Use the Internet to find out what the literary definition is of 'tragedy', 'comedy' and 'history play'.

b Suggest three or four reasons that could support each view of the play and use the table below to record your ideas. Look at various photographs in this edition to help you form ideas about what kind of play this is.

	Reason 1	Reason 2	Reason 3
Tragedy	Richard, the main character, dies at the end		
Comedy			
History			

c Give your own view about the genre of the play and suggest what aspects (for example, what episodes or what feature of Richard's character) you would need to emphasise in order to support that interpretation of the play in performance. Share these ideas with others in your class.

Perspectives and themes

What is the play about?

The obvious answer to this question might seem to be that this is a play about the rise and fall of a man who will stop at nothing to gain power. However, since the play was first performed, a number of different interpretations have been proposed – and there is no 'correct' way of thinking about any work of literature. How you personally read or interpret *King Richard III* may depend upon your own values and beliefs, the society in which you live, or even the way you have been taught to think about Shakespeare at school. For example, references to sin and redemption abound in the play, but how you understand and respond to these ideas will be shaped by your own religious faith (or lack of it). It is unlikely that many people watching a modern performance of this play believe in the divine right of kings (that a monarch is God's representative on Earth), but in Shakespeare's day, almost everyone held that belief.

This section investigates some of the different ways of thinking about *King Richard III*.

Themes

Themes are important ideas or concepts that recur throughout the play and help link all the different elements into a coherent whole. Themes may be developed both verbally and/or visually. For example, the boar image repeatedly linked to Richard contributes to our understanding of the savage nature of his power. This image recurs in the language and is often visually represented on stage. Themes can emerge through imagery, characters and events, adding texture and complexity to the play, with the result that *King Richard III* becomes much more than 'just' a story about a man who murders his way to the throne.

Main themes of *King Richard III* include:

- the pursuit of power
- appearance and reality
- attitudes to women
- sin and salvation

- Church versus state
- nemesis, fate and free will
- dreams and the supernatural
- words as weapons.

◆ In small groups, choose one of the themes listed above. Look through the play and locate an example of the following that illustrates your chosen theme and its importance to the play:

- an event
- a character and a character's action
- an image or other quotation from the script.

Record your ideas on large sheets of paper, add visual images (for example, search the Internet for production photographs) and then share your presentation with other groups. Display the sheets on your classroom wall.

The pursuit of power

The play could be seen as a study in the harsh realities of power politics: what life is like under a brutal King ruling a deeply corrupt state. Richard exploits the historical divisions caused by feuding political factions, manipulates individuals and the system, seizing the opportunity to make himself King. He is a Machiavellian figure – a cynical politician who uses any method to gain and maintain power, even to the point of eliminating friends and allies. Richard's antithesis is Richmond (Henry VII), a monarch apparently divinely appointed by God whose reign promises lasting peace and stability. Because Henry VII's reign marked the beginning of the Tudor dynasty, Shakespeare is likely to have been flattering Queen Elizabeth I, Henry's granddaughter.

Some commentators see in Richard parallels with political figures in more recent times, whose huge ambition has led them to use ruthless means to achieve their goal. From this viewpoint, Richmond could be seen, for all his talk of peace and unity, as yet another politically ambitious figure, staging a coup to gain control of a profoundly unjust state.

In small groups, compose a series of three or four tableaux to illustrate your understanding of the contrasting types of power held by:

- Richard
- Richmond
- Queen Elizabeth.

Think about the nature (physical or not), the extent (individual or collective, personal or political) and the effect (harmful or protective) of the power held by each character.

Discuss key differences between your tableaux, making direct reference to specific characters and events in the play to support your ideas. Find a key quotation from the script to use as an appropriate caption for each tableau.

Appearance and reality

Richard is an arch-deceiver. His skills as actor and manipulator enable him to use false words and appearances to fool other characters. His enthusiasm for sharing these skills with an audience – while other characters are on stage and unaware of what is happening – provides much of the play's entertainment. However, Richard is not the only character who hides true feelings beneath an outward show. Other figures, including Stanley, Queen Elizabeth and the Bishop of Ely, all successfully hide their true motives from Richard. Acting is a recurring motif in the play, creating a double layer of deceit, as real actors portray characters who are dishonestly performing a role.

Compile notes on the way in which Elizabeth, Stanley and the Bishop of Ely (a female character, a member of the nobility close to Richard, and a representative of the Church) all consciously set out to deceive others. Note down in three columns their deceptive words or actions, their apparent intention in saying or doing these things,

and the effects of their deception. Consider the following lines as a starting point:

- Elizabeth: Act 4 Scene 4, lines 197–436
- Stanley: Act 3 Scene 2, lines 17–18; Act 4 Scene 4, lines 463–505; Act 4 Scene 5
- Bishop of Ely (Morton): Act 3 Scene 4, lines 1–78; Act 4 Scene 3, lines 43–57.

◆ Write at least three paragraphs outlining the ways in which these three characters contribute to the theme of appearance and reality in the play. Include embedded quotations in your writing.

Attitudes to women

Richard introduces this theme in Act 1 Scene 1, by referring to women as a source of trouble for men, as if possessing a malevolent power: 'Why, this it is when men are ruled by women' (line 62). The position of women in the play has been vigorously debated by critics over the past fifty years. Are women merely powerless victims (for example, grieving mothers and widows) or do they provide emotional strength in the play, in direct contrast to Richard and his male followers?

The diagram opposite suggests a number of roles that women fulfil in the play. Below it and on the page opposite are a number of quotations from the play that refer to, or are spoken by, women. Look at the diagram and the quotations and then carry out the activities below.

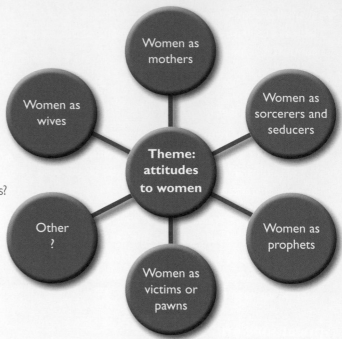

◆ Identify who says each quotation and when. Find some other quotations to add to this list.

◆ Match the quotations to the different female roles. Some might fit in more than one category. One circle has been left blank in case you feel that another role needs to be included.

◆ Take each category one by one, and discuss what aspects of that specific role or 'type' seem to be proposed in the play. For example, motherhood is not presented as a straightforward concept: mothers love and grieve for their children; equally, a mother may wish a child dead. Investigate each category, locate conflicting views and suggest where one category overlaps with another.

◆ In groups, select one category of womanhood and create a movement piece that encapsulates the various aspects you have discussed. The only words you speak must be the relevant quotations. Make sure all group members are involved, both in speaking and moving.

Why, this it is when men are ruled by women.
'Tis not the king that sends you to the Tower.
My lady Grey, his wife … 'tis she
That tempts him to this harsh extremity.

Then be your eyes the witness of their evil.
Look how I am bewitched. Behold, mine arm
Is like a blasted sapling, withered up.
And this is Edward's wife, that monstrous witch,
Consorted with that harlot, strumpet Shore

*   … Oh, let her live,*
And I'll corrupt her manners, stain her beauty,
Slander myself as false to Edward's bed

The jealous, o'er-worn widow

Naught to do with Mistress Shore?

ANNE *Oh, wonderful, when devils tell the truth!*
RICHARD *More wonderful, when angels are so angry.*

O my accursèd womb, the bed of death.
A cockatrice hast thou hatched to the world

Ah, my poor princes! Ah, my tender babes!
My unblowed flowers, new-appearing sweets!
… hear your mother's lamentation.

Oh, would to God that the inclusive verge
Of golden metal that must round my brow
Were red-hot steel, to sear me to the brains.
Anointed let me be with deadly venom
And die ere men can say 'God save the queen.'

Thou protector of this damnèd strumpet,
… Thou art a traitor.

Relenting fool and shallow, changing woman.

RICHARD   Who intercepts me in my expedition?
DUCHESS   Oh, she that might have intercepted thee,
                    By strangling thee in her accursed womb

For then I'll marry Warwick's youngest daughter.
What though I killed her husband and her father?

To hear the lamentations of poor Anne,
Wife to thy Edward, to thy slaughtered son,
Stabbed by the self-same hand that made these wounds.
Lo, in these windows that led forth thy life,
I pour the helpless balm of my poor eyes.

Play the maid's part: still answer nay and take it.

A care-crazed mother to a many sons,
A beauty-waning and distressèd widow,
Even in the afternoon of her best days,
Made prize and purchase of his wanton eye,
Seduced the pitch and height of his degree
To base declension and loathed bigamy.

Bear with me, I am hungry for revenge

From forth the kennel of thy womb hath crept
A hell-hound that doth hunt us all to death

Oh, now let Richmond and Elizabeth,
The true succeeders of each royal house,
By God's fair ordinance conjoin together.

If ancient sorrow be most reverend,
Give mine the benefit of seniory,
And let my griefs frown on the upper hand

Earth gapes, hell burns, fiends roar, saints pray,
To have him suddenly conveyed from hence.
Cancel his bond of life, dear God, I pray,
That I may live and say the dog is dead.

… the queen hath heartily consented
He should espouse Elizabeth her daughter.

Sin and salvation

Elizabethans believed that the soul lives on after death and may be rewarded or punished by God. All hope of salvation depended on the individual's spiritual state at the moment of death. If sins were confessed and then forgiven by a priest (shriven), or the sacrament of bread and wine celebrated, then the person died in a state of grace and the soul enjoyed an eternity of peace in heaven. Dying with sins unconfessed and unforgiven damned the soul to everlasting suffering in hell. Those who had not fully confessed before dying went to Purgatory, where they suffered until the unconfessed minor sins were burnt away (purged) by remorse.

Characters in the play are constantly reminded of their past sins. Richard recalls Margaret's cruel acts against his family (Act 1 Scene 3). Margaret's curses and prophecies remind the feuding nobles of their past crimes (Act 1 Scene 3). United in suffering, Queen Elizabeth, the Duchess of York and Queen Margaret lament wrongs committed against them (Act 4 Scene 4). Reminded of past sins and fearing everlasting damnation, characters attempt last-minute salvation for their terrible deeds. Clarence, Grey and Rivers, Hastings and Buckingham all refer to the importance of prayer, confession of sins and divine forgiveness before they die.

◆ Look back at the last (or almost last) words of Clarence (Act 1 Scene 4, lines 170–257), Buckingham (Act 5 Scene 1) and Richard (Act 5 Scene 3, lines 180–209). In pairs, discuss which lines or phrases offer the most striking glimpse of that character's vision of what awaits him. Select four or five of these lines and create a dramatic presentation in which you are only able to use those words (although some can be repeated).

◆ Consider how these final words work in the context of the play's themes and characters. For example, does the acknowledgement of sin help us (as readers or viewers) to sympathise with certain characters? Does it give the play a moral centre (reassuring the audience that sinful people will ultimately be punished)? In your opinion, which characters are most likely to gain salvation? Compile some notes based on your ideas, quoting some of the words or phrases used in the drama activity as evidence.

◆ Draw up an essay plan in response to the following essay question: How important is the theme of sin and salvation in *King Richard III*? If you are studying the play for an examination or other form of formal assessment, remind yourself of the assessment criteria before you start. Share your essay plans with other students in your class and discuss key differences.

Church versus state

The play exposes the tension between Church and state. The belief in the 'divine right of kings' held that the monarch was God's representative on Earth. As such, a crime against the King was a crime against God. The crown, orb and sceptre and anointing with holy oil at the monarch's coronation symbolised the bond between the secular and the spiritual.

The play constantly reminds the audience of the power and powerlessness of Church against state when the King is evil. Richard's hellish origins ('cacodemon', 'hellhound') contrast with references to heaven, angels and saints that resonate throughout the play. In addition to the named archbishops, bishops and priests who are present in crucial scenes, a director has many opportunities to include churchmen in the several processions, executions and crowd scenes.

Priests have to please both God and man. Witnessing a succession of churchmen lending their holy office for Richard's advancement creates episodes rich in irony. The Bishop of Ely, anxious to gather strawberries for his monarch (Act 3 Scene 4), and two churchmen supporting a 'pious' Richard (Act 3 Scene 7) reveal a Church impotent against Richard's power, as well as how Richard manipulates the Church for his own purposes.

The powerlessness of the Church is forcefully realised on stage in Act 3 Scene 1, which examines the right to sanctuary. A person accused of crimes could be protected from civil justice by sheltering in a church. Queen Elizabeth and the young Duke of York seek this sanctuary, but Richard and Buckingham successfully persuade the Church to yield up 'sanctuary children'.

◆ Improvise a conversation between the Bishop of Ely and the two bishops who appear on either side of Richard when he is pretending to be reluctant to take the throne (Act 3 Scene 7, lines 94–220). The conversation takes place after Richard has been defeated at the Battle of Bosworth. What do the clerics have to say about their roles in Richard's rise and fall. Could they have behaved differently? How do they defend their various actions?

Nemesis, fate and free will

The play examines political and religious issues, but nemesis and the working of fate are also major themes. Nemesis is retribution (the punishment for wrongdoing), and fate is the power that makes such punishment inevitable. This was the defining pattern of Greek drama, in which the inevitable workings of fate brought suffering and death.

In *King Richard III*, lamentation, cursing, dreams, prophecies and omens – often written in stylised and ritualistic form – express the hatred and desire for retribution that dominates many events in the play. The 'prophetess' Queen Margaret is the 'voice' of nemesis as she remembers past bloody deeds that call out for revenge. She prophesies that vengeance shall fall on the house of York for the wrongs done to the house of Lancaster (Act 1 Scene 3), and each victim remembers Margaret's prophecy at their moment of death.

But if Margaret is the voice or 'chorus', Richard is the agent of nemesis. He has the political power to destroy his enemies. Richard is at the centre of the action as death follows death, but he fails to see that he, too, is part of the pattern and it is inevitable that he too must die.

◆ In Richard's opening soliloquy, he says that he is 'determinèd' to be a villain (line 31). This can either mean that Richard is predestined to be a villain, or that he has made up his mind to be one. Prepare a class debate. Is Richard merely behaving according to fate and predestination, or is he a Machiavellian character enacting his free will? Find evidence that supports both readings, then decide which side of the argument you are going to support.

◆ Once you have discussed this as a class, consider how a director could suggest either reading on stage. If you wanted to emphasise the role of fate, are there any episodes or characters you would choose to cut? Similarly, if you wanted to present Richard as a man exercising his own free will, are there any episodes or characters you would cut? Write at least five paragraphs outlining your editorial/directorial decisions and explaining the reasons for them.

The contexts of *King Richard III*

Shakespeare's sources

One way of thinking about *King Richard III* is to set it in the context of its time. This involves looking at the world that Shakespeare knew and the way history was interpreted to make sense of this world.

Historical accounts of English history were vital sources for Shakespeare as he wrote *King Richard III*. Raphael Holinshed's *The Third Volume of Chronicles* (1587) and Edward Hall's *The Union of the Two Noble and Illustrate Famelies of Lancastre and Yorke* (1548) were particularly important. Shakespeare took these narrative accounts of English history and turned them into compelling drama. *King Richard III* is just one of the many history plays he wrote, and it shows the free use of historical sources that characterises them all. Shakespeare followed in Holinshed's footsteps when he represented Richard III as an evil King, but he goes further in his dramatic portrayal of him as a murderous usurper and tyrannical ruler.

The Tudor myth

Under Henry VII (Richmond – the man who killed Richard and established the Tudor dynasty) and his son Henry VIII, successive historians and writers established the now-traditional view of Richard as an evil, unpopular King. Such writers described him as a usurper (a person who wrongfully seizes power) who murdered Henry VI, the princes in the Tower and his wife Anne. Sir Thomas More's *History of Richard III* (written 1513–18) describes Richard as 'deformed' and evil from birth. Another 'history' claimed that Richard was born with teeth and with hair down to his shoulders. Other histories written during the reign of Henry VIII were responsible for the popular image of Richard as a hunchback.

The Tudor point of view also emphasised their right to rule. It focused on the horrors of civil war and praised the Tudors as the bringers of peace and prosperity to England. Polydore Vergil's *Historia Anglia* (1534) claims that Henry IV's illegal seizure of the crown from Richard II broke the God-given order of the universe.

This supposedly resulted in all the disasters that followed: the early death of Henry V, the bloody civil war known as the Wars of the Roses and Richard III's murderous, despotic reign. According to Vergil, England was rescued by Henry Tudor, who was God's instrument on Earth and who brought peace and plenty by uniting the houses of York and Lancaster.

The claims of the new King Henry VII to the throne were insecure and it was essential for Henry to destroy Richard's reputation. Under Elizabeth I, the historians Edward Hall and Raphael Holinshed incorporated the interpretations of More and Vergil so completely into their history books that by the end of the sixteenth century, this negative portrayal of Richard's appearance and actions was almost universally accepted. This version of history was Shakespeare's major resource as he wrote his play.

▼ Portraits of Richard III are believed to have been altered in Tudor times to make him look more sinister and evil.

Whatever his own views about Richard, Shakespeare was more interested in creating drama that would grip and thrill his audience. To achieve that dramatic intensity, and to give Richard his magnetic stage personality, he compressed historical events and made many alterations to produce fast-paced action. He invented Richard's wooing of Anne, the imprisonment of Hastings, Clarence's dream and murder. He also included Queen Margaret in the events of the play (even though she died in 1482) and compressed Richmond's invasion (November 1483), Buckingham's execution (August 1485) and the Battle of Bosworth (22 August 1485) into five scenes.

◆ **What evidence do we have today that might help us to rewrite history and see Richard III from a different perspective? Research the recent discovery of Richard III's skeleton beneath a car park in Leicester to see what evidence that presents for a different understanding of the last Plantagenet King of England. Below are some points to start with:**

- **The skeleton was found with significant battle wounds – eight in the head.**
- **The skeleton had a contorted spine (suggesting a disease called scoliosis).**
- **The frame of the skeleton indicated a slender build.**
- **The arms of the skeleton were crossed, which could indicate the wrists were still tied at burial.**
- **The teeth of the skeleton were ground down (possibly from anxiety or stress) and showed extensive tooth decay.**

Shakespeare's inspiration

Layers of interpretive possibilities within the script are also built on past dramatic performances as well as on contemporary accounts of the Wars of the Roses. Shakespeare was influenced by classical dramatists such as Seneca, a first-century Roman much loved by Elizabethan audiences for his use of violence, bloodshed and physical horrors in his plays. Ghosts and the supernatural, omens, prophecies and vivid descriptions of the underworld often appear in Seneca's plays, together with descriptions of bloody deeds committed offstage or in the past.

English dramatic traditions also influenced Shakespeare as he wrote *King Richard III*. The medieval mystery plays were religious dramas that told the story of the Bible from creation to the end of the world. One character from these plays that was imprinted in the popular imagination was Herod – the tyrant king who was brutally violent and responsible for the massacre of innocent children. This character, shouting and stamping across the stage, spoke directly to the audience, telling them what he was going to do and revelling in his own wickedness.

Shakespeare was also influenced by medieval morality plays, which personified a range of vices (including the seven deadly sins) and virtues in stories of temptation and ongoing conflict between good and evil.

By the mid-sixteenth century, the character Vice had become the star turn of morality plays, and audiences relished his theatrical delight in his own malice and trickery. Vice (sometimes called Iniquity) was a representative of the devil, whose function was to entrap people into sin through charm, wit and double-dealing. When he says 'Thus, like the formal vice, Iniquity / I moralise two meanings in one word', Richard invites the audience to see him in the same way they see this character from the morality plays.

In one of Richard III's soliloquies in *Henry VI, Part 3*, Shakespeare elaborates on this aspect of his character. Richard shows his craftiness and his ability to deceive and betray when he says:

> I can add colours to the chameleon,
> Change shapes with Proteus for advantages,
> And set the murderous Machiavel to school.
> Can I do this and cannot get a crown?
> Tut! Were it farther off, I'll pluck it down.
>
> Act 3 Scene 2, lines 191–5

Richard refers to Proteus (a Greek god who was said to constantly change his shape) as he revels in his ability to hide his intensions and to deceive others for his own advantage. He also refers to Machiavelli (whose name is synonymous with deception and manipulation) as he boasts that he will surpass him in his murderous schemes. Like the character Vice, Richard also revels in his own machinations and reveals his intentions to the audience in soliloquies and asides.

It is evidence of Shakespeare's dramatic genius that he was able to create such a magnetic and compelling stage personality out of historical accounts of the last of the Plantagenet kings and out of past performances of charismatic evil on the English stage.

Characters

Character study as an approach

One traditional way of interpreting Shakespeare's plays has been by closely examining the main characters: what they say and do, how they behave and how they relate to one another.

This approach to literary criticism was developed over one hundred years ago by A. C. Bradley (*Shakespearean Tragedy*, 1904), but has remained a popular way of thinking about the plays, particularly in school. It tends to treat dramatic roles as if they are real people who have lives beyond the world of the play. One advantage of focusing on characters is that it helps readers to make connections with the world of the plays, sympathising with human problems and emotions.

However, in recent years approaches to 'character study' have undergone significant revision. Some critics have argued that character-based approaches focus attention too much on emotions rather than ideas, and may give the impression that Shakespeare's dramatic scope is rather domestic and narrow. Furthermore, it has been argued by theatre historians that Elizabethan and Jacobean playwrights were not concerned with constructing psychologically consistent characters. Instead, certain character traits would be conveyed to audiences on Shakespeare's stage through 'stock' gestures and signalled by types of costume. Therefore, achieving realistic characterisation (as we might get in a modern novel or a television drama) was unlikely to have been Shakespeare's aim.

It may be that the fascination with tragic heroes emerged some time during the nineteenth century – the time of the great Victorian actor-managers, famed for their starring roles – and was further influenced by the kind of characterisation developed in the novels of the time. Some critics and historians have suggested that Victorian moralists were interested in using Shakespeare's characters as examples for moral guidance.

This section offers a number of activities that will help you explore different views of 'character', combining more traditional ideas about characterisation with broader considerations of the thematic, dramatic and political functions of the various roles in *King Richard III*.

Richard – a man of many parts

Although there is a huge cast of characters in this play, Richard dominates. Unusually for a Shakespeare play, there are no sub-plots, and this enables Richard to appear in fifteen of the twenty-five scenes overall (and, arguably, to be essential to the remaining ten). In his soliloquies, Richard frequently refers to plays and acting ('part', 'tragedy', 'pageant'), as if drawing attention to the fact that he is play-acting in order to deceive those around him. Consider some of the various parts or roles Richard adopts in the course of the drama:

Richard the actor Part of Richard's enduring fascination lies in his great acting skills. He pretends to be the caring brother, devoted lover, the innocent who is unjustly accused, a pious man of God, and the simple man who is too modest to become King.

Richard the charmer Richard's delight in his own abilities is infectious and gives him great audience appeal. He can, for example, charm the audience as he shares his plots with them in language that is often mocking, sardonic and full of wit.

Richard the lover Anne regrets succumbing to Richard's 'honey-words'. We observe Richard making two boldly persuasive marriage propositions in the course of the play.

Richard the brave warrior Richard's intellectual energy is matched by his physical vitality. He is constantly planning and always busy, restless in mind and body, fearless on the battlefield.

Richard the physically disabled man

Despite his proven prowess on the battlefield, at times Richard goes out of his way to draw attention to his disabilities, downplaying the extent of his power in order to manipulate people's reactions to him.

Richard the solitary man In *Henry IV, Part 3* (Act 5 Scene 6, line 83), immediately after he has murdered King Henry, Richard declares 'I am myself alone'. *King Richard III* starkly portrays how he puts that self-centred philosophy into action.

Richard the machiavellian politician

Niccolo Machiavelli (1469–1527), in *The Prince*, stated that politics must be separated from ethics, that the end justifies the means, and decisions based on the needs of the state come above conscience. This idea of a cunning, manipulative ruler was taken up by Elizabethan dramatists, who created self-centred, immoral villains like Richard.

◆ As a class, divide into seven groups. Look at the photographs in this edition and select at least one image that your group believes illustrates an aspect of Richard that is described above. Each group takes one of the listed roles to focus on. Create a presentation for the rest of the class that explores the way in which Richard plays this particular role. Your presentation should last three to four minutes. Use the following points to help you shape your presentation:

- Find a key episode or scene in which Richard plays this role. Summarise Richard's actions in words, mime, or a series of tableaux.
- Pick out key quotations – things Richard says that emphasise the characteristic you are exploring.
- Choose relevant photographs and other images from this edition and/or from the Internet.
- evaluate how successful Richard is at playing that particular part – what does he achieve by acting in this way?

On the psychiatrist's couch

◆ One branch of literary criticism that developed in the late twentieth century is concerned with using psychology as a tool to help us understand particular characters, their motivation and the way they act. Put Richard on the psychiatrist's couch. One person takes the role of Richard before the Battle of Bosworth, the other becomes the psychiatrist, asking questions about his relationships, desires and fears. Use the bullet points below to help you prepare, then role-play the encounter and show it to others in your class.

- How does Richard feel about what his mother says about him? Does this make him feel resentful about his favoured brothers? Is he jealous? (Look at Act 2 Scene 2, lines 49–56; Act 4 Scene 1, lines 54–6; Act 4 Scene 4, lines 136–96.)
- Richard gives the impression that he is very self-conscious about his physical appearance. Was his childhood difficult? What are the most hurtful things people have said about him? Has he ever felt pressure to prove himself capable of doing things that other people take for granted? (Look at Act 1 Scene 1, lines 14–30; Act 1 Scene 3, lines 47–53; Act 1 Scene 2, lines 34–67 and 105.)
- How would Richard describe his love life? What kind of relationships does he enjoy with women? Does he have women friends or does he just see women as sex objects? (Look at Act 1 Scene 1, lines 62–100 and 154–61; Act 1 Scene 2; Act 4 Scene 2, lines 52–64.)
- What are his greatest fears? What do Richard's dreams say about his subconscious fears? (Look at Act 5 Scene 3, lines 121–223 and 284–9; Act 1 Scene 3, lines 202–39).

Richard's social media profile

◆ Imagine Richard lived in the digital age. Create his profile and home page as it might appear on a social media website. Your mocked-up page(s) will probably contain some of the following:

- friends
- likes (for example, music, TV programmes, films, hobbies, favourite historical figures, political affiliations, religious beliefs)
- pictures from key moments in Richard's life
- comments
- notifications (who might have liked Richard's comments or replied to them)
- messages from others to Richard
- friend requests from people who want to be Richard's friends.

◆ As an extension, create a similar profile for Richard's brother Clarence, and include messages he might have sent to Richard following his imprisonment.

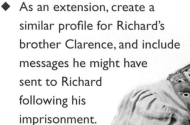

Richard's relationship with Buckingham

Although Buckingham appears to adopt a politically neutral position at the beginning of the play, he goes on to sustain a relationship with Richard longer than any other character. In the end, however, Buckingham becomes a victim of Richard's merciless plotting, just as Clarence and Hastings did before him.

◆ With a partner, trace the relationship between Buckingham and Richard. Look at the way Buckingham responds to Margaret's warnings early on in the play (Act 1 Scene 3, lines 280–304). At what point do we begin to see Buckingham and Richard forming an alliance?

◆ Pick a memorable episode or scene that shows Buckingham and Richard working closely together. What role does Buckingham adopt in his relationship with Richard? What qualities of Buckingham effectively complement those of Richard? In what ways is he different? Where does it all start to go wrong?

◆ Study the photographs of Richard and Buckingham in this edition. Make some suggestions about how you would present Buckingham on stage and give reasons for your choices.

◆ Using the notes and ideas generated by your discussions, write an essay with at least five paragraphs outlining the way Buckingham's relationship with Richard develops. Make sure you include quotations from the play to support your points in each paragraph. You might find it helpful to use the scaffold below:

- **Paragraph 1:** introduce the important role that Buckingham plays and how he relates to Richard.
- **Paragraph 2:** what kind of man does Buckingham appear to be at the beginning of the play. How is he drawn to Richard?
- **Paragraph 3:** give an example of the way Richard and Buckingham operate as a team; how do they complement each other? How do their antics contribute to the dramatic qualities of the play?
- **Paragraph 4:** describe what goes wrong. Does Buckingham change (or is it Richard)? Who is to blame for Buckingham's downfall? Does Buckingham repent at the end? Is Richard a changed man without Buckingham?
- **Paragraph 5:** sum up what Buckingham's relationship with Richard contributes to the play (such as dramatic tension, humour, tragedy, themes, development of Richard's character).

The women in the play

Feminist approaches to literary criticism attempt to focus on the contribution female characters make to a text, to consider the role of women as portrayed in a piece of work and to expose the way traditional readings of plays (often from a male perspective) represent women. In the early twentieth century, the female characters in *King Richard III* tended to be regarded as powerless victims. This view has been challenged by many critics in the past fifty years.

Queen Margaret

Margaret is the French wife of the murdered Henry VI, who is bitterly opposed to the house of York. In *Henry VI, Part 3*, Margaret led armies and had great power. Here she has lost all, and is reduced to using only the power of words to curse and prophesy the doom of others. She is chorus, prophetess and nemesis, cursing all whom she believes have plotted against her. She fiercely and passionately denounces and curses Richard, who has killed her husband and son. Like the other women in the play, Margaret is a victim of misogyny in a state where men have all the power. But it seems that Margaret influences the women so that they finally support each other, and it is Margaret who inspires Elizabeth to stand up to Richard in Act 4.

In many productions of *King Richard III*, Margaret's part is heavily cut. In the 1995 film version, Margaret is omitted completely. However, some recent directors have argued strongly that Margaret's role in the play is crucial, both dramatically and thematically. For example, like Richard, at times Margaret is a character who is given the privilege of speaking directly to the audience.

◆ Imagine you are about to direct a new film version of *King Richard III*. The script editor and the producer both think that Margaret's part should be omitted. You disagree. Prepare an argument for preserving the part of Margaret and then suggest a short-list of actors who you think would be good for the role.

◆ To help you consider Margaret's importance, draw a table like the one opposite and collect evidence for each of the roles Margaret fulfils.

Role	Explanation of role	Evidence from the play
'Chorus' (a figure from classical drama)	Comments on events; provides historical background…	Her asides Act 1 Scene 3…
Prophet		
'Nemesis' (a figure from classical drama)	Figure of divine retribution, demanding justice	
Motivator to the other women		
Dramatic counter-balance to Richard	Strong female figure; represents house of Lancaster…	
Other…		

◆ Using your notes from the table, write a letter to the script editor explaining why you believe the character or role of Margaret to be essential to an understanding of the play overall.

◆ Look through the various photographs in this edition showing Margaret in different productions. What aspects of her role does each emphasise? Propose the names of two or three well-known actors who you might want to cast in the part. Explain what appropriate qualities they have.

Queen Elizabeth

Elizabeth Woodville married Edward IV and used her power to ensure that her family achieved high-ranking positions. The promotion of her relatives caused resentment among the traditional nobility. The only occasion on which Richard and Margaret agree is when they mock the *parvenu* (people who rise above their original status through sudden wealth or position) Woodvilles (Act 1 Scene 3, lines 255–65). Richard uses the unpopularity of the Woodvilles to gain the support of Hastings and Buckingham, and he orders the executions of Elizabeth's son (Grey), brother (Rivers) and supporter (Vaughan), but he does not harm Elizabeth.

When husbands lose power, so do their wives. After King Edward's death, Queen Elizabeth is forced to face the consequences of the loss of her personal and political power. She foresaw her future powerlessness as King Edward lay dying: 'I fear our happiness is at the height' (Act 1 Scene 3, line 41).

Grieving the death of her two young sons (Act 4 Scene 4), she joins Margaret and the Duchess of York in a highly patterned lamentation as the three women remember their dead. Elizabeth bravely stands up to Richard ('Tell me, thou villain slave, where are my children?'), outwits him as he woos her for her daughter, and is rewarded when her daughter marries Richmond, the new King Henry VII.

The Duchess of York

The Duchess is the widowed mother of Richard, King Edward and Clarence. Her husband had been humiliated and killed by Margaret (in *Henry VI, Part 3*). In *King Richard III*, she suffers the deaths of Clarence and her two male grandchildren on the orders of Richard, and has to endure Richard spreading rumours that she was unfaithful and her eldest son is illegitimate. The Duchess joins the grieving of Margaret and Elizabeth, but she is vilified by Margaret for giving birth to Richard. Her final words to Richard are a curse and her desire for his death and defeat in battle: 'Bloody thou art, bloody will be thy end'.

Lady Anne Neville

Anne was betrothed to Prince Edward, the son of Henry VI. Both Edward and Henry were killed by Richard. In Act 1 Scene 2, she mourns over the corpse of Henry. Richard engages her in a war of words, resolved only when she agrees to become his wife. Later in the play, Anne shows courage and determination when she visits the princes in the Tower (Act 4 Scene 1), challenging Brakenbury to allow her to enter. About to be crowned Queen, she reveals that the curse she placed on Richard's future wife is ironically upon herself, seduced by his 'honey words'. Richard's 'timorous dreams' deny her sleep and, in almost her last utterance, she fears he will 'shortly be rid of me'. She is all too right. He arranges her death so that he can marry the young Elizabeth.

◆ In small groups, consider the following statements about the female characters in the play (Anne, Elizabeth, the Duchess of York and Margaret). Discuss the statements in turn and select those with which you most strongly agree and disagree:

- Men hold all the power in the play.
- Anne's role is the only important one; the rest of the women's parts could all usefully be cut in a production.
- The women are bound by a sense of feminine solidarity.
- The women provide a dramatic contrast to Richard and his male followers.
- The women all hate one another as much as they hate Richard.
- By the end of Act 4, the women gain strength by supporting each other, acting collectively.
- Women help change the course of the play.
- Men and women are portrayed as socially equal in the play.
- Although we never actually see Jane Shore, she is an important female character.
- The audience gets to hear Richard's innermost thoughts at different points of the play, but all the women remain as one-dimensional, 'flat' characters.

◆ Prepare to explain your choices to the rest of the class, making reference to events in the play. What are the sharpest points of disagreement?

The men in the play

Clarence, Hastings and Buckingham in turn become victims of Richard's merciless plotting. Shakespeare exposes the ironies implicit in appearance and reality, as each is fooled and blinded by Richard's false friendship. Finally, just before execution, each man is forced by his conscience to examine his own moral nature.

Clarence

Clarence's first appearance emphasises his trusting faith in a scheming brother who is about to have him executed. His gullibility generates situations where irony is at once funny and macabre. He tells the two Murderers whom Richard has sent to kill him that Richard is loving and kindly and 'would labour my delivery', not realising that Richard's 'delivery' means death. Shakespeare's transforming imagination underplays Clarence's involvement in past events (perjury and murder in *Henry VI, Part 3*), focusing instead on his dream; in an episode rich in imagery (Act 1 Scene 4, lines 9–74), Clarence finds belief in Christianity and understands the power of conscience, repenting his past crimes.

Hastings

Imprisoned through the intrigues of the Woodvilles ('By the suggestion of the Queen's allies'), Hastings is a faithful supporter of the house of York. His overconfidence and blindness to the real motives of others, allied to his bitter opposition to the Woodvilles, make him an easy victim of Richard's plans. He rejoices at the executions of Rivers, Grey and Vaughan, and is convinced of his own invulnerability. But Hastings's misinterpretations of every warning sustain the humour and grim irony that characterise the play. He fails to take the advice of Stanley to flee north, and he refuses Catesby's appeal to support Richard's bid for the crown (Act 3 Scene 2). In a deeply ironic episode at the council, he believes that Richard is incapable of hiding his true feelings, and intends harm to no one present (Act 3 Scene 4). Realising his mistakes too late, he recalls Margaret's curse as he prophesies 'the fearful'st time' for England under Richard.

Buckingham

Buckingham's ability to dissemble almost rivals Richard's own. He possesses great political awareness and diplomatic skill, and appears first as peacemaker (Act 1 Scene 3), bringing messages from Edward IV to appease the various rivalries. He stands aloof from the bitter family arguments. Buckingham is the only important person not cursed by Margaret, but his neutrality evaporates (Act 2 Scene 2) when he seizes the opportunity to join with Richard in isolating Edward, Prince of Wales, from his family. He becomes Richard's right-hand man, and much of the humour and irony of Acts 2 and 3 derive from the energy and verve Buckingham and Richard generate as they embark on a spree of outrageous play-acting and stage-management that has lethal outcomes. They order the imprisonment and execution of Rivers, Grey and Vaughan (Act 2 Scene 4). They send the princes to the Tower (Act 3 Scene 1) and contrive Hastings's execution (Act 3 Scene 4). Persuading the citizens of London there is a plot against them (Act 3 Scene 5), they fool the Lord Mayor and aldermen into making Richard King (Act 3 Scene 7).

When Richard refuses to grant him the promised earldom of Hereford, Buckingham does not hesitate. He raises an army against Richard, but a storm disperses his troops. Before his execution, he recognises the justice of his punishment and reflects that 'Margaret's curse falls heavy on my neck'. Margaret's curse is a persistent reminder throughout the play of the power of nemesis and fate (see p. 235) as characters face the inevitable consequences of their actions. Buckingham's fall marks the beginning of Richard's own decline in fortune. The 'deep-revolving witty Buckingham' is replaced by the sinister figure of Ratcliffe. Richard will rely increasingly on several unprincipled men to carry out his brutal plans.

Lord Stanley, Earl of Derby

The husband of Margaret Beaufort and stepfather to Richmond, Stanley is the only character to play Richard at his own game – his words hiding his true intentions. Stanley's loyalty is first challenged by Queen Elizabeth (Act 1 Scene 3), who knows Stanley's wife hates all the Woodvilles. His reply is both tactful and politic, an approach he uses successfully throughout the play to avoid suspicion. His plea to Edward IV to save the life of his servant establishes Stanley as a caring master who is respected by the King. He gradually emerges as an important focus for opposition to Richard, aware almost from the beginning of Richard's true nature.

Stanley shows some of his true feelings when he warns Hastings to be suspicious of Richard (Act 3 Scene 2) and when he encourages Dorset to join Richmond (Act 4 Scene 1). Powerless to stop Richard from becoming King, Stanley waits for the opportune moment. When Richard holds his son hostage and threatens him with execution, Stanley promises the tyrant military support, but he secretly intends to support Richmond. Using Richard's own weapons of double-dealing and hypocrisy, Stanley joins Richmond to defeat Richard, and by good luck his son's life is spared.

Richmond

Richmond – the future Henry VII – appears very late in the play, addressing his troops in Act 5 Scene 2. He seems the all-conquering hero, a *deus ex machina* (god who intervenes in the nick of time) who ends Richard's evil reign. He appears to have all the right credentials: he is highly principled, honourable, moral and righteous, a fighter who wants only his country's good. Believing God will support his just cause, he puts his fate in divine hands. He is not part of the bloody legacy of the Wars of the Roses, and his innocence is acknowledged by the ghosts. An astute tactician who realises the importance of Stanley's forces, he shows genuine affection for his stepfather and is magnanimous in victory.

While some commentators argue that Richmond is the hero saving England from Richard's oppression, others disagree. They claim that the play has been starved of moral language for so long while Richard has delighted audiences with his Machiavellian cunning, that the contest is not a fair one. Such transparent moral righteousness as Richmond possesses seems naive and dramatically unconvincing compared to the much more interesting Richard. What is your view of Richmond?

◆ Imagine Lord Stanley has arranged Richmond's first press conference following the victory at Bosworth. This is a chance for the press to get to know the new King and to glimpse the way Stanley is managing the regime. In groups, two people take roles as Stanley and Richmond; the rest become journalists. Separately, journalists prepare questions while Stanley and Richmond prepare statements for the press (explaining, for example, how the battle was won, what England can look forward to, and so on).

◆ As a whole class, select one Stanley/Richmond pair and improvise the press conference, with the rest of the class in role as journalists. The challenge is for Stanley and Richmond to answer questions in a way that is consistent with the play, and to incorporate some of their original language in the responses.

Exploring themes through character

References to appearance abound in the play, particularly concerning Richard's physical looks and disability. A traditional trick of story-telling in a number of cultures is to portray villains as ugly or disfigured, and this seems to be one way Shakespeare is inviting us to regard Richard: his interior sinfulness is exhibited in his outward features. The discovery of Richard's buried remains in 2013 settled the long-running debate as to whether the real historical figure was disabled or not, but attitudes to disability and disfigurement have changed considerably since Shakespeare's day.

How to present Richard to a modern audience, and how to deal with offensive disability-related language ('bunch-backed', 'elvish-marked', 'hedgehog') presents a challenge to directors and actors. Below are some views on Richard from actors and directors.

I became very interested in the fact that Richard is a severely disabled man. Some actors underplay this – but if you read Richard's opening speech about himself, he is clearly disabled, and has experienced a lot of prejudice, a lot of hatred. This, in turn, has filled him with self-hatred. It's this that enables him to do such evil to other people. He was used to hatred as a disabled man in an un-PC society. There were no Paralympics then.

Actor Antony Sher

I've always been struck by his anger as a character, and in the play he explains that this is because he was born so physically disadvantaged. That wasn't something Shakespeare invented – and so perhaps the play isn't the Tudor propaganda hatchet job that people often assume … When you play Richard on stage, you have to decide how you want him to look. I had a withered left arm, my left leg was in callipers, and I had a huge birthmark across my face, because there's a lot of talk in the play about the circumstances of his birth. The idea was that from one side he'd look almost completely normal, and then he'd spin around and everything would be twisted.

Actor Jonathan Slinger

In Richard, Shakespeare created a monster – but he is a monster in a world that is equally monstrous. Medieval politics can't have been fun: it's a vision of a world of violence and lack of moral scruple … I wanted him to have the shape of a retired American footballer: very big and heavy, with a huge upper body compared to his legs, and a tiny bald head. People said I looked like Shakespeare's 'bunch-backed toad', as his mother calls him. His disability is incredibly important to the play – it's a motor for his fury.

Actor Simon Russell Beale

Richard III is a supercharged panto/tragedy … Although Richard III is frequently attacked as a melodramatic and simple-minded play, it is psychologically very acute – … in the way that it shows how a sociopath can move through normal society with terrifying ease.

Director Dominic Dromgoole

We don't see Richard as a 'wink-wink, I'm a villain' character … Richard is just a normal guy who has had enough … like any disabled member of our society even today.

Director Stephanie Barton-Farcas

◆ What similarities and differences are there between the various viewpoints expressed in the statements? Which do you most – or least – agree with?

◆ In four out of the five productions referred to above, able-bodied actors were cast as Richard. Discuss whether it would make a difference if Richard was played instead by a disabled actor – or if other cast members were disabled. You might find it useful to look back at some of the production photographs of Richard in this edition.

The language of *King Richard III*

The first thing that might strike you about the language of *King Richard III* is that it is highly patterned and often formal. Its style reflects many of the techniques Shakespeare had learned at his school in Stratford-upon-Avon, where Renaissance rhetoric (the art of using language persuasively) was at the centre of the curriculum. As a schoolboy, he imitated classical models, practising many different ways of using language that he later employed in his plays. Richard's curses, lamentations, entreaties and warnings use language in many ways.

Repetition

Shakespeare's use of **repetition** gives his language great dramatic force. Repeated words, phrases, rhythms and sounds add to the emotional intensity of a moment or scene, heightening theatrical effect. The play is full of examples of highly patterned repetition, and many episodes have a ritualistic quality because of the symmetrical repetition of particular phrases and rhythms. This can be seen most in the following language devices.

Anaphora is the repetition of the same word at the beginning of successive sentences:

> *Was ever woman in this humour wooed?*
> *Was ever woman in this humour won?*
>
> Act 1 Scene 2, lines 231–2

Epistrophe is the repetition of a word or phrase at the end of a series of sentences or clauses:

CHILDREN	*Ah, for our father, for our dear lord Clarence.*
DUCHESS	*Alas for both, both mine Edward and Clarence.*
ELIZABETH	*What stay had I but Edward? And he's gone.*
CHILDREN	*What stay had we but Clarence? And he's gone.*
DUCHESS	*What stays had I but they? And they are gone.*
ELIZABETH	*Was never widow had so dear a loss.*
CHILDREN	*Were never orphans had so dear a loss.*

> Act 2 Scene 2, lines 72–8

Polyptoton is repetition of words derived from the same root word, but with different endings or forms. In Act 4 Scene 4, the women lament, expressing their sorrow in stylised formal language. In lines 39–46, there are seven uses of 'killed' or 'kill':

> *I had an Edward, till a Richard killed him;*
> *I had a husband, till a Richard killed him*
> …
> *Thou hadst a Clarence, too,*
> *And Richard killed him.*

Other examples of repetition are **alliteration** (the repetition of consonants at the beginning of words) and **assonance** (repeated vowel sounds). Both are evident in the single line:

> *And with a virtuous visor hide deep vice.*
>
> Act 2 Scene 2, line 28

◆ **Turn to a scene you particularly enjoy. How many examples of repetition can you find in it?**

Other language devices

Antithesis

King Richard III is full of conflicts, and Shakespeare's language powerfully expresses conflict through its use of **antithesis**: the opposition of words or phrases. Every page of the play contains antitheses. For example, 'Your grace attended to their sugared words / But looked not on the poison of their hearts' (Act 3 Scene 1, lines 13–14) sets 'attended to' against 'looked not on', 'sugared' against 'poison', and 'words' against 'hearts'. Richard's first soliloquy, which opens the play, contains many antitheses – for example, from the first sixteen lines:

> *winter/summer*
> *smoothed/wrinkled*
> *bruisèd arms/monuments*
> *stern alarums/merry meetings*
> *dreadful marches/delightful measures*
> *mounting/capers*
> *rudely stamped/love's majesty*

At the end of Act 2 Scene 4 (lines 60–2), the Duchess of York laments her sufferings in tightly packed dramatic antitheses:

My husband lost his life to get the crown,
And often up and down my sons were tossed
For me to joy and weep their gain and loss.

Before the final battle, Richard urges on his troops 'If not to heaven, then hand in hand to hell.' His final words are an ironic antithesis, expressing what his ambition has dwindled to: 'my kingdom for a horse!'

◆ **Choose a particular scene and work through it, identifying how each antithesis adds to the dramatic tension in that part of the play.**

Stichomythia

Another source of conflict and dramatic tension is Shakespeare's use of rapidly alternating single lines spoken by two characters to increase pace and tension in a scene. This is known as **stichomythia** and can be seen in Richard's 'wooings' of Anne and Elizabeth in Act 1 Scene 2, lines 197–205, and Act 4 Scene 4, lines 347–71.

Lists

One of Shakespeare's favourite devices was to accumulate words or phrases rather like a list. He knew that 'piling up' item on item, incident on incident, can intensify description, atmosphere, character and dramatic effect. Shakespeare would probably have known this language device as 'copiousness'. Act 3 Scene 5, lines 1–9 list at least a dozen things that a deceitful actor can do. There are many other kinds of list in the play, often in a single line containing four items ('Deep, hollow, treacherous, and full of guile' Act 2 Scene 1, line 38), and sometimes as a much longer catalogue – for example at Act 4 Scene 4, lines 168–73, when the Duchess of York describes Richard's life:

A grievous burden was thy birth to me.
Tetchy and wayward was thy infancy;
Thy schooldays frightful, desperate, wild, and furious;
Thy prime of manhood, daring, bold, and venturous;
Thy age confirmed, proud, subtle, sly, and bloody

◆ Read through any act, collecting as many lists as you can. Then work with others to act out a few of the lists.

Blank verse

With the exception of the episode with the Murderers in Act 1 Scene 4, the play is written entirely in **blank verse**. Each ten-syllable line has five alternating unstressed (×) and stressed (/) syllables (**iambic pentameter**), as in:

× / × / × / × / × /
A horse, a horse, my kingdom for a horse!

◆ To experience the rhythm of iambic pentameter, speak a few lines from any verse speech. As you speak, beat out the five-beat rhythm (clap your hands or tap your desk). When you have a feel for the rhythm, invent a few blank-verse lines describing your response to the play.

◆ *King Richard III* is an 'early' play, and as in other works written by Shakespeare at the start of his career, many of the lines are 'end-stopped' – that is, they make sense as a line: the meaning does not 'run-on' over into the next line (enjambement). All actors face the problem of whether they should pause, however briefly, at the end of each line. What do you think? Select a long speech and speak it with a pause at the end of each line, then say whether you think actors should always 'signal' the end of the line in some way.

Imagery

Imagery is the use of emotionally charged words and phrases to conjure up vivid mental pictures and associations. Such images intensify the dramatic and emotional impact of the play. They give insight into characters' feelings and thoughts, and help to create the play's distinctive atmosphere and themes. *King Richard III* is rich in imagery and certain images recur through the play, helping to create its distinctive atmosphere.

Animal imagery

Richard is described in metaphors using animal imagery throughout the play. He is called a 'dog', 'hedgehog', 'hell-hound', 'bunch-backed toad', 'cur', 'rooting hog', 'cockatrice', 'bottled spider'. But the imagery is extended to the many characters who are imprisoned – for example, Clarence and Hastings are 'mewed up' (confined) like captive birds of prey, while those who are free and in power are 'kites and buzzards' or 'eagles'.

Theatrical imagery

Shakespeare's fascination with his own profession provided him with a recurring theme: the world as a stage. On this stage, humans make brief appearances to play their parts and take on different roles in different contexts. Richard is the epitome of the consummate actor who delights in trickery and duplicity – and invites the audience to delight in it, too.

Similes and metaphors

Shakespeare's imagery uses **metaphor** or **simile**. A simile compares one thing to another using 'like' or 'as': Richard claims he is 'like the formal Vice, Iniquity', and declares he will be led by Buckingham 'as a child'. A metaphor is also a comparison, but suggests that two dissimilar things are actually the same or have much in common. For example, the first two lines of the play compare the 'winter' of past battles with the 'summer' of the present time of peace. Richard uses a metaphor when he speaks of the dead King Edward and his sons: 'The royal tree hath left us royal fruit'.

The house of York's family tree is full of fruit (sons who will become King and continue the royal line) when the play opens. But this powerful visual image shows the tree is bare when Richard enters for his final confrontation with Richmond. Here, the verbal imagery of the play is reinforced by the visual imagery of the stage set.

Personification

Personification is a particular type of imagery. It turns things or ideas into humans, giving them human feelings or body parts. The two Murderers call conscience 'blushing, shamefaced'; Richard speaks of 'dull delay' and 'snail-paced beggary'. The Duchess of York tells of England's earth being 'made drunk'.

◆ Turn to two or three pages at random. Identify the images on each page and suggest how they add to the dramatic appeal of the scene.

Playing with language

Puns

A **pun** is a clever or humorous play on the meaning of words that sound or look similar. Richard is a master of the pun as he turns meaning on its head to ridicule, embarrass, sneer at or attack his opponents. Richard reveals his hatred for the Woodvilles by punning on 'noble' (Act 1 Scene 3, line 81), meaning 'one of the nobility' but also 'a coin of little worth'. He puns on 'son' / 'sun' in the second line of the play. The 'son of York' is King Edward, but the 'sun' was also the Yorkist emblem that would bring light and warmth to Richard's family. Throughout the play, 'blood' can refer to family, gore, rage or the Yorkists in general and Richard in particular. Look out for the many other puns as you read through the play.

Keywords

Certain words echo through the play, often repeated: 'blood', 'grace', 'God', 'hate', 'hell', 'Lord', 'murder'. Richard frequently turns an oath (a formal promise made in the name of a god or holy person) into an irreverent and blasphemous expression.

◆ Look back through the play and make a note of the oaths used by Richard and others, and the dramatic contexts in which they are used. A few examples to get you started are:

- The old Queen Margaret's curses in Act 1 Scene 3, include the an invocation of God's power
- In Act 3 Scene 1, Richard says to the young princes: 'God keep you from them and from such false friends'.
- In Act 4 Scene 4, Richard searches for an oath strong enough to convince Queen Elizabeth to allow him to marry her daughter. He finally says 'Why then, by God', but her answer exposes his hypocrisy and blasphemy.

Dramatic language

Soliloquies and asides

A **soliloquy** is a monologue, a kind of internal debate spoken by a character who is alone (or assumes they are alone) on stage. It gives the audience direct access to the character's mind, revealing their inner thoughts and motives. An **aside** is a brief comment or address to the audience that shows the character's unspoken thoughts, unheard by other characters on stage. The audience is taken into this character's confidence or can see deeper into their motivations and experiences. Asides can also be used for characters to comment on the action as it unfolds. You can see how Richard uses both soliloquies and asides throughout the play.

Irony

King Richard III is a play much concerned with false appearance. Shakespeare fills it with two types of irony: verbal and dramatic. In both, the audience knows something that a character on stage does not. Richard is a master of **verbal irony**, saying one thing and meaning another. Everything he says to Clarence and Hastings in the first scene is charged with double meaning. When he tells Clarence 'I will deliver you or else lie for you', Clarence thinks his brother is promising to free him from prison or take his place there. But Richard has murder ('deliver' from life) and telling lies in mind.

Dramatic irony occurs when what is said contrasts with what happens elsewhere in the play. The young York calls Richard 'gentle uncle' and 'kind uncle', unaware that his uncle wishes him dead. There is huge dramatic irony in the appearance of the wicked Richard between two churchmen: the contrast of all he has said and done with his pretended saintliness.

◆ Choose two examples of dramatic irony in the play and write notes in your Director's Journal about how you would want the set design, lighting, sound effects and actors to highlight the contrast between what is being said and what is actually happening or intended.

◆ Use an online version of the play to copy and paste all Richard's soliloquies and asides. Read through them to identify what Richard confides in the audience and how he creates a confidential relationship with them.

King Richard III in performance

King Richard III was probably written and first performed around 1592 or 1593. It is almost certain that the play was performed at the Globe Theatre while Shakespeare was alive. According to contemporary reports and anecdotes, it was a great success for both Shakespeare's playing company and for Richard Burbage – the first actor to play the part of Richard III.

Performance on Shakespeare's stage

During Shakespeare's lifetime, plays in outdoor amphitheatres like the Globe were performed in broad daylight during the summer months. So, at 2 p.m. people would assemble with food and drink to watch a play with no lighting and no rule of silence for the audience. There were high levels of background noise and interaction during performances, and audience members were free to walk in and out of the theatre.

In the Globe, the audience was positioned on three sides of the stage: the 'groundlings' stood in the pit around the stage while those who paid more were seated in three levels around the pit. Actors would see around three thousand faces staring up or down at them. The positioning of the audience made it difficult for everyone to hear all that was going on. Inevitably, the actors would have their backs to sections of the audience at times. The best place for actors to stand, especially for a soliloquy or an aside, was at the front of the stage so that they could directly address almost all of the audience. However, it would be tedious if all the action occurred here!

Shakespeare's use of repetition helped to overcome this problem. There are times when the same idea is stated or developed in three ways in order to allow an actor to address each section of the audience. These repetitions were never simply word for word, but were used to create rhythm, accumulate details and build on an idea through different metaphors and imagery. If you spot significant repetition, it may be a clue that Shakespeare intended the character to move around the stage and engage different parts of the audience.

This illustration from 1647 shows the Globe Theatre, built for the second time in 1614 after the first one burnt down.

'Blocking' is a term used to describe actors' positions on the stage, and on Shakespeare's stage a character's position gave the audience clues about their role or authority in the play. Upstage is furthest away from the audience and downstage is closer to the audience. Characters absorbed in their own lives, or characters who played out literary or conventional stereotypes, were often placed centre-stage or upstage – furthest away from the audience. Characters who had a comic role, who performed many roles or commented on the action on stage were often played closer to the audience or at the edge of the stage. In this way, they existed on the intersection between stage and audience.

◆ Actors at Shakespeare's Globe often comment on how effectively its stage layout can be made to work dramatically, and especially on the way it encourages a close rapport with the audience. What parts of *King Richard III* do you think would work well on this stage, with the audience so close to the actors, and why? Which parts do you think it would be difficult to stage convincingly, and why?

The popularity of Shakespeare's play is evident in the anecdotes about Richard Burbage in the role of Richard. Burbage was well known for his charismatic and powerful acting, and his portrayal of Richard III was very popular with audiences at the Globe Theatre.

The popularity of the play is also evident in its printed history. It was so popular that six Quarto editions of the play were published before it appeared in the Folio edition of Shakespeare's plays in 1623. 'Quarto' and 'Folio' refer to the paper size: Quarto editions were smaller as well as cheaper and quicker to publish than Folio editions. Often, the Quarto version was written from an actor's memory of the performance or by piecing together a few of the actor's lines with the prompt book. As a result of all these editions, there are different versions of the script in existence today. For example, there are thirty-two lines in the First Quarto that are not in the Folio, and the Folio has about 200 lines that do not appear in the First Quarto.

King Richard III in the eighteenth century

From 1700 until 1877, all performances of *King Richard III* were based on an adaptation of Shakespeare's play written by Colley Cibber. Cibber was Poet Laureate, as well as a playwright and actor, and his version of the play placed the focus firmly on the character of Richard. It was a star vehicle for him as an actor, and this was the version that many other actors chose to display their virtuosic acting abilities for more than a century and a half.

In Cibber's version, Richard has more than forty per cent of the play's lines – two hundred lines from Shakespeare's other history plays were inserted and Cibber put in over a thousand lines of his own. He cut the parts of Queen Margaret, Edward IV, Clarence, Hastings and the Woodvilles. His Richard was a melodramatic villain to the end, and Cibber captured this with the now-famous line he inserted into the play: 'Off with his head. So much for Buckingham!' Cibber gave his villainous hero another famous line on the eve of the Battle of Bosworth:

'Conscience avant; Richard's himself again'. There is no room for ambiguity or remorse: this Richard shakes his sword at fear and sallies forth to battle.

David Garrick was another star actor who played Richard in Cibber's version of the play. He first performed the role in 1741, using a more naturalistic acting style than was favoured at the time. He brought a new expressiveness to the role, using naturalistic voice, gestures and facial expressions to portray Richard as a human being rather than a stage monster. William Hogarth captured the horror and vulnerability of Garrick's portrayal of Richard just before the Battle of Bosworth in a theatrical portrait in 1745. Garrick's approach was both shocking and inspiring for his audiences, and his performances as Richard were a great success. During his time as actor and stage manager at the Theatre Royal, Drury Lane (between 1747 and 1776), the play was performed 213 times in twenty-nine years!

Hogarth's painting of David Garrick in the title role of *King Richard III*.

King Richard III in the twentieth century

Since 1700, nearly all productions of *King Richard III* have cut characters, scenes and lines in order to focus attention on Richard. However, most productions in the twentieth century have returned to the early Quarto and Folio versions, and perform the play with few cuts. Richard III remains a star role that attracts star actors, all of whom want to give a definitive performance of the character. However, the individualistic melodrama of Cibber's script is now replaced by considerations of the more psychological interpretations of Richard and the political potential of the play in performance.

In 1984, Antony Sher played Richard III in a production with the Royal Shakespeare Company (RSC). His portrayal involved an exploration of the character's motivations and past experiences, and his performances are remembered for his striking mannerisms and costume choice. He used two crutches and the dangling cloth of his costume to create the image of Richard as a 'bottled spider' and 'bunch-backed toad' scuttling around the stage like an insect. The mobility and speed of this obviously handicapped character was shocking and unsettling for the audience. Sher's performance provided a glimpse into Richard's manic and evil nature while also attempting to explore some of the reasons why he was like this.

▲ **Aidan McArdle's 2001 portrayal relied less on physical disability and more on purity and saintliness to fool his victims.**

In 1996, David Troughton played Richard as Mr Punch, a grotesque clown figure who used disguise and false identities to hide the hollowness within.

◆ Carry out some research into the character of Mr Punch and use your findings to analyse how playing Richard in this way adds to the dramatic effect.

In 2002, Kenneth Branagh emphasised Richard's physical limitations; the actor wore an ungainly and confining leg-brace strapped to his torso.

Henry Holden is a disabled actor who needs crutches to walk in his own life. His 2007 production presented Richard's story as similar to that of any disabled person's story in society today – a struggle to get the things that rightfully belong to them.

◆ The pages in this section all portray very different interpretations of Richard. Which comes closest to your own view of Richard? Discuss the reasons for your choice/s with a partner.

◆ Write notes in your Director's Journal to describe how you would want to see Richard portrayed on stage. Compare these past performances with your own ideas.

The reconstruction of Shakespeare's Globe Theatre, on London's Bankside, allows many of the productions there to show the style and costumes that would have been familiar to Shakespeare's audiences. In Shakespeare's time, boy actors played the women's parts, and modern performances at Shakespeare's Globe have experimented with having an all-male cast for this play.

In 2003, the Globe also made a daring experiment in its production of *King Richard III* when all the parts were played by women. In the photograph top right, Kathryn Hunter portrays a crafty and devious Richard who attempts to persuade a reluctant Queen Elizabeth that her daughter should be his next wife. A similar moment is captured in the photograph on the right from a Shakespeare's Globe production with an all-male cast, with Mark Rylance as Richard III and Samuel Barnett as Queen Elizabeth.

◆ Look at the images on the right from performances with an all-male and an all-female cast at Shakespeare's Globe. What – in your opinion – are the gains or losses when the play is performed by actors all of the same gender?

A production of *King Richard III* in Arabic (with English subtitles) was commissioned by the Royal Shakespeare Company as part of its Complete Works Festival in 2007. This adaptation was called *The Baghdad Richard* and it set the play in the modern world of the Arabian Gulf. According to a synopsis of this performance:

> *The play unfolds within the hothouse, feudal atmosphere of desert places in an oil-rich kingdom. In this world of tribal allegiances, family in-fighting and absolute power, the questions of leadership, religion and foreign intervention that are at the heart of Shakespeare's play, take on powerful new meanings in a modern context.*

A more recent performance at Shakespeare's Globe was given by the National Theatre of China as part of the World Shakespeare Festival in 2012. In this production, Richard was portrayed without the physical disabilities or bodily impairments that audiences have come to expect. Instead, the actor playing Richard was tall and athletic with an imposing physical presence on stage. And yet there were elements of mental impairment in this portrayal, especially in the mental anguish and psychological turmoil of Richard on the eve of the Battle of Bosworth. The director, Wang Xiaoying, said in an interview with the Chinese newspaper *Xinhua*:

> *The real Richard in history was not handicapped at all. We don't want to make his disability a reason behind his desire for power. In other words, we don't want to make him starkly different from ordinary people.*

◆ What inspiration do you get from reading about these two recent productions of *King Richard III*? Imagine you have been invited to the next 'World Shakespeare Festival' – which country would you like to represent and how would you like to perform Richard? Think about the language and cultural context as you do so. For example, you might like to think about specific points of history and/or tyrannical regimes that might offer interesting interpretive contexts for a new production of the play.

▼ This is a performance of *King Richard III* at a festival in Portugal.

257

King Richard III on film

A silent, black and white film from America in 1911 shows an actor adopting the characteristic appearance for Richard that had developed over the years: Elizabethan doublet and hose, a fur-lined coat and a black wig with shoulder-length hair.

In his 1955 film, Laurence Olivier had the same look, but he added a large and unmistakable nose. The cinematic techniques available to Olivier enabled him to create a character who was at once fascinating and repellent. He took viewers into his confidence through the use of extreme close-ups, yet created a sinister atmosphere as the camera lingered over Richard's misshapen shadow moving through the scenes. Olivier's direct speeches to the camera left no doubt about Richard's evil intentions and power to dissemble, but he was still charismatic and mesmerising.

The film emphasised the importance of the crown as a symbol and Richard's lack of right to rule. It began with an added scene of pomp – the coronation of Edward IV, in which Richard's own coronet falls to the floor. Richard's coronation later was a much less grand affair, and Queen Anne fainted as Richard ascended the throne. At Bosworth, the crown is trampled in the mud before Richard is killed and his body flung over a horse.

Olivier added lines from *Henry VI, Part 3* to the opening soliloquy, to express Richard's duplicity and devious ploys:

> *Why, I can smile, and murder whiles I smile,*
> *And cry, 'Content!' to that which grieves my heart,*
> *And wet my cheeks with artificial tears,*
> *And frame my face to all occasions.*
>
> Act 3 Scene 2, lines 182–5

He also added lines from Cibber's version to emphasise Richard's deformity, and included a silent yet influential part for Jane Shore, who appears in dramatic and amorous scenes with both King Edward and Hastings.

◆ Watch Olivier's film of *Richard III*. Give your response to each of Olivier's inventions and additions, saying how helpful you find them.

Ian McKellen's filmed version of *Richard III* (1995) was an adaptation of Shakespeare's play set in 1930s England. The directors used the cinematic techniques and realistic settings of a contemporary action movie, with fast-paced scenes of violence and war. This, together with Shakespeare's language modernised for contemporary audiences, made the film a box-office success. McKellen hoped that by putting Richard's story in a modern setting, it would help the audience see it as more than just 'old-fashioned Shakespeare'.

McKellen's Richard is a slightly handicapped and stiff-backed officer, who rises to power to become a fascist dictator. The film opens with flashbacks of the recent war in which Richard has cold-bloodedly and violently killed Henry VI and his son Prince Edward. It uses the full opening soliloquy from Act 1 Scene 1 (with additional lines from *Henry VI, Part 3*), spoken first as a public speech and finished as private thoughts spoken aloud in the lavatory. McKellen uses the same technique as Olivier, directly addressing the film audience.

The film ends with an ambiguous and unsettling confrontation between Richmond and Richard. As they face each other towards the end of the Battle of Bosworth, Richard refuses to surrender. Richmond raises his pistol to shoot him, but Richard jumps from the roof of a bombed-out building into the flames below. His final line (taken from the scene that precedes the battle in Shakespeare's play) – 'Let us to't pell mell / If not to heaven, then hand in hand to hell' – is set to jaunty music as he holds out his hand to Richmond. Richmond's smile as he watches Richard fall to his death is hard to decipher. The audience is left with an unsettled feeling: it is unclear what the future holds for England.

▶ **Ian McKellen has played Richard on stage and on film.**

In the docudrama *Looking for Richard* (1997), Al Pacino played Richard. as well as providing a commentary on his experience of playing the role.

The film merged scenes from Shakespeare's play (in medieval costumes) with episodes in which the actors talked about their characters. Academics were also interviewed about the play. Pacino brought Shakespeare to a modern American audience and raised questions about who has the authority to make interpretive statements on Shakespeare – American actors or British academics.

Pacino's use of the docudrama form allowed him to switch roles from Richard to director, reflecting on his performance (and on the performances of other actors, as well as different interpretations of the play). In his commentary, he talked to viewers and explained his motives and actions in much the same way Richard does in his use of soliloquies and asides in Shakespeare's play.

Throughout history, performances of *King Richard III* have shown a wide range of interpretations and possibilities for dramatic portrayals on stage and on film. In part, this is because the role itself is extremely theatrical. Richard is not only a tyrant king or heroic villain. He is also a consummate actor who plays many parts and revels in each role that allows him to hoodwink his enemies and get rid of those who stand in his way to the throne.

◆ In groups, think about how you would want to stage *King Richard III* for a new production in a city of your choice and with an unlimited budget.

- Describe the setting and time (i.e. the present, the past or the future) and think about how lighting, costume and music could contribute to the overall effect.
- Cast your production with known actors, or other celebrities, and explain your choices. Then identify several speeches you think are particularly important and write instructions on how they should be delivered.
- Draw some costume designs, or use pictures taken from magazines or the Internet.
- Programme notes that are sold at performances of the play might include information on how the stage set links to the director's interpretation and characterisation. Write your own programme notes, in role as a director, using your ideas for a set design above and your knowledge of the play, along with its language, events and characters.

Writing about Shakespeare

The play as text

Shakespeare's plays have always been studied as literary works – as words on a page that need clarification, appreciation and discussion. When you write about the plays, you will be asked to compose short pieces and also longer, more reflective pieces like controlled assessments, examination scripts and coursework – often in the form of essays on themes and/or imagery, character studies, analyses of the structure of the play and on stagecraft. Imagery, stagecraft and character are dealt with elsewhere in this edition. Here, we concentrate on themes and structure. You might find it helpful to look at the 'Write about it' boxes on the left-hand pages throughout the play.

Themes

It is often tempting to say that the theme of a play is a single idea, like 'death' in *Hamlet*, or 'the supernatural' in *Macbeth,* or 'love' in *Romeo and Juliet*. The problem with such a simple approach is that you will miss the complexity of the plays. In *Romeo and Juliet*, for example, the play is about the relationship between love, family loyalty and constraint; it is also about the relationship of youth to age and experience; and the relationship between Romeo and Juliet is also played out against a background of enmity between two families. Between each of these ideas or concepts there are tensions. The tensions are the main focus of attention for Shakespeare and the audience; this is also how the best drama operates – by the presentation of and resolution of tension.

Look back at the 'Themes' boxes throughout the play to see if any of the activities there have given rise to information that you could use as a starting point for further writing about the themes of the specific play you are studying.

Structure

Most Shakespeare plays are in five acts, divided into scenes. These acts were not in the original scripts, but have been included in later editions to make the action more manageable, clearer and more like 'classical' structures. One way to get a sense of the structure of the whole play is to take a printed version (not this one!) and cut it up into scenes and acts, then display each scene and act, in sequence, on a wall, like this:

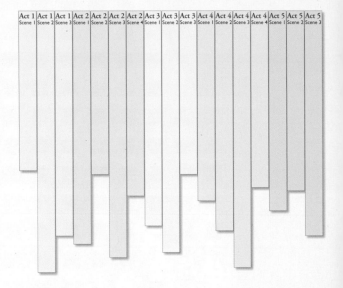

As you set out the whole play, you will be able to see the 'shape' of each act, the relative length of the scenes, and how the acts relate to each other (such as whether one act is shorter, and why that might be). You can annotate the text with comments, observations and questions. You can use a highlighter pen to mark the recurrence of certain words, images or metaphors to see at a glance where and how frequently they appear. You can also follow a particular character's progress through the play.

Such an overview of the play gives you critical perspective: you will be able to see how the parts fit together, to stand back from the play and assess its shape, and to focus on particular parts within the context of the whole. Your writing will reflect a greater awareness of the overall context as a result.

The play as script

There are different, but related, categories when we think of the play as a script for performance. These include *stagecraft* (discussed elsewhere in this edition and throughout the left-hand pages), *lighting*, *focus* (who are we looking at? Where is the attention of the audience?), *music and sound*, *props and costumes*, *casting*, *make-up*, *pace and rhythm*, and other *spatial relationships* (e.g. how actors move around the stage in relation to each other). If you are writing about stagecraft or performance, use the notes you have made as a result of the 'Stagecraft' activities throughout this edition of the play, as well as any information you can find about the plays in performance.

What are the key points of dispute?

Shakespeare is brilliant at capturing a number of key points of dispute in each of his plays. These are the dramatic moments where he concentrates the focus of the audience on difficult (sometimes universal) problems that the characters are facing or embodying.

First, identify these key points in the play you are studying. You can do this as a class by discussing what you consider to be the key points in small groups, then debating the long-list as a whole class, and then coming up with a short-list of what the class thinks are the most significant. (This is a good opportunity for speaking and listening work.) They are likely to be places in the play where the action or reflection is at its most intense, and which capture the complexity of themes, character, structure and performance.

Second, drill down at one of the points of contention and tension. In other words, investigate the complexity of the problem that Shakespeare has presented. What is at stake? Why is it important? Is it a problem that can be resolved, or is it an insoluble one?

Key skills in writing about Shakespeare

Here are some suggestions to help you organise your notes and develop advanced writing skills when working on Shakespeare:

- Compose the title of your writing carefully to maximise your opportunities to be creative and critical about the play. Explore the key words in your title carefully. Decide which aspect of the play – or which combination of aspects – you are focusing on.
- Create a mind map of your ideas, making connections between them.
- If appropriate, arrange your ideas into a hierarchy that shows how some themes or features of the play are 'higher' than others and can incorporate other ideas.
- Sequence your ideas so that you have a plan for writing an essay, review, story – whichever genre you are using. You might like to think about whether to put your strongest points first, in the middle, or later.
- Collect key quotations (it might help to compile this list with a partner), which you can use as evidence to support your argument.
- Compose your first draft, embedding quotations in your text as you go along.
- Revise your draft in the light of your own critical reflections and/or those of others.

The following pages focus on writing about *King Richard III* in particular.

Writing about *King Richard III*

Any kind of writing about *King Richard III* will be informed by your responses to the play. Your understanding of how characters, plot, themes, language and stagecraft are all interrelated will contribute to your unique perspective. This section will help you locate key points of entry into the play so that your writing will be engaging and original.

How do you find your unique perspective? You may want to start by considering this play in the context of Shakespeare's other history plays. *King Richard III* dramatises the final events of the Wars of the Roses, and ends with the marriage of Henry VII (Richmond) and Elizabeth, marking the start of the new Tudor dynasty. The play is coloured by perspectives on Richard that are informed by a Tudor viewpoint: he is represented as a malignant and violent tyrant king who murders eleven people (including his own family members and innocent children) in order to seize the throne.

The real Richard III was not as evil or sinister as Shakespeare has imagined him to be, and his reputation has changed much throughout the centuries since he died. Shakespeare and other sixteenth-century writers embellished this historical figure with dramatic and sensational characteristics, many of which are pure fiction. Shakespeare's Richard III is not only a representation of Tudor perspectives; he is also an inherently theatrical character who delights in his own machinations and in his many performances on stage. He acts out several parts and plays to the audience, seeking its approval and complicity. His many soliloquies and asides that comment on what is happening around him and on his own plans – especially in the first half of the play – are typical of his invitations to the audience to join him in delighting in his own mischief.

In this, Richard is like the Vice character in medieval morality plays and, indeed, Richard makes this comparison himself in Act 3 Scene 1. The Vice character was associated with the Devil and linked to sin, hell and damnation, as well as being the source of much comic

energy on the stage. Shakespeare's Richard uses similar verbal trickery and punning, shows the same triumphant glee in his deceptions and has a similar relationship with the audience as did the Vice character, who moved easily from the world of the play to the world of the audience.

Although Richard dominates the play, the other characters also shape our response to him. Richard's colloquial and informal language is contrasted with the formal rhetoric and elaborate language of the women in the play. The triad of women – all of them queens – who clearly see Richard's evil intentions, are brought together in scenes of grief and madness. The former Queen Margaret's mad curses, Richard's mother's shame at having borne such an evil son and Queen Elizabeth's grief-induced insanity are all testimony to another perspective on Richard. Their highly rhetorical speeches create patterned and rhythmic sequences, and offer a contrast to Richard's informal language.

While thinking through the range of possible written responses, you may find it helpful to consider the performance possibilities offered by the play. Your own perspective will develop as you make connections between its dramatic, contextual, linguistic and thematic features.

Creative writing

At different times during your study of *King Richard III*, you may be writing about the play and about your personal responses to it. Creative responses, such as those encouraged in the activities on the left-hand pages in this book, allow you to be as imaginative as you want. This is your chance to develop your own voice and to be adventurous as well as sensitive to the words and images in the play. This is a rich, multi-layered text that benefits from many different approaches, both in performance and in writing. Don't be afraid of larger questions or implications that cannot be reduced to simple resolutions. The complex issues are often the most interesting.

◆ Richard's asides and soliloquies allow him to engage with the audience in a sophisticated yet informal manner. Try to write asides and soliloquies for another character so that they also develop a relationship with the audience. What difference does this make to your understanding of the character?

◆ What happens to the characters who live on after the play has finished? Choose one of the characters and write their version of events. Write this as a first-person narrative, a monologue or a script.

Essay writing

Other responses, such as essays, have a set structure and specific requirements. Writing an essay gives you a chance to explore your own interpretations, to use evidence that appeals to you, and to write with creativity and flair. You can approach the play from a number of critical perspectives or in relation to different themes. You will also need to explore the play in the social, literary, political and cultural contexts of its production (Shakespeare's day) and reception (today or at any point since Shakespeare's day).

An essay can be seen as an exploration of the play in which you chart a path to illuminate ideas that are significant to you. It is also an argument that uses evidence and structural requirements to persuade your readers that you have an important perspective on the play. You must integrate evidence from the script into your own writing by using embedded quotations and by explaining the significance of each quotation and reference to the play. Some people like to remember the acronym PEA to help them here. P is the POINT you are making. E is the EVIDENCE you are taking from the script. A is the ANALYSIS you give when using this evidence, which will reflect back on the point you are making and contain your own personal response and original ideas.

The following titles are typical essays based on *King Richard III*:

1 Shakespeare's representation of Richard III is influenced by historical accounts of the last Plantagenet king and by dramatic characters from medieval drama. How do you understand this character and the impact he has on the stage and in the events of the play?

2 Choose two or three central themes and explain how each is developed linguistically and dramatically through the play.

3 Write about an aspect of language that interests you in *King Richard III*.

4 The figure of Vice (and other representations of evil on stage) from medieval drama is an important influence on the character of Richard. Discuss the effect this has on your understanding of characters and events in the play.

5 Do you see Richard as the play's hero or as its villain? What evidence can you find in the play that suggests you could argue that he is both?

◆ Pick at least two of these essay titles and sketch out an essay plan for each. Swap plans with two other students in your class, giving constructive feedback and making suggestions for improvements.

◆ Select the two essay titles that you think are the most difficult to answer. Try to pinpoint which aspects of the questions you find most challenging. Then get together with a partner and share ideas about how to address these challenging aspects.

Royal family tree

m = married

 House of York    House of Lancaster   House of Tudor

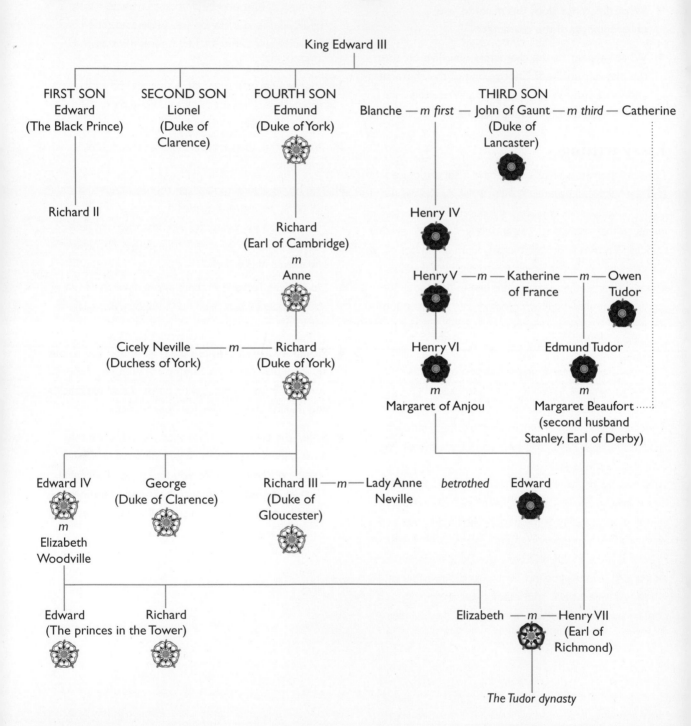

Acknowledgements

Cambridge University Press would like to acknowledge the contributions made to this work by Rex Gibson and Pat and Tom Baldwin.

Extracts from 'Richard III: Shakespearean actors rake over the remains', The Guardian, 4 February 2013 on p. 247 copyright © Guardian News and Media Ltd 2013. Extract from programme notes from Nicu's Spoon Theater Company production of Richard III, 2007, on p. 247 reproduced with permission of Stephanie Barton-Farcas.

Picture Credits

p. iii: John Douglas Thompson as Richard in a Shakespeare & Company production 2010. Photo by Kevin Sprague; p. v top: Crucible Theatre, Sheffield 2002, © Donald Cooper/ Photostage; p. v bottom: Richard III: An Arab Tragedy, RSC/Swan Theatre, Stratford-upon-Avon 2007, © Donald Cooper/ Photostage; p. vi top: Shakespeare's Globe, London 2012, © Geraint Lewis; p. vi bottom: RSC/Barbican Theatre, London 1985, © Donald Cooper/Photostage; p. vii top: Richard III: An Arab Tragedy, RSC/Swan Theatre, Stratford-upon-Avon 2007, © Donald Cooper/Photostage; p. vii bottom: RSC/Barbican Theatre, London 1996, © Donald Cooper/ Photostage; p. viii top: Richard III: An Arab Tragedy, RSC/Swan Theatre, Stratford-upon-Avon 2007, © Donald Cooper/ Photostage; p. viii bottom: RSC/Barbican Theatre, London 1996, © Donald Cooper/Photostage; p. ix top: Jason Asprey (Hastings) and Ryan Winkles in a Shakespeare & Company production 2010. Photo by Kevin Sprague; p. ix bottom: RSC/ Swan Theatre, Stratford-upon-Avon 2012, © Geraint Lewis; p. x: RSC/Barbican Theatre, London 1996, © Donald Cooper/ Photostage; p. xi top left: RSC/Royal Shakespeare Theatre, Stratford-upon-Avon 2003, © Donald Cooper/Photostage; p. xi top right: RSC/Royal Shakespeare Theatre, Stratford-upon-Avon 2003, © Donald Cooper/Photostage; p. xi bottom: RSC/Courtyard Theatre, Stratford-upon-Avon 2007, © Geraint Lewis; p. xii left: Northcott Theatre Company/ Ludlow Festival 2008, © Donald Cooper/Photostage; p. xii right: RSC/Royal Shakespeare Theatre, Stratford-upon-Avon 1984, © Donald Cooper/Photostage; p. 14: © Donald Cooper/Photostage; p. 22: RSC/Young Vic Theatre, London 2001, © Donald Cooper/Photostage; p. 26: Leia Espericueta (Anne) and John Douglas Thompson (Richard) in a Shakespeare & Company production 2010. Photo by Kevin Sprague; p. 38: Bridge Project/Old Vic Theatre, London 2011, © Geraint Lewis; p. 46: RSC/Royal Shakespeare Theatre, Stratford-upon-Avon 1980, © Donald Cooper/ Photostage; p. 60: Shakespeare's Globe, London 2003, © Donald Cooper/Photostage; p. 67: RSC/Royal Shakespeare Theatre, Stratford-upon-Avon 2003, © Donald Cooper/ Photostage; p. 70: RSC/Royal Shakespeare Theatre 1980, © Donald Cooper/Photostage; p. 78: A Noise Within, Los Angeles 2009, © Craig Schwartz Photography; p. 88: Judah Piepho (Duke of York) and Anne Miller (Duchess of York) in a Shakespeare & Company production 2010. Photo by Kevin Sprague; p. 95 top: RSC/Swan Theatre, Stratford-upon-Avon 2012, © Geraint Lewis; p. 96 bottom: A Noise Within, Los Angeles 2009, © Craig Schwartz Photography; p. 102: Northcott Theatre Company/Ludlow Festival 2008, © Donald Cooper/Photostage; p. 108: Richard III's boar emblem, © PA Photos/Topfoto; p. 116: Temple University, Philadelphia 2009. Photo by Ian Paul Guzzone; p. 120: RSC/ Royal Shakespeare Theatre, Stratford-upon-Avon 1995 © Donald Cooper/Photostage; p. 126: Richard III: An Arab Tragedy, RSC/Swan Theatre, Stratford-upon-Avon 2007, © Donald Cooper/Photostage; p. 132: RSC/The Other Place, Stratford-upon-Avon 1992, © Donald Cooper/Photostage; p. 136: Lyttelton Theatre/National Theatre, London 1990, © Donald Cooper/Photostage; p. 147: 'Children of Edward' by Paul Delaroche, © DEA/G. DAGLI ORTI/Getty Images; p. 156: RSC/The Other Place, Stratford-upon-Avon 1992, © Donald Cooper/Photostage; p. 158: © Donald Cooper/ Photostage; p. 160: 'The Murder of the Princes in the Tower', © Getty Images; p. 172: RSC/Swan Theatre, Stratford-upon-Avon 2012, © Geraint Lewis; p. 176: RSC/Royal Shakespeare Theatre, Stratford-upon-Avon 1984, © Donald Cooper/Photostage; p. 197: Apollo Theatre, London 2012, © Nigel Norrington/ArenaPAL; p. 204: A Shakespeare & Company production 2010. Photo by Kevin Sprague; p. 210:

Produced for Cambridge University Press by White-Thomson Publishing
+44 (0)843 208 7460
www.wtpub.co.uk

Managing editor: Sonya Newland
Designer: Clare Nicholas
Concept design: Jackie Hill